Talking with Sartre

10 Mai 70

Mon cher Gerassi
Je suis tout à fait d'accord
avec votre projet d'écrire ma
biographie. Je vous fournirai tous
les renseignements et les documents
dont je dispose et je m'engage
à vous en assurer l'exclusivité.
Il va de soi que mon adhésion à
ce projet implique que je refuserais
quel que soit la personne qui me
le propose, tout projet de retracer
ma vie dans un livre

    Bien amicalement à vous

Talking with Sartre

Conversations and Debates

Edited and translated by

JOHN GERASSI

Yale University Press/New Haven & London

Designed by Mary Valencia
Set in Scala and Scala Sans type by The Composing Room of Michigan, Inc., Grand Rapids,
Michigan
Printed in the United States of America.

Library of Congress Cataloging-in-Publication Data
Talking with Sartre : conversations and debates / edited and translated by John Gerassi.
    p.   cm.
  Includes bibliographic references and index.
  ISBN 978-0-300-15107-7 (cloth : alk. paper)
  ISBN 978-0-300-15901-1 (paperback : alk. paper)
  1. Sartre, Jean-Paul, 1905–1980—Interviews.   I. Gerassi, John.
  B2430.S34A5 2009
  194—dc22   2009022455

A catalogue record for this book is available from the British Library.

This paper meets the requirements of ANSI/NISO Z39.48-1992 (Permanence of Paper).

10 9 8 7 6 5 4 3 2 1

For Catherine Yelloz

Contents

CONTENTS

Preface

When the ninety-year-old British philosopher Bertrand Russell launched the International War Crimes Tribunal in 1966—basically as a propaganda weapon to investigate and, inevitably, condemn the United States for its aggression against the Vietnamese people—he realized he was too old and frail to act as its president. So he asked the century's most important novelist-playwright-philosopher-activist, Jean-Paul Sartre, to be its chair. But Sartre refused. So Russell asked me to intervene.

As head of the Bertrand Russell Peace Foundation in New York, I had made various suggestions about such a tribunal, and Russell was aware that I knew Sartre well. This was partly because before World War II, my father, the Spanish painter Fernando Gerassi, had been his best friend, and Sartre had written about him in his trilogy, *The Roads to Freedom*. "Gomez," as Sartre named him, is a crucial character in the novel; he abandons his wife and child to go fight for the Spanish Republic during the Civil War of 1936–39 and becomes a general, the last top warrior to defend Barcelona, which indeed is what happened in real life.

But to Sartre at the time this was not commendable: nothing must interfere with artistic endeavor, he insisted. By going to fight against fascism, Fernando had betrayed his artist's commitment. And Sartre often prodded me on why my father did go fight, even after Fernando knew that the Republic would lose. In the novel, Sartre has my father say, "You don't fight fascism because you're going to win. You fight fascism because it is fascist." A perfectly logical explanation to any political animal. And to Sartre later, but not at the time.

Also, my mother, "Sarah" in the trilogy, had been one of Simone de Beauvoir's closest friends when both were students at the Sorbonne, and it was she who had introduced Sartre to her lover, my father-to-be. "Castor" (as Simone was nicknamed) and my mother maintained their friendship after the war, and she always stayed with us when she came to the United States. Thus, whenever I went to France, it was natural that I would spend time with Sartre and Beauvoir.

And I had established my own reasons for spending time with them. I was writing my doctoral dissertation at Columbia University, first on Sartre's aesthetics, then, when that topic invited too much absurd criticism from the philosophy department, on Sartre's feud with Albert Camus. So I kept asking him questions, which he apparently quite enjoyed, though we inevitably discussed politics more than aesthetics or Camus (indeed, I eventually switched to writing my dissertation on revolutionary theory for my Ph.D. at the London School of Economics).

It was at one of these discussions, upstairs at the Falstaff bar, off Montparnasse Boulevard, that at the age of twenty-three I behaved like a wise-ass punk. I arrogantly told Sartre that he would never be able to combine his philosophy, Existentialism, with Marxism, which he was vehemently trying to do, unless he gave up his notion of "man's project," which was at the heart of his philosophy of free will. When he finally did agree and abandoned Marxism, I apparently gained his trust, at least on political matters.

Since I had written a few articles here and there with many direct quotes from Sartre, Russell assumed that I had easy access to him, and on December 23, 1966, he called me in New York while I was decorating a Christmas tree with my six-year-old daughter Nina, and asked me if I wanted to go to North Vietnam with the first investigating committee, which was leaving Paris on December 26. How could I refuse? In that case, Russell asked, on the way could I please stop in Paris and persuade Sartre to join the tribunal as its president?

I saw Sartre on that Christmas day. We talked for almost two hours without a resolution. Finally he said, "OK, you've done your duty. You spelled out every possible argument. Now, as a friend, tell me why you are abandoning your family at Christmas to join this ersatz tribunal and travel to North Vietnam."

"You're right, it won't do any good politically worldwide," I answered. "But I'm going because the Vietnamese are the victims. They need to know—even if it doesn't stop a single U.S. bomb—that we are with them, that people like you, Sartre, and Russell, and Dave Dellinger [an influential American pacifist] are on their side, that we know the United States is the aggressor and that the Vietnamese people are the courageous victims fighting for their freedom. That's why I'm going, even if the biased press of America and England never carry a word of this, yes, ersatz, tribunal."

Sartre smiled, then said, "OK, good reason, count me in."

That was the greatest moment I spent with him.

But there were many others, some not so great. In 1970, no longer a professional journalist and blacklisted from an academic job in the United States because of my antiwar activities, I was teaching at the University of Paris VIII, Vincennes, and talked politics every Sunday over lunch with Sartre and Beauvoir at the noisy, degenerating art-nouveau Montparnasse restaurant La Coupole or at La Palette, a more quiet one a block away. On one such occasion, a rude yokel managed to dodge the protective waiters and approach our table to ask Sartre when was he going to continue his autobiography. Sartre had indeed started to tell his own story in *The Words,* but it went up only to age thirteen. He had no intention of going further. By the end of our lunch, however, as I described in *Jean-Paul Sartre: Hated Conscience of His Century,* I had agreed to write his biography, and Sartre had handwritten out an exclusivity contract-letter.

We began our conversations for his biography in November 1970 and kept them up, on and off, for four academic years, through 1974, meeting in his apartment every Friday, with numerous updates at random intervals after my union lawyers won my trial and got me reinstated in academia in the States. Our talks were often heated arguments, sometimes so belligerently discordant that I feared the project would end.

Once, after I published an article in the prestigious French yearly magazine *Obliques* claiming that his relationship with my father had to deteriorate since he surely felt extremely guilty about not being more active during the Spanish Civil War, Sartre actually shouted at me that he had never felt guilty about anything in his whole life, and that I would never understand the real meaning of literature. Another time, when I defended then-president Charles de Gaulle because, I said, he was the only conservative world ruler who wanted the United States out of NATO since its goal was to dominate the world, he sort of called me a "reactionary pimp" like de Gaulle ("vous n'allez pas devenir un macreau réac comme lui?"). He hated de Gaulle with a rabid passion, and he punished me the following Friday by pinning a note on his door saying: "I had to go to the dentist. I think."

But we always made up, or rather ignored our previous disagreements, and continued to have lunch together every Sunday, usually with Beauvoir and my girlfriend, Catherine. It was at one of these lunches that I had my worst moment with Sartre. For a few years I had been living with Catherine, a beautiful, warm, sympatica student who had absolutely no interest in Sartre's philosophy but liked to tease him about his enormous appetite (though he never gained weight), and argue with him about the current cinema. Once, when we were all staying at the house near Nîmes, in the South of France, that Sartre had bought for Arlette, his adopted daughter, and Arlette and I had gone shopping, we returned to find Sartre and Catherine on all fours staring at the ground.

"Did you know," Sartre explained contentedly, "that ants always greet each other by bumping heads and then go to their left to pass?"

"Does that prove that nature is left-wing?" quipped Catherine mischievously.

So when, for lunch at La Palette months later, I showed up late, and obviously shook up, Sartre asked, "Where's *la petite*?" That was what he always called her, because she was half an inch shorter than he (five feet). I hesitated. Beauvoir noticed my teary eyes and said so. "We broke up," I finally admitted.

Sartre looked hard at my face through his walleyes, then said: "Well, I envy you. I have never cried for a woman in my life."

Beauvoir was crushed. Sartre sensed it, so he quickly tried to explain: "When Castor and I decided to have what you call an open relationship, we realized that passion inevitably leads to possessiveness and jealousies. So, as you know, we decided that our relationship would be 'necessary' but that we would be free to have others, which we called 'contingent.' That demanded that we eliminate passion, the kind of hard emotions which often manifest themselves with tears. But now I realize . . . well, I envy you—you can cry at forty, and I never have at seventy."

I could see that Beauvoir was suffering deeply. Obviously, she had often shed a tear for her lover, Sartre or another, and obviously was hurt that he had not.

It was extremely painful for me, too. Especially because by then Catherine was part of my setup with Sartre. She didn't transcribe the conversations I had with him; that was done by a professional. But she corrected the names, described the places Sartre mentioned that I knew nothing about, took me to some of them, and told me stories, hers or what her parents had said, about the events Sartre described, making them so much more human. She used to mark with a green felt pen, on the copy of the transcriptions, one set of which I kept, the sections that interested her most, and they were indeed the most fascinating. She was always eager to listen to the tapes, especially because Sartre and I had agreed not to dwell on his philosophy. "Let's let the academicians do that," Sartre said, betraying his contempt for that breed, which spent a lifetime dissecting the works of others. "So we'll focus on the lived [*le vivant*]," I quipped.

"*D'accord,*" he had agreed.

My interviews with Sartre, therefore, were more like conversations. I was and am a political animal, an internationalist, especially a third-worldist. I had traveled all over the world, usually as a journalist, often as an anti-imperialist militant, inevitably also as an ordinary tourist. Sartre had probably traveled as much, but as a celebrity, met at the airport by high officials, accompanied by translators. By the time our conversations began, I had published a dozen books on Latin America, Vietnam, the Spanish Civil War, and, with a friend, the firm connection between organized crime and capitalism in the United States. Sartre had written literature, plays, essays, novels, and his brilliant autobiography of his youth, *The Words,* and won the Nobel Prize for it. We brought our baggage with us to the table.

But, without being Marxists, we had one indisputable fact in common. We agreed that, no matter what the pragmatic scholastics ranted, no matter what almost every American high school teacher droned into the heads of their gullible students, no matter how often the fat cats of the developed world shouted that they care about the poor, that everyone benefits from the wealth of the few (the trickle-down theory), the world is at war, a class war: the poor versus the rich. And we agreed that until the poor can rise up and expropriate the wealth of the rich, and then distribute it equally to all, the class war will be a shooting war, periodically at least.

So our task was not to discern who did what or when. But why. We would search for the political causes of our actions ("our" because Sartre hoped to gain insights into my father's behavior by probing into my own reactions). We would stick to the existential motto that the personal is political, and the political is always personal. Under no circumstance, Sartre and I agreed, would we rehash what he had so eloquently written in *The Words*. Except if I thought that he had lied, as he sometimes had. I had committed myself to write his political biography—to describe the roads he traveled on that led him to become, as I named the book, the Hated Conscience of His Century. Our conversations were to give me the tools for understanding both—that is, why he was hated and why he remains the conscience of the world's students, intellectuals, and militants.

Our conversations amounted to seventy-odd cassettes, quickly transferred to a dozen top-quality professional reels and transcribed to more than two thousand single-spaced, legal-size pages. Obviously much that we talked about is now redundant, repetitious, even incoherent, and often refers to incidents that no longer interest either the academician or the fidgety reader. So in translating our conversations I have edited those parts out. Some of the events mentioned, however, were, and perhaps still are, historically important. If they need explanations, I have added these as notes. And I have added bits of dialogue that took place at our lunches, for which I have notes jotted down after we parted, carefully gone over by Catherine (until that fateful day when we split up), but no tapes. For those who are curious about what I have cut out or added, or who don't trust me, or who just want to hear Sartre's forceful basso voice, all the original reels and all the unedited transcriptions are available at the Beinecke Library of Yale University, which bought them from me the year I came back from Europe, penniless and unemployed.

I have separated the conversations herewith under monthly headings, but that is not totally accurate because our conversations were not chronological. We would talk about a particular subject one month, then sometimes come back to it many months later. So I have often combined and included them under the month in which the most important part took place. The researcher who wants to hear the original must do as I did: listen to all the tapes (or read all the transcripts), jot down the subject and attribute to it a number, and then piece them together. It means a lot of work; it did to me. But the result is worth it: a more or less chronological document of a great literary figure's life and interpretation of his times.

Talking with Sartre

November 1970

GERASSI: How young were you when you first realized that you were different from your friends, your peers and classmates? Your father was dead. Your maternal grandfather—who was the master of the house, the bearded titan who played god in the local school production, the benevolent tyrant who treated your mother as your sister, even made you share a room with her in his house—must have colored your vision of the world very early.

SARTRE: Yes and no. His care, his appreciation of my literary fantasies—I spent all my free time at home reading and writing adventure "novels," which he assiduously read—his devotion to "his children," me and my mother, certainly made me feel important. But not different. At school, I was no more of a standout than any of my mates. At eleven-thirty, when we broke for lunch, my mother came to fetch me just like the other mothers, but after the afternoon session, at three-thirty, I dallied in the streets like the others. We played football in the streets and became sort of a gang, which often got us into fights with the kids from the other schools.

You told me those other kids were poor, from bad neighborhoods. Did that inject a notion of class war in your battles?

No. It's true, as you know, that rich kids live in rich neighborhoods, which means that their local school will be fancier. That's not because the government will give them more money. In France, where education is centralized, every school is allocated an equal amount per student, unlike your schools in America where, you tell me, schools depend on property taxes, hence have a built-in class structure. Still, in France as everywhere, rich kids live in rich neighborhoods. Mothers often don't work, and they devote some of their time, and money, to making the school more attractive, better decorated, sponsoring plays and concerts and whatnot. In poor neighborhoods, mothers work, and fathers don't have time or the inclination to ask their kids how they're doing, or to scold them if the headmaster reports that their children misbehaved. So in that sense there was a very marked class distinction between our street gangs. But when you fight an opponent over turf, turf that neither could claim anyway, the opponents are sort of equal—enemies, yes, but equal fighters, so to speak. So while I went to school in Paris, despite my background and family situation, I never felt different or class conscious.

Despite the fact that your lycée then, Henri IV, was one of the best.

True, but we all roamed Paris as we wished. (Streets were safe then.) The others might have felt class antagonisms, but we didn't, and they didn't insult us by yelling Hey Richies! or whatever.

But when your mother got remarried to an engineer and you moved to La Rochelle, that must have changed things.

And how. But not because of class. First of all I was a Parisian, and they hated Parisians. The nifty kids from the capital. Sure, that was a class distinction, but neither they nor I felt it that way. I was an outsider. And don't forget, I switched in the middle of the school year. My classmates simply did not like me. But they were bourgeois kids too. What made things worse is that I soon became a very good student because I had read more than they did. That was mainly because Charles [Schweitzer], my grandfather, had constantly suggested that I read such-and-such a book, and when he read my "novels" he'd make comparisons to some other major author. While always praising me, mind you. The result at La Rochelle was that I became the teacher's pet in literature class. Boy, did my classmates tease me for that. But we were all the same class. Not rich-rich. Those went to private schools, religious schools. We never fought them since we never saw them. I say "we" because when it came to fighting, I was part of the gang. Only for fighting.

With sticks or just fists?

Not even. Just a lot of pushing and slapping. No one got really hurt. But when the fights were over, I was ostracized by my classmates for a long time, maybe a whole year. Our battles were with the kids from the other schools, and they were mostly bourgeois, too. Not like in America, I guess, where you had both classes in the same school, yes?

By and large. The very rich also go to private schools. But growing up in my neighborhood, on the Upper West Side of Manhattan, was a mixture. I was obviously a bourgeois kid. Yet I ended up roaming around with the poor kids, especially the foreigners, in part because, like them, I was constantly attacked as a dirty foreigner with a funny accent. I used to come home in tears with my clothes torn, but Fernando always reacted by asking me if I had fought back and how. One day, I'll never forget it, I came home in tatters, bleeding, and hurting, but laughing, and Fernando, before asking me what happened, immediately congratulated me.

That's a very important difference. You grew up a rebel. You had the subjective experience of the class struggle, even if at the time your enemies were racial, sort of, anti-foreigners, and when you went home, your father put it in an objective perspective. I had none of that. Both at Henri IV in Paris, where most of us were children of bureaucrats or functionaries—Charles after all was a teacher, of German—and in La Rochelle, where most families had something to do with the sea and the port, but not as fishermen, as some kind of administrators, there was no class antagonism. I was never a rebel. You said so yourself when you insisted that you would try to answer, in your biography of me, how a solid bourgeois who never rebelled against his class could end up a revolutionary. And that's true. Whatever contradictions in society I discerned, I got from noting the difference between what people said and what they did. But I have never fought or actually even been with proletarians, and my life has always been fundamentally bourgeois.

Yet your reading and writing were acts of rebellion, weren't they?

Not quite. It's complicated. You see, my mother and grandmother wanted me to read childish books, you know, the kind of books normal ten-year-olds read, and they tried to get Charles to impose better habits for me. And Charles knew that the "novels" I wrote were all derivative, inspired by what I read, and mind you, rarely understood. Certainly when I read *Madame Bovary* at ten—or was it eight?—I understood nothing. But I took out of it some thread, which I then composed into one of my tales. Theoretically my whole family disapproved. But I knew that my mother took the notebooks— each "novel" was one school notebook—and gave them to Charles, supposedly as proof of my weirdness. Charles read them carefully and even corrected my grammatical and spelling mistakes. And indeed, I guess, to some extent, I wrote them for him, knowing of course that he disapproved. In sum, my whole family disapproved of my reading—not everything, mind you, since I also read everything that [Michel] Zévaco and [Pierre] Ponson du Terrail wrote, and these popular writers, though basically anarchists, appeared weekly in the local press, with garish illustrations. Nor did they like my "novels," but I knew that they actually admired me for writing them.

That's your childhood at home, but it clashes severely with your life outside.

Complicated. Charles convinced me that I was special, a prodigy, without ever saying so of course. That meant I was special. But out in the world, only gods like Charles would be able to see what I was. To everyone else, I was, well, like everyone else.

You said that as a child you were convinced that the world was perfectly balanced, that everything was in order, stable, established. Isn't that contradicted by the fact that when you wanted to play with the other kids in the park at Luxembourg Gardens, you were unceremoniously told to beat it, so much that your mother intervened and asked the other parents to help? Not so well ordered after all.

Hold on. I objectified the situation. These kids were used to each other and were in the habit of playing together. Without me. So the order of things meant that I was not of that group. At Henri IV it was different. They knew me and I knew them, so I was part of their group. Those kids in the Luxembourg didn't turn me down because I was small or ugly, but because I was not of their group.

But in *The Words* [Sartre's autobiography] you admit to feeling frustrated, rejected. Why didn't that make you understand that you were different?

It did, in a way. It reaffirmed the fact that I was a prodigy. That, Charles had firmly established. At home I was the center. My grandfather was extremely authoritarian, but not with me. Why? Because I was a prodigal boy. In the Luxembourg, I was nothing, and that was normal. And in school too, at the beginning. When I entered high school in La Rochelle (I was twelve or thirteen), I was a very bad student because my classmates didn't realize that I was brilliant. So bad, in fact that my mother had to have a chat with both my French and Latin teachers, asking them to pay a bit of extra attention to me, which they did. That made everything normal, in order again. But Charles was

not around at La Rochelle. Still, I had the same reaction as when I tried to join the group in the park. They were a unit, I was an outsider. That was normal.

Really? On the one hand you spend your time reading books and writing stories of which Charles and the two women in your house disapprove. That's an act of rebellion, yet you want Charles's approval and admiration. On the other hand, you get rejected by your peers, which you admit is hurtful, but you think that's normal. It doesn't jibe.

Didn't you do the same? Castor told me of a session you and Fernando and she had in New York where you argued with her for two hours, pushing your Marxist view on her, while your father, who was always anti-, or at least non-Marxist, simply listened, not saying a word—very rare for Fernando—whose approval you wanted.

Oh yes, I remember that well, but I was older, fifteen. It was at the Menemsha Bar on Fifty-seventh Street. I had problems dealing with Fernando, the man of action. So I had taken the opposite stance: read, study, talk, argue, but no action. That was my rebellion. I wanted his approval at the same time that I was taking a point of view opposed to his. And when he told me later that evening that I had not argued it very well, it hurt.

So there you have it. You rebelled and wanted his approval. A contradiction? Not at all.

But you're claiming that you never rebelled against Charles.

That's right, I didn't have to. Unlike Fernando with you, Charles had convinced me I was special.

Yet you then became fascinated by what he was not, a man of action. So you focused on the only friend you had who was one, Fernando. That's why, of all your friends, Fernando was the only one you went way out of your way to see. Like when you traveled to the South of France whenever he came across the border, and that fascinating conversation you, represented by Mathieu [in *The Roads to Freedom*], had with Gomez, who is Fernando. Why, Mathieu asks Gomez, are you going back to fight when you know the war is lost?

That was a question of logic.

Not quite, since you have Gomez answering Mathieu so politically on the button that one fights fascism not because one is going to win but because fascism is the ideology of fascists.

That's what your father did say.[1]

But you chose to repeat it because you knew it was what a committed man of action would say, and because you, as Mathieu, was guilty of not having been a man of action.

But Mathieu does become a man of action.

Not quite. He ends up in the army and goes through the routine of being a soldier, eventually a prisoner, like you, but uncommitted, simply because France is at war and you, Mathieu, are French. That's not the same as volunteering to fight in another country and—as you asked me when I was going to North Vietnam, proving that such an act still troubles you, "Why are you abandoning wife and child?"

Hold on. First of all, your father was Spanish, even if he was born in Constantinople and was twenty-seven when he first went to Spain to copy Velázquez at the Prado. Spanish, or Ladino, was his native tongue, and he certainly had the character of a Spanish anarchist. Second, Mathieu may not have been a committed revolutionary before the war, but he certainly had a social conscience, and he gains commitment when he discovers the collective in the stalag.

Come on, that's not the same thing. Neither you, nor Mathieu, had to face the reality of having to kill a human being, no matter how terrible that being may be. And when Mathieu gets discharged from the stalag he reverts to his usual habits, writing at the café, like you.

You're approaching the dilemma of commitment from the wrong angle. The point I was raising in that conversation between Mathieu and Gomez was abandoning the real commitment of an artist—in other words, how can a writer or a painter give up his or her calling, even for a just war?

You're referring to Fernando's letter to Stépha [Fernando's wife, my mother], whom he left behind to go to fight in Spain?

That was crucial, absolutely crucial. He had sent her a letter saying, "I am not an artist. An artist does not kill. I have just killed a man. Forget me." He was right. That's why Picasso told you in 1954 that your father would be as famous as he if he had not gone to Spain.

Did you know that Fernando had written such a letter to Stépha when you wrote *The Roads to Freedom*?

She showed it to me before she went to Spain herself to work in the propaganda bureau.

But you didn't use it in the novel.

It was too melodramatic, typical of Fernando.

But you remained fascinated with my father.

He was the only friend I had who was like me, or so I had assumed. I once heard him say, "First I paint, then my family. I don't care if Stépha and Tito starve, first I paint." [Tito is my nickname.] That was how I felt then too, even though I had no family: first I write. Castor felt the same way. That's probably why neither of us ever even thought of having a family. And then here comes one of our closest friends, who always claimed to have the same commitment to his art that we had to ours, who goes off just like that, with no suitcase, no change of clothes, to war. Do you know that when I brought you home to Stépha and explained, she became hysterical and started repeating, "But he was wearing silk socks," silk socks, over and over.

Was there a connection in your mind, do you think now looking back, between Gomez and Pardaillan, Zévaco's swashbuckling hero, whom you had so admired—more, revered—as a child? And you put Charles in there too, the towering man of action, although he was not one, was he?

Correct. I really am not sure what he was. That's why I did not define him in *The Words*. To this day, I wonder. I know he was afraid of death. I think that's why he played that comedy of loving me so much. He wanted to accept everything, nature, life, death, but he needed something else to make him accept death as normal, and that was me, so he played it out, a role, to convince himself that I would be his extension, his survival so to speak, or his continuation after he died. So in fact he was the very opposite of the man of action.

Was he that tormented, that riddled with anxiety about death that he hoped to turn you into his extension in life?

I don't think he ever understood or came to terms with his monsters. But I must have picked up the vibes, and in trying to be like him, rejected the act of rebellion, discarded the notion of the man of action, although as you correctly said, I made him out to be one in *The Words*. That was wrong. He was a voyeur.

And so were you, no? Despite your battles with other kids in the streets of Paris. For all your denials, you too were afraid of death. Which is why you said that one writes for god or for others but not to be read. In other words, you wrote to cheat death because you were afraid too. Or better put: you wrote to avoid death. You wrote to gain eternity.

And that's why I was fascinated by your father, who became the very opposite, not the least bit afraid of death.

You're wrong. There's a wonderful passage in [Ilya] Ehrenburg's memoirs where he visits Fernando at the siege of the Alcazar of Toledo. Fernando guides him to the top of a building with a very slippery tile roof, from which they could indeed see the children playing inside, behind the walls, which is why Fernando had refused to bombard the fortress. Then Ehrenburg notices that Fernando is white as a sheet and shaking. "It's one thing to die in battle," Fernando explains; "it's an incredible stupidity to die falling off a roof."

Ah yes, Fernando the macho anarchist.

No, that absurd Spanish sense of honor, of pride, if you wish, but also a wonderful notion that death must make sense. But fear of death nonetheless.

Fear of death perhaps, but not fear of being forgotten.

Quite. And that's what Charles feared, and passed on to you.

But let's not scoff at that. Such a fear is what makes us become creative, or do-gooders, or men of action. It's all a way of ending up as more than the few years we roam this planet.

And you certainly said exactly that in that wonderful story "Erostrate," where your hero, noting that no one remembers who built the temple of Ephèse that he burnt down, decides to murder six people at random to create such an absurd event that no one will ever forget him. But your examples are not equal. Of the sixty thousand non-Spanish anti-fascists, volunteers of the International Brigades, who went to Spain to fight Franco, Hitler, and Mussolini, at least half were under fake names with no traceable ID. The world would never know who they were, and those volunteers knew that they would never be identified. They went to Spain, they fought, and they died because that's what a genuine humanist does. Period.

"One fights fascism because they are fascists."

Exactly.

That's why you went to North Vietnam, and sacrificed a happy marriage.

That's why you agreed to become the tribunal's president. And that's why you loved Zévaco's stories. His heroes always fought for the poor, the downtrodden, the exploited. And at formidable odds, twenty to one, thirty to one. But that's not Charles. Yet you admired him because, why? Because he was an atheist who played the role of god. And why didn't you love your mother? Mothers don't have to achieve greatness to be loved by their children; they simply have to be present.

She let herself be bullied by Charles. He would scold her, in front of me.

8

Don't do that. No that's wrong. Be quiet. And she would take it. But eventually, at La Rochelle, that changed. My mother had caught me stealing a bit of money from her purse. I was still trying to get my classmates to like me, and I stupidly thought that by buying candy and giving it to them, they would begin to like me. My mother not only caught me but, when Charles came to spend some time with us, told him about it. He would understand, I thought. He would be on my side. He said nothing then. But the next day, we went to the store together and he dropped a coin, which I rapidly bent down to fetch for him. With a great grandiloquent movement of his cape and cane he stopped me. You cannot touch honest money, he said, since you have become a thief. With his bones cracking, he then slowly, painfully I thought, bent down to pick up the coin. That was the rupture. He no longer was my defender. I never admired or mimicked him again. But that did not make me closer to my mother. She had betrayed me. She had married a man I didn't like. A graduate of [the Ecole] Polytechnique. She had taken me to a town I despised. And she had put me in a school where they hated me. Yet I could never tell her that I was unhappy. Why? Perhaps because until that day in the store—it was a pharmacy, I see it clearly still today—I had a solid rock behind me to make me understand that life was as it should be, and a mother that didn't count. Then, after being betrayed by god, by the rock, I was left with nothing. My mother ended up part and parcel of that package.

Was your stepfather that bad?

Objectively, not at all. He was the son of a railway station attendant, studious, determined. A man of duty. He drove himself to the top of his classes and got into one of the most prestigious institutions in France. The epitome of bourgeois achievement. And he was proud of it. Subjectively, he was a stuffed shirt. A bore who stole my sister (that is, my mother) and never considered me a prodigy. But he was not my father, so he didn't really count and I never rebelled against him.

My grandfather was a poseur, a fraud if you wish, but he made me think he admired me. Do you know that we communicated—until his betrayal, that is—by verse? Yes, verse. I wish I had all that to show you. Just imagine his patience and indulgence. To read my terrible poems, full of mistakes and cheating rhymes, and then bother to answer them in correct iambic pentameter!

At eight, ten, twelve? How did you get to that point?

No, no, much younger. I guess I decided very early that since my god, and the two women in the house, read in their free time, reading must have a great value, so I started by making believe that I was reading. I would sit on a box or something imposing in front of the family and make like I was reading, turning pages, stuff like that. To save me from boredom, I would often invent stories in my head as I "read," which I derived from the illustrations that had accompanied Zévaco's or Ponson du Terrail's stories in the papers. That, too, I began by faking it, seeing that Charles always read all the newspapers, though not the stories mind you. Actually, I think he didn't really like or even approve of fiction, but he read the classics because "one should." So after a while of making believe, I began to decipher what I was not really reading, and in effect taught myself how to read. It was a case of having his values. Eventually I began to write my own stories, with heroes like Zévaco's Pardaillan, who of course was very much like Charles. My first "novel" was called *The Banana Merchant,* and the hero had a beard just like Charles. But there was one book that Charles adored and gave me with such fanfare that I knew he wanted me to like it. And I did, skipping pages of course, the pages that would bore any child. Victor Hugo's *Les Misérables.* And of course it has its Pardaillan, right? Namely, Jean Valjean. I wonder why I didn't include *Les Misérables* in the list I gave you of what I read then. Strange. Funny that I would forget the most important book, yes?

Take it up with [Jacques] Lacan when you see him next.[2]

Are you kidding? He'd love it, but I'll never give him that satisfaction.

By making you read *Les Misérables,* was your grandfather trying to begin to edge you into some kind of political consciousness?

Oh, no—well, maybe somewhat. It never occurred to me, but now that I think about it, he never objected to Zévaco, even if he didn't read the weekly installments. He knew very well who he was, and that he was an anarchist. Pardaillan—meaning of course Zévaco—used to say, "I am superior to no one." But of course he was. Yet I accepted that notion, which was immediately confronted, in effect, when my cousins showed up. Charles treated them differently. He was not pleasant with them. I didn't like them much either, but I felt it was unjust for Charles to discriminate, since we were all equal. They were part of large families. So it didn't matter what Charles thought about them, or the way he talked to them. But it made me conscious that I did not have such a family. I think it is very important for a child to have a father, good or bad. I didn't have one. Charles may have been a god, but he certainly was not my father. So I lived basically in solitude. Yet I was happy because I was spoiled. I would say to myself what luck to be born in France with

such grandparents and a mother. Of course, it didn't quite click. I knew I was being judged by others, folks outside my family, and they judged me according to what I did.

No Exit? "Hell is other people"?

Exactly.

And Charles is really an extension of yourself in your eyes.

Precisely, and since I know that I'm a fraud, he's a fraud, and I don't respect him for that. Yet I admire him. Some contradiction, eh?

Is that the root of your insecurity?

Complicated. I think I am insecure precisely because Charles treats me differently than he treats my cousins, other children. Sure I want to be special, sure I revel in the fact that Charles and my immediate family think I'm special, sure no one, including me, understands that Charles treats me that way because he's afraid of death, and wants me to be him by extension after his death. But something's wrong. Is it because I am alone, I mean a child in a family of adults? Is it because my sense of equality, derived from Zévaco, jars my reality? Can one become enamored with the concept of liberty, equality, fraternity, just from reading?

Tough question, because the idea of solidarity that is the basis of liberty, equality, fraternity, is a gut feeling—it's what made us socialists without ever knowing what the word meant. It's what disturbed you when you saw that Charles did not treat your cousins as he treated you. No capitalist-in-the-making would think that strange. If he was on the up side of that difference he'd be pleased. On the down side, jealous.

Absolutely. Yet at the same time that I thought I should be equal to my cousins, I also knew that they had a more integrated family structure and, on the other hand, that I was superior. That said, I was aware that there were students in my class who said things much more interesting than anything I could say. But that did not affect my profound conviction that there was no original difference between people. That's an emotional conviction. Like you said in your article in *Les Temps Modernes* [a monthly magazine started by Sartre and Simone de Beauvoir and others in 1945 and edited by Sartre; it is still being published], if you have an IQ of 20 and I have an IQ of 120, our experiences are nevertheless equivalent. [The article Sartre is referring to was called "Revolution by Lifestyle," or "Vivre la révolution" in French, and was published in the June–July 1969 issue of *Les Temps Modernes.*] Without that understanding, no one can be a genuine socialist. Do you know that in 1955

when I was in China, Chou En-lai said that the notion of equality is a petit bourgeois notion. That really shocked me. I guess party communists must believe that, so as to justify their central committees running everyone's lives. It's very hard for people to understand that equality does not mean that we are all as intelligent; it means that our joy, our pain, our need to be relevant, are equal.

So where did we get this notion of equality? Was Charles political?

Charles voted Radical-Socialist. That was a centrist but anticlerical party that was the mainstay of the bourgeoisie.

You say that in *The Words,* namely that he voted for a conservative party thinking it was for progress. But that didn't influence you, did it? First of all, you remained totally apolitical before the war. And second, when you began to get interested in politics, you were not a real leftist—I mean you were an armchair leftist.

True. Despite Fernando's pressure, I never joined the Writers and Artists Committee Against Fascism, or against the war. Whatever its title. And I was never very active.

Was that because those committees were run by communists?

Perhaps. Although [André] Malraux was the president of one of them, and your father was a member. He had come back from Spain violently anti-communist, didn't he? And that's why you were pro-communist at fourteen, yes?

I don't think so. Maybe. I knew that communists from all over the world had smuggled themselves to Spain to fight fascism. Unknown and unheralded heroes, in my mind.

But by the time you had a discussion about that with Castor in New York, you had witnessed that terrifying dinner with Ehrenburg, hadn't you? That should have made you anti-communist, or at least against the party. But no—why? Was that your rebellion against Fernando?

Perhaps. Yet I will never forget when Ilya Ehrenburg visited the United States as a correspondent for *Pravda,* in 1945, and spent all his time when he was in Manhattan with my parents. At one of the dinners, my mother asked him whatever happened to [Marcel] Rosenberg, the Soviet ambassador to the Spanish Republic, whom both my parents adored. Ehrenburg lowered his face and mumbled one word: "Stalin." Then my father asked about a Russian general who fought with the International Brigades. "Stalin." Then another. "Stalin." For at least an hour, name after name, the explanation was

"Stalin." My mother was crying. My father fighting tears. The dinner was, and is, so ingrained in my mind that I described it to every political friend I had. But also true I had been impressed by all those who had fought for the Republic and were communists, friends of my father since at one time he commanded the International Brigades. People like [Ales] Bebler, later Marshal [Josip Broz] Tito's foreign minister; [Henri] Tanguy, whose tank was the first into Paris in 1944; the Italian communists Luigi Longo and Palmiro Togliatti, and the pro-communist socialists Pietro Nenni, and especially Kantor and . . .

You mean [Alfred] Kantorowicz, the political commissar of the Thäl-mann Battalion, who wrote that great novel, *Chapayev*? But he defected.

Later, much later, and you know what Fernando said when an immigration agent, who was secretly CIA, asked him why Kantor would not talk to the West? Kantor had been vice minister of culture in the East German Communist government before defecting to Bonn. The CIA tried to grill him, but he would not say a word. So they asked Fernando, and he said: Because he is a real communist. That got Fernando harassed by the CIA for twenty years, despite the fact that he was a veteran of the OSS. He had been submarined into Spain to set up an underground to blow up bridges, roads, et cetera, should Franco allow the Germans to cross Spain to attack the Allies when they landed in Africa. When the war ended, the United States refused to legalize his status (he had arranged for us to come to the United States on fake diplomatic passports), so he could not legally work. Carmelita Hinton, the founder of Vermont's famed Putney School and a co-founder of Women's Strike for Peace, hired my parents and at first paid them on an honorarium basis, which was legal, but my parents had to report every month to a so-called immigration officer, but really CIA agent, until their friend the sculptor Alexander Calder asked his pal Abe Fortas, then a close aide to President [Lyndon B.] Johnson, to intervene. Fortas got Bobby Kennedy, then attorney general, to demand the files from INS, which turned out to be at CIA because they were blackmailing him, trying to get him to work for them, which he would not do. Apologizing "in the name of America," Bobby got my parents citizenship by executive order in 1964.

Still, to stay pro-communist after that dinner with Ehrenburg can only be explained as a way of rejecting your father's convictions.

Maybe. But then your praise, in effect, of Zévaco's anarchism was a rejection of Charles's "humanism."

Hold on. First, there's the age difference. As brilliant as I may have been, ha-ha, I certainly did not understand in political terms the difference between collective action led by a party and the work of a single individual against the bad guys in society. Charles was king, emperor, dictator, true, but like every respectable bourgeois, in awe and praise of France's revolution, exemplified by liberty, equality, fraternity. Neither he nor most bourgeois adherents to humanism understood that there can never be liberty, equality, or fraternity without socialism. That allowed him to think that Pardaillan was a good guy fighting for his own brand of humanism. Don't forget, he never read Zévaco. Still, he couldn't object since my stories always ended with society being better off, like in Zévaco, with less poverty, the good guys in power, the bad ones in jail. So I certainly was not rebelling against him or his notion of democracy, and he didn't take it as such.

So where or what began your understanding that bourgeois humanism was a cover-up for domination by one class over another?

Very hard to say. I have to try to figure out—just when did I realize that not only was my life at home a series of comedies, in the sense of play-acting, but also that I didn't like them? When did I realize that I wanted to be with my peers, my classmates, my comrades? Because to be with comrades is to be equal. The trouble is that the reverse side of the coin of that realization was that I felt lonely at home, or rather that I was conscious that I was alone, since loneliness is a state of mind whereas alone is a fact, and if I was lonely, I got out of it by writing. Charles didn't care that I was alone. I don't think he ever thought of it. But the women, my mother and grandmother, kept saying "that boy is alone too much, he needs friends."

And friends, of course, meant comrades, and there can be no superior or inferior among comrades. Comrades mean equals.

That's all in Paris. But at thirteen you move to La Rochelle, where you have no comrades, and your peers ostracize you. So then what? What happens to your notion of equality?

Everything changes there. First there's my mother's betrayal, her remarriage, which is why we move to that city in the first place. Then there's Charles's betrayal over the coin. Then there's my grandmother's death. That triggers an important revelation, because I was very fond of her. We used to play piano together. Stuff like that. But when she died I was totally neutral. She was eighty-two. But that's not the explanation. I simply do not put death into a living context. In other words, I disassociate death from life. I've done that all my life. I have been seriously criticized for that too, like when [Claude] Lanzmann's sister died. [Evelyne Lanzmann, an actress who went by the stage name Evelyne Rey, became one of Sartre's mistresses in 1953. Sartre wrote the role of Johanna in his play *The Condemned of Altona* for her. She committed suicide in 1966, shortly after Sartre broke off their affair.] When I was told she had killed herself, I had a short asthma attack, but then nothing. Since I am absolutely certain that after one's death there's nothing, I cannot grieve. Now, is that because I have identified my survival with my literature, even though intellectually I know that's all meaningless? Let the shrinks debate that. For me, it's simple: death is nothingness, hence not part of life, so I do not think of death.

But you did, when you wrote in *The Words* about your father's death. In fact I have it here, I underlined it: "He loved, he wanted to live, he saw himself die. That's enough to make a man total." Aren't you making a value judgment there on how one dies?

But the way one dies means one is still existing.

So why did you take dying—not death, dying—out of *Being and Nothingness?*

That was a mistake. I was writing against [Martin] Heidegger then, because he claimed that life is a mere delay, a reprieve, in one's own death. I was trying to explain that life is a series of projects, and projects do not encompass death, so why mention it? Think of death, and the project is destroyed. Philosophy is the imitation of life, as [Baruch] Spinoza said, not the other way around.

So, as you wrote, since books don't die, to read is to be an optimist?

Exactly.

So, since you write books, *you* won't die.

Precisely.

So, loneliness, or solitude rather, depression, being ostracized, all that disappears when one writes.

Correct. And the product is a rarity. That's why in its survival it is life itself. Everything is rare. Air, land, water, production, consumption, matter, space, all rare. The book then personifies life, as immortal as matter or air.

So, if that is what we do when we write, copy life in effect, then life is absurd.

Of course life is absurd, since it is made up of rarities.

The more absurd, then, the more death is intolerable.

So ignore it. Make another project, which by definition excludes death.

Besides volume four of *Flaubert,* what are the projects that will exclude your thinking of death? [Sartre published a three-volume biographical study of the French novelist, titled *The Family Idiot: Gustave Flaubert, 1821–1857,* in 1971. He was working on a fourth volume, which he never finished.]

Ha! Projects don't exclude death—projects are the antithesis of death. That's an important difference. The project is an act. Writing is an act. My projects right now: the next part of the *Critique of Dialectical Reason.* Then I think I want to write my political testament.

But to come back to my question about your consciousness of equality, where is it in your projects? And in La Rochelle, where your comrades hate you and ostracize you. And in any case, writing as an act is solitary; where does your notion of solidarity fit in?

Don't mix different stages. First of all, whether my classmates hate me or not does not change the fact that in La Rochelle, after being betrayed by Charles and my mother, I am aware very quickly that my enemies are my equals because they judge me by what I do. Writing may be a solitary act, but it posits solidarity because it responds to the society we live in. Good or bad, the book is in play, so to speak. And whether the author wrote it out of ambition, vengeance, fear, whatever, determines the author, not the book. And writing it is like any other project—building a house, murdering one's neighbor, stealing a best friend's wife, whatever.

There's nothing special about that act in itself; its value is determined by others. People talk of talent after the fact. But talent is drawing the chair to the table.

If it's an act like any other, why did you choose writing?

To feel superior. Superiority eliminates culpability.

You felt guilty that you were human?

Not guilty, which is defined after the fact, but culpable, which implies conscious responsibility. Every human is culpable. That's why he fears death. To avoid that fear one must be superior. And superiority comes only in total commitment to the act. Or, better put, to be one's project.

I smell the original sin. Is the "project" faith?

Not bad. Now you see why Christianity is so powerful. Everyone is a sinner. How to live with that? By total commitment to god. Right? No. If that was the escape, the church would lose all its faithful. So it introduces the mystery, the dogma that no one can be sure of salvation, no matter how good and hon-

orably one lives. That solves the question of why did that innocent child next to me get hit by the stray bullet while I went unscathed. If one cannot predict god's ways, one can never be saved, or committed, hence we all stay sinners. And as sinners we dread what will happen after we die. We remain frightened. Very nicely done. But it doesn't work with those who do not fear death. And they don't fear death because they are totally committed to their act, their project.

OK, so why did you choose writing instead of being a gangster?

Upbringing. Family. Class. Education.

If only those who are totally their project do not fear death because that totality makes them superior, why don't I fear death?

You're a writer.

Not your kind. I write to battle, to change the world, not to gain immortality. I see writing like you define your love life: some are necessary, some are contingent. My novel, which I wrote when I was seventeen and was never published, thank god, was necessary. *The Great Fear* [a book I wrote about Latin America] was contingent.

Very good. I like that. But your *Great Fear* was total commitment to battle, like your father going to fight in Spain. He wasn't afraid of death then, just as before, painting away in his studio, he wasn't afraid then either. The commitment is what makes each of us in our way immortal, then and there, now and here, with each project. And that's just as true for the gangster as it is for the philosopher. The value? That is decided by others, by society. It has nothing to do with death, or immortality.

What about the writer who writes for god? Like [Claude] Mauriac?

When Mauriac writes, he is immortal and, believe me, does not even think of his death, no matter how much he writes about it. He may tell you afterward that he wrote god's will, but that's afterward, when he is searching for salvation instead of living it.

So the totally committed who commit suicide, who obviously are not afraid of death, reflect a failed project?

It's more complicated. First of all, there's the gesture. A gesture is done for others. A statement. I don't think most suicides really expect to die. [The communist author Michel] Leiris, for example. He was absolutely decided, supposedly, since he had saved a barbiturate from each prescription his doctor gave him, for years, and then, ten years ago, he decided the time had come. He took all that he had saved. Then he laid down next to his wife, who

was waiting for him to go to sleep. But he said, "I think I took a bit too many barbiturates." She called a neighbor and rushed him to the hospital, where they pumped him out. Why did he tell his wife? He gave himself one last chance. They had both drunk a lot that night, so he could have fallen asleep perfectly normally, and she would not have been suspicious. But even the ones who kill themselves alone. They're calling out. Unless of course they're suffering terribly. Like from cancer. But that's a different issue completely.

In the case of [Catherine] Von Bulow, who tried to commit suicide "because she had no way out" of the relationship she was having with an older but very rich and powerful man, Claude Gallimard, your publisher. After I got her to the hospital and she was OK, the doctor asked me if she had tried before. "You know," he said, "it's a myth that those who talk about wanting to commit suicide don't really try it. Eventually, they talk themselves into it."[3]

Suicides are people who judge life, who think it has a value or message or purpose, and for some reason they are not in the soup [an expression of Sartre's that means fully engaged, down in the trenches, getting one's hands dirty]. Life is a fact. It has no value in itself. It's not even a question of accepting or not accepting it. It is, period. Those who are not their project seem unable to understand that. They expect this or that. And when it doesn't come out as they expect it, they judge it. Good or bad or whatever. I was once very close to someone who always expected something from life, as if life did or did not do, as if life was an active something. You know about her, yes? Lanzmann's sister. Were you with Von Bulow when she came to?

Yes.

What did she say?

"I'm sorry."

Perfect: a reaffirmation of life.

I thought life is, period. So what's this mystical-sounding "reaffirmation" bit?

Ha-ha-ha . . . just an expression. You're absolutely right: life has no value in itself, only to people. And that's relative to each circumstance.

Like de Gaulle. You hated him, we kinda liked him.

That's baffling to me. How can you have any respect for that antiquarian monarchist who thought he was a king? Anyway, his death seems to me totally unimportant, except that I like the fact that he died alone, playing solitaire.

For those of us who worry that the United States is trying to dominate the world, who know that the United States has a first-strike policy against Russia, which in turn did not, hence for us who worry that the United States is willing and is perfectly capable of starting World War III, which would destroy the planet, the fact that de Gaulle had similar worries and kicked NATO out of France was very significant.

He did that as a gesture, meaningless, propaganda.

When I was an editor at *Newsweek,* we had lunch one day with General [Pierre-Marie] Gallois, de Gaulle's chief of nuclear defense, what was called La Force de Frappe, and I asked him in French, which way were his missiles pointing? After asking me if anyone else at the table understood my question and I said no—actually I lied, since Kermit Lansner, the managing editor, spoke French fluently and in fact was a secret correspondent for *Le Nouvel Observateur* [a leftist weekly newsmagazine]—he made a gesture with his two hands showing that the missiles were pointing both ways—that is, at Russia and at the United States.

Hey, I don't want to accuse you of naïveté, but you can be sure that le Gallois knew that *Newsweek* was then liberal-left and wanted to impress you. De Gaulle's policy was always to appear nationalistic and independent. But it was baloney, pure propaganda, to get his reactionary party elected. France under de Gaulle gained a tremendous amount of American investments, so much that de Gaulle's economy depended on them. Forget the word, look at the facts, you know—like we say, It's what we do that matters.

Well, [Jean] Ripert once told me that de Gaulle had ordered him to prepare a plan for the total nationalization of the electrical industry, which was an American monopoly in France.[4] And nothing happened. So when Ripert asked de Gaulle why not, the old boy replied, because the left is not demanding it. "I was ready," he said, "but the left was not making it an issue."

That's true. Our left stinks. Always has. Just think back, how the socialists and communists supported the war in Algeria, even when the Algerian Communist Party was for Algerian independence and its leaders were being tortured by [General Jacques] Massu's goons.[5] But don't blame the left, as de Gaulle and, I guess, Ripert do. De Gaulle would never have nationalized the electrical industry. American pressure was too strong.

Still, remember when [British prime minister Harold] Macmillan stopped in Paris in February 1963 on his way to meet Kennedy in Barbados and asked de Gaulle, "What can I do to stop the United States from treating England as an obedient pawn?" De Gaulle answered: "Too late, England is an aircraft carrier for American goods."

Just words, no importance. Politicians are like people; it's what they do that matters.

You don't think that it was important that de Gaulle closed the U.S. bases in France, that he stopped the United States from being in charge of NATO in Europe, that he said: "No nation is free if it has some other nation's base on its soil!"

Bullshit! De Gaulle was a nineteenth-century royalist who thought he was the king. How could you stomach that "La Grandeur de la France" crap he spewed all the time? You really surprise me, Gerassi, falling for that shit.[6]

You don't think he understood the danger of America, that America wanted to dominate the whole world?

Damn it! Maybe. So what! He certainly didn't understand that America wanted to dominate it through trade, that it was all about money. You didn't have to put up with that pompous ass every day, since you were living in London then.

But you did keep coming to Paris, since we had lunch once a week. Paris really is your city, isn't it?

Absolutely. Like you. You too were born here, right?

Yes, but I left at eighteen months when my father died. My mother and I went to live with my grandparents in Meulon, where he taught German, then back to Paris, on rue Le Goff, as I described in *The Words*. My mother remarried when I was eleven. I remember she came with him to school to introduce him as "a man of great qualities." I didn't understand what she wanted, and he left the next day. She sat me on her knees and asked me if I had any objection to the three of us making a home together. I said no, but didn't mean it. In fact, I thought it was a betrayal right then and there. She had met him in Cherbourg, where my father, a naval officer, was stationed, and he was a naval engineer. I gather he was taken with my mother already then, and when he heard that she was a widow with a ten-year-old child, he showed up. She was obviously not in love with him, but she felt tremendous pressure to become independent from her parents. Charles had reached the age of retirement, but couldn't take care of us all materially. And this Mancy guy [Joseph Mancy, Sartre's stepfather] was now quite solvent. But my life changed drastically, and I resented my mother, not him. I didn't like him; he was big, very big, with

a black mustache and a big nose. He tried to make me good at math, which I hated, and once, because I had answered him curtly, and she had heard me, she came rushing out of the kitchen and slapped me. He didn't understand why. And I never forgot it.

Seems even today, your recollection is flavored with jealousy . . .

You have to understand. For ten years my mother belonged to me. My grandparents didn't have a big apartment, so we slept in the same room. I never saw her naked—she was always careful—but I did see the hair under her arms, and combined with drawings I saw, I ended up telling my classmates about pubic hair, without calling it that of course. She would take me to the Luxembourg, shopping, movies, you know, she was all mine. Then all that stopped. Mancy was nice with me and I didn't hold it against him, but she betrayed me, or at least betrayed the unwritten compact we had between us. And I changed. I became what school authorities call a "troublemaker." When Mancy was transferred to La Rochelle, she went with him and I stayed to finish that school semester in Paris. He had been . . . [At this point a nurse showed up, interrupting our talk. Although he was only sixty-five, Sartre was already suffering from all the amphetamines he had taken his whole adult life and needed to receive special injections once a month. After the nurse left, he continued.]

She's a real petit bourgeois. I gave her this book to read, *The Trial of Geismar,* with my preface, and I told her it was a book about the May '68 student rebellion, but she was shocked.

Why the shots?

I had dizzy spells during the vacation, and the doctors concluded that my veins had hardened somewhat, so the shots are to enlarge them.

The consequence of speed?

I guess. But even if it kills me tomorrow, it was worth it. I mean, I never slept more than four hours a day for the past forty years. If you add that up, it means I'm already ninety, consciously at least.

Anyway, as I was saying, Mancy had been a director of a joint that built ships, and then he was made boss of the outfit's operations in La Rochelle. I was badly received in that town. It's a hard place. Very Protestant and closed. I was seen as a stranger, and as a Parisian, as a ruffian. I tried to integrate myself, but without success. I tried to gain acceptance by yelling louder and more often than my classmates, and the professor would throw me out of class, which made my mother cry. You know the worst, when I tried to join a group that always played around the port. I went up to a group of four guys and one girl who was gorgeous. She was not in my class but I had seen her with some of my classmates many times and I was very attracted to her. So I said something to try an opening. Dead silence. They all stared at me, then she asked the others: "Who's this guy with one eye that says shit to the other?" As I turned and walked away, I heard them laugh like crazy.

Is that when you decided that you would have to seduce women by your intellectual brilliance and never by your looks?

Ha ha. Perhaps. But I reacted by becoming a thief. I stole money from my mother to buy candy, as a bribe to be accepted by my classmates. And I fought hard in the local battles.

School battles?

My lycée, which was a public school, against kids from the other schools. And to become part of the warriors I had to fight hard. But my main tactic was the bribes. And then came that disastrous theft of fifty francs, a lot of money then. Disastrous because I was caught. I was sure that Charles, who came to visit about then, would understand. That was my second betrayal. I now had two enemies, my mother and my grandfather, the only two people I had loved as a child.

But you didn't break with them?

Oh no. I pretended that nothing had happened, and my mother did the same. I needed some normalcy at home to offset my disgust and hatred of La Rochelle.

And you continued to write and read a great deal, right?

Mostly I read or reread my old favorites, Ponson du Terrail and Michel Zévaco . . .

The great swashbucklers, solitary heroes against the world, heh?

Yeah, but all kids like that stuff. You're trying to imply that my anarchistic traits date back to those books. I don't think so.

Well, not just the books, but also your social life. A stranger in the streets and school, unless you fought the enemy, which by the way was a class enemy, since you were with the rich, and those you fought were the poor.

I think you're pushing. First of all, I also read traditional books— mediocre, granted, like Pierre Loti—but considered "literature," in quotes and . . .

But you liked Zévaco, who was a confirmed anarchist, one against all . . .

I didn't know that. I just liked the adventures.

Which you carried over in the "novels" you kept writing, yes?

True. All my novels were about *cape et épée*—you know, swashbucklers. My hero was named Goetz, based on a history that I read when I had the mumps, about a Goetz von Berlichingen, a popular crusader who was imprisoned in a big clock with his head sticking out through the dials; the hands were sabers meant to cut off his head, but he escaped. He always escaped, alone, to carry on the good fight for the poor.

Sounds like both class consciousness and the beginning of an alone-against-all anarchism . . .

If you want. But remember, if these kinds of stories ran in the regular press—and Zévaco's novels were serialized too—then you have to say that all kids were class conscious and anarchistic.

OK, I'll give in here. But the point could be made that most kids were, indeed, and I think still are, instinctively class conscious and fantasize a hero who would crush all the bastards of the world and make things right. Except for the snobs of your private school, the rich who show disdain for the poor, most kids are on the side of the downtrodden. And then they adapt to society and enter the system.

Actually, I think you're right. Kids are selfish, egocentric and egotistical, but they side with the poor until the system's propaganda, which includes their parents, mind you, makes them conformists and then cogs in the system.

And in your case, that self-centeredness made you survive La Rochelle.

Actually, I used to show my "novels" to my classmates. They would laugh, especially at the subtitle, which was always "the true story of a hero." They would say "but it isn't true" and laugh their heads off, and never read them.

Your mother did, though.

Yes, and always offered some changes, usually of words, like don't say strong, say sturdy or whatever.

Since you started writing to impress Charles and he was no longer with you in La Rochelle, you didn't have to continue writing and she didn't have to read what you wrote.

True. For me by then it was an act of salvation. For my mother, I think, it was a form of showing me that she cared. In both cases it helped make me survive that horrid port, La Rochelle.

You stayed there three years, right?

Yes, through twelfth grade, sixteen, when I went back to Paris to live with my grandparents and continue my studies there. The second part of pre-mière and philo at Lycée Henri IV, and khâgne and hypo-khâgne at Lycée Louis-le-Grand.[7] I passed the exam [for admission to L'Ecole Normale Su-périeure], finishing number seven, and stayed there the four years, up to the *agrégation* exam.[8] I flunked the first time. Then I passed, as you know—number one on the second try.[9] Then I got drafted, like everyone else, and en-joyed a year and a half of boredom. Because of my eyes, I became a meteorol-ogist; they apparently don't have to see the weather, just smell it. Once dis-charged, my first job was teaching philosophy at a lycée in Le Havre.[10]

When did you renew your relationship with your mother?

I would see her occasionally in Paris, after she and Mancy returned. Neither of them approved of what I was doing or writing, especially after I gave her to read "L'enfance d'un chef," the last story in *The Wall* [published in 1939]. Charles simply sent it back to me, unread. My mother read to page 30, and "couldn't go on." She was quite religious, although she often com-plained, when children or poor people suffered or died, that "God was not just." She could take my anti-religious stuff. But sex was something else. Like her own mother's dictum, it was never to be discussed. And Mancy, a reac-tionary functionary after all, was disgusted by what I wrote. Nor would any-one in my family officially meet Castor except my mother, who would arrange for the three of us to meet periodically in some patisserie and never told her husband. And as you know, since you met her there, she moved into my apartment after her husband died.

Why? He died very early, no? Your grandparents were still alive; she could have moved back with them.

Mancy died in 1945. She never wrote me that. I was then in America, as you remember since I stayed with you all when I was in New York. By the way, Fernando never understood that I did that out of friendship, because the newspaper alliance that had invited me and was paying my way wanted to put me up in a nice hotel. I remember that you and I were on the same side of an argument at the Museum of Modern Art. Remember? The three of us went to see the big constructionist show at the museum and your father was not very moved, while we both liked it a lot, and you said that Mondrian's *Broadway Boogie Woogie* was like a dance. You were fourteen, and that impressed me a lot. In fact, I put that into *The Roads to Freedom*, when Gomez and Richie go to see the show.

You know, years later, when I was an art critic at *Newsweek* and I reviewed the huge Modern Museum show of Op Art, which credited Mondrian and the constructionists as their roots, I reviewed it with the headline "An Adventure Without Danger." I thought of that discussion you and my father had back then in 1945, and I remembered Fernando saying, "Yes, but Mondrian does not ask difficult questions." It took me a long time to understand what he meant. But to return to your mother: her husband had died while you were in America?

Yes, and she didn't want to ruin my stay. I had called her after arriving, or a few days after, when the press association set up the calls, and told her I loved America (of course I meant I loved New York, as I hadn't gone anywhere else yet), so she didn't say a thing about Mancy. When I got back and she told me, I gained tremendous sympathy and respect for her again. So I decided a sacrifice was in order. After all, she had sacrificed herself for us, my grandparents and me, by marrying him in the first place. So I gave up my hotels. As you know, I loved living in hotels, which I did ever since I came back from Berlin, and I hated the idea of living in a bourgeois apartment. But I got used to it.

Ah yes, Berlin. In 1933, you and the Nazis got to Berlin about the same time, right?

That's right. I got the same fellowship to go study there that Raymond Aron had the previous year. He helped me get that deal and so he also gets the credit for introducing me to phenomenology, but as you know it was your father who did that.[11]

But there were no phenomenologists in Berlin then, were there? And you didn't speak German anyway, did you?

Well, I could read it . . .

[Edmund] Husserl and Heidegger?

Not very well, true. Some. After all, Charles had been a teacher of German and often cursed in German, thinking I would not understand, but of course kids pick it up.

What? You picked up Husserl's swear words from Charles?

Ha-ha ha. You know, I always wanted to study English, but Charles insisted on German, so I had a fairly good basis. But for Husserl . . . Actually,

your father visited me twice for two weeks and translated a lot of it. Still, yeah, I was just having fun . . .

With the Nazis?

Ah, come on, don't be mean, it was a boondoggle. I was supposed to feel German culture, and I did. And I didn't like it. But it was a very happy year.

December 1970

GERASSI: When I went over our last session, I was struck by your very last statement, that you had a "happy" year. You were unhappy in La Rochelle but happy in Berlin? I thought that, to you, "happiness" was a reactionary concept.

SARTRE: Shit—ha-ha, I have to be careful with my words with you. As an individual I was miserable in La Rochelle in public, but mind you, perfectly contented alone with my writing. La Rochelle was a bigoted, foreigner hating, reactionary, Protestant, closed hole. As an individual, I was perfectly at ease in Berlin, a musical, agitated, fun-loving, open society, until the Nazis shut it down, but they didn't do it while I was there. The women were beautiful, sexy, and available. So as an individual it was a great year for me. That I didn't understand the significance of the Nazis goose-stepping down the Ku-damm, yeah, OK. But most of the Berliners I knew laughed them off, as I did.

Did Fernando, when he visited you?

No, to be honest, he warned me, but I didn't take him seriously. He had spent years under some form of fascism already in Spain, a monarchy with an extremely reactionary Catholic clergy that wanted to kill all nonbelievers, and he saw parallels in Germany. He warned me, I remember, that anyone who says "If you're not with me, you're against me" wants to execute all those against. But I thought he was a typical Spaniard, always exaggerating. Still, his two visits were great. For one thing he spoke perfect German, and philosophical German at that. And he loved women as much as I did.

Stépha wasn't with him, I take it?

No, but don't jump to more conclusions. Your parents had an open relationship . . .

Not to my mother . . .

Hey, just because she didn't exercise her right of openness doesn't mean that she hadn't agreed on the terms. She did.

OK, so you weren't politically aware of what was going on in '33. But when you say you were happy, you're eliminating the social element of . . .

OK, I said I was happy. That's not the issue we were discussing at lunch last Sunday. I said that the quest for happiness is reactionary. The goal of revolution is not to make everyone happy. It is to make everyone free and unalienated while dependent on each other. That's the contradiction we were discussing. If you want to define being free as being happy, fine, but what do you do with being dependent? That's the communal aspect of a social revolution, right? The difference between revolt or rebellion and revolution is its conscious communality, which is totally free.

Cannot revolt or rebellion lead to revolution?

Of course, but only when that spirit of communality dominates the rebellion.

Do you think that happened in 1968?

It began to. At first the students rebelled against the so-called educational reforms that de Gaulle's minister wanted to impose on them, to force them to decide what they wanted to do in life at sixteen or eighteen or whatever. They refused. They wanted to be able to read Goethe as well as study Riemann's anti-Euclidean physics. But as they joined forces, their rebellion became a rejection of the state, and the original motive for their demonstrations disappeared into a class war, sort of, where the class was youth facing unemployment. Then as the workers joined them, it became the alienated against the rulers, alienated being anyone who was fed up at having to behave according to a code defined by "them"—the grandees, the rich, those who graduated from the "great schools," the media, the trendsetters, the church, all churches—in fact, all those who considered themselves "the establishment." Wasn't that what the hippie-yippee movement was all about, as you wrote in our magazine? Except in France—maybe because it is a small country, but I think because it suffered two major wars in this century, betrayals, racism, Gestapo repressions—our youth is much more politically conscious than yours, even if they were born after, as most were. In any case, once attacked by the state, they coalesced into a single communal body. No one remembered what the original rebellion was about. They were now fighting for each other, for all. You got here in May '68, in time to see, no? The young helping the old, shielding them from the cops, pissing on their handkerchiefs to cover the faces of octogenarians to protect them from the tear gas. It was films like that which made de Gaulle run off to Baden-Baden to ask General Massu to invade France and Massu to refuse—the same Massu who had ordered his troops to torture Algerian rebels a few years earlier. If the Communist Party hadn't betrayed the revolution, we would have a communal state today. That would have been social happiness.[1]

But you never sought happiness?

No. To seek happiness means to believe that one can attain the meaning of life. As a kid I never asked what is the meaning or the goal or the reason of life. It is, period. But I was aware that my class, the bourgeois, always sought something.

What did you understand?

At ten years old, I understood that it was money. That's what defined the bourgeois.

But not you?

I was a bourgeois, of course. Raised and taught by bourgeois. But somehow I did not identify with that class. Maybe because I had no father. Maybe because, once we moved to La Rochelle, I was an outsider. I remember that I thought that life was fine. There were a lot of poor people, I could see that. But I thought that's why there were the rich, made to save the poor, and those not-so-rich, to help as much as they could. And that was fine.

Yet you wrote in *The Words* that you wanted to fight the bad guys and were upset that there weren't any. But the bad guys in your eyes were only the big ones, the dictators, the Napoleons. And since there weren't any . . .

All was good. Until we went to La Rochelle, that is. There I lost my angelic quality. I became a punk. I fought and I stole. I had no remorse, mind you, because it was my way of having a life. I expected my mother to understand. I expected Charles to understand. They didn't.

So you were unhappy?

As an individual, yes, but not because life was no good. I didn't suddenly think that the meaning of life was something else. I never changed in my being: I am what I am and I write.

And you were the hero of your novels. But you also understood the absurdity of that, since you tried to link Pardaillan to Don Quixote?

Starting in ninth grade, the literary contradictions began to set in. Corneille was no problem; his heroes, Horace, le Cid, Rodrigue, were real heroes; but Racine made me hesitate. His heroes are really anti-heroes. And that sort of fitted with what I read about the war. It reinforced my suspicion that happiness is objective and communal—hence, in the bourgeois world, nonexistent. I understood the difference between happiness and joy. Joy is subjective. If you feel joyous, no one can tell you you're not. But happiness is a state, not about this or that. Of course you can think you're unhappy, but concretizing it, like I did with my first major affair, which began when I was at Normale, at twenty. I fell madly in love with a woman, Simone Jolivet, who later would become the mistress of Charles Dullin, the great director who directed my first play. I considered it an "unhappy liaison" for three reasons: first, because she lived in Toulouse; second, because I was at Normale and limited in my days off; and third, I couldn't afford to travel down for two days very often, in fact I had to borrow money from my classmates. And when I complained that she wasn't available when I decided to go see her on the spur of the moment, she answered that how dare I complain when I come down at the best once a month, saying, "What am I supposed to do, sit here, staring at my navel, waiting . . ."

Aha! You were normal then? Jealous!

Hey, I was twenty. And it was my first great love affair. It lasted three or four years. I learned. But as you know, women want you to be jealous.

But not society.

True. But I found in all my affairs that if I wasn't jealous, the woman would say, "So you weren't jealous—that means you don't love me." I got into the habit of making believe that I was jealous—except with Castor, of course.

Why did that relationship become so special and so different?

It's complicated. You have her version in her memoirs. And you should interview her and get her to be more candid than in her books. For me, I think our relationship developed intellectually at first. We were both studying for the agrégation. She was at the Sorbonne and I was at Normale, and one of her classmates was René Maheu—you know, the guy who is now head of UNESCO . . .

Yes, I interviewed him already . . .

You did! And what did he say?

When I told him that I knew he had been Castor's first lover, he jumped and asked me if it was Castor who had told me. I told him no, that we had decided that I was going to spend a whole month interviewing Castor next February, and that it was my mother who had told me. "Ah yes," he remembered, that "lovely Stépha, the Ukrainian, her best friend. Everyone was in love with her, including Sartre," he said.

That's true. But your mother was a puritan; she believed in being faithful to Fernando.

The way she put it was that she and Fernando had the same kind of relationship as you and Castor but that she didn't need to have "unnecessary" affairs.

Ha-ha-ha! Wonderful. Nicely said. She was a tremendous flirt, however.

I know. Castor in her memoirs admits that it was Stépha who taught her how to dress more seductively, how to take care of her nails, in order to pick up those gorgeous Hungarians at the library.

Did Stépha know that it was Fernando who deflowered Poupette [Hélène de Beauvoir], Castor's sister?

Sure. But let's go back. Why did your relationship with Castor become "necessary," as you both have claimed, while all the others were "contingent"?

Well, not for Castor, you know—her affair with Nelson Algren was very serious.

Yeah, I asked her about it and she told me she really hoped he would come to Paris to be with her, but he said, No! Stay here in Chicago! Castor told me she then said, Look, you have nothing here except your work. I have my work and Sartre in Paris, so you come to Paris. And he said that's the point, either me or Sartre. And she chose you. When I asked her why, since she was really in love with Algren, she said, "Because Sartre doesn't ask me to choose."

Algren was a friend of your father, wasn't he?

Not really, just an acquaintance. I mean, they never saw each other without other people.

But Castor met Algren at your place, no?

At a sort of get-together with a bunch of leftist politicos. I remember that Joan Miró was there, and he was a friend and not political, except anti-Franco, of course. But the others had been brought by Meyer Shapiro, the art historian. He was a sort of Trotskyist, or so my father said, and he came with three or four writers from *Partisan Review,* which was somewhat Trotskyist then, and Algren was among them. Castor was there because she was staying with us. By the way, let me tell you a story about Shapiro. When my parents moved to Vermont, to teach at the Putney School, and I was visiting them, Fernando asked me if I would help him take a big canvas that wouldn't fit in the car off its frame, so we could roll it up and bring it to New York for Shapiro. We did, and once in my apartment Fernando had to make some calls, so I re-stretched it and fixed it to the siding. But I miscalculated and stopped when I saw that two inches would overlap. "Oh, don't worry about it, just tuck it into the side," said Fernando. When Shapiro showed up with a student he stared at it for a while, then turned to his student and asked him: "Can you see why Fernando is a great painter?" When the student was silent, Shapiro said, "You see those two inches which are now eliminated? That made the painting off balance. Gerassi's genius was to notice that and get rid of them. Now the balance is perfect."

Ha-ha ha. I love art critics!

OK, so Castor was willing to push the concept of contingency a bit, but were you not in love with each other?

Sure, but not the way the bourgeois world defines love. She was sleeping with Maheu, but our minds were having real intercourse. We fell in love with each other's intuition, imagination, creativity, perceptions, and eventually for a while bodies as well, but just like one cannot dominate a mind (except through terror, of course), one cannot dominate taste, dreams, hopes, et cetera. Some things Castor was better at, some I was. Do you know that I would never allow any writing of mine to be published, or even made public to anyone, until Castor approved? And she was a rough critic. She made me rewrite my play *Nekrassov* five times, for example.

Can I ask you if it's true that you and Castor stopped having sex from 1947?

1946, '47, '48, I don't remember, but yes. How did you know?

She told me.

Boy, she didn't even write that in her memoirs.

Well, she did say that you were "not a copulator but rather a masturbator."

It's true that I prefer the game, the seduction to the act, or as you put it, "the input was not worth the output," correct? Speaking of seduction, are things OK with Catherine?

Yeah, just fine.

You know that Castor and I like her a lot. She's really wonderful.

Anyway, so Wanda [Kosakiewicz], Olga [Kosakiewicz], Michelle [Vian], even Sally Shelly were all contingent affairs?

You know about Shelly?

I know her personally; we're friends. I've read some of your letters to her . . .

Oh my god, really? Wow, she kept them all these years, eh? Well, I'll tell you, that was a really wild, and I admit very deep, affair.

But still contingent? Yet you did ask her to marry you, didn't you?

OK, I see you know the story. She wanted to go back to America. That was the only way I could hold her in France.

But would you really have married her?

Ah, who knows. You know how we met?

She told me she came to France in 1948 and tried to get a job to stay. So she went to the *International Tribune,* and they told her, prove that you can write, go do a few obituaries of well-known people. She forgot all about it until one day she saw you sitting in a café in St. Tropez and came up to you and said: "Excuse me, Mr. Sartre, I have to write your obituary." You laughed your head off, and invited her to sit down, and off it went.

She was eighteen and stunning. I was forty-something. Ultimately contingent, perhaps. But marvelous, absolutely marvelous.

She ended up working for the United Nations and eventually became head of the law of the sea, or something like that. I see her now and then. I have copies of all your letters to her. I'm trying to persuade her to write a book about your affair. But what amazes me is that the great Sartre couldn't hold her, huh?

All men are mortal, Gerassi, you and me too . . .

Which is why you write? To cheat death?

Once one decides to be a writer, one's conception of life, one's whole being, changes. The decision implies one of two modes of behavior. To me it

demanded both. The first, I admit, I toyed with. Give me a small pension, a room in a convent, three meals a day, and I write. That's it. Just write. The other: travel, experience as many different circumstances as possible. Go into every world. Go see how the pimps live in Constantinople. Why Constantinople? There are pimps right here, around the corner. Because travel, experiences, give a richness to the writing. All adventures help, including sexual adventures, love, et cetera. They are all the meat of the writer, hence not as important in themselves as the act of writing. Either way, writing is a total commitment (as is any art). That's why now I say that I broke with my mother, when she got married, not because I was jealous and fearful of being unhappy, as was the interpretation back then, but because even the act of being jealous, of breaking with one's mother, is valid to a writer. That's what I would say now if I wrote the sequel to *The Words*. Of course a writer doesn't need to actually do the things he describes or go to the places he makes come alive. He can be stimulated by what he reads and use his imagination. Brunet in *The Roads to Freedom*: is he me or is he [Paul] Nizan, my best friend then? Actually, neither. It's fake, right? But I knew enough communists so that Brunet is real. It's like my "true story" when I was eleven. A writer has to choose the false against the true. When you decided to be a writer, you couldn't make that choice because you wanted a revolution, you worked for a revolution. I was nothing but what I wrote. You had a goal. I was my goal.

Meaning that you were god. Reminds me of when I was fifteen and my best friend asked me why I wanted to write. "Because there is no god," I said. "What does one thing have to do with the other?" he pressed. Because, since there is no god, I answered, life is terribly unjust. So I want to create a world that is just. In books, everything ends according to a certain logic, with a beginning, a middle, and an end. So I create a perfect world. I am god. "But if you want to be god," he said, "it means you believe." And he was right. I mean, not that I believed in god, but that I believed in something above human—namely justice, like a Platonic idea.

You were almost there. Change your Platonic idea to freedom and you have it. Writing implies belief in freedom, total freedom. All arts consist in rendering a world imbued in freedom, a world that is wanted, mediated, conceived by a conscience, a free conscience.

And terminated, complete in itself.

Absolutely. That's the key. You have it perfectly. Self-contained. But when your friend said that it meant that you believed after all, you should have answered no, because when I write, I create the imaginary.

And the glory is for creating heroes who fight for that justice, which is freedom to you? But the real hero is the writer, no? [André de] Chénier decapitated. [Victor] Hugo exiled to Guernsey. [Emile] Zola. You complain that Charles was a Dreyfusard but never talked to you about it. The man of action who dies a martyr. Isn't martyrdom a religious concept?

Absolutely. There's no doubt that as a kid, seven or eight, missing from my life was religion. So I created one for me; that was literature. And the martyrdom of that religion was the writer who produces and suffers. All my great literary heroes were miserable, at least in part of their lives, dying unhappy, like Chateaubriand, dying in desperation. But the work lives on.

You got a lot of that from Charles, but he was happy, or, let's say, satisfied with himself, was he not?

I thought so. He had a sort of equilibrium that projected, if not happiness, at least contentment. He loved his wife, yet she didn't want to sleep with him, except to make children, four of them; well, one died, so he slept with his students. He would have liked a bourgeois life, with a nice bourgeois family. His sons hated him. My mother loved him but suffered from his contempt for all his grandchildren, except me. I think he really loved me, in his way, or at least he made believe that he did, and I liked it. But ultimately, he could not have been a happy man. He was afraid of dying.

But he didn't show it, did he? He pretended to be a sort of god.

And how. You remember how I described his great entrance in the play. Where he played God?

With his long beard and thunderous voice and his allure; he was over six feet tall and quite massively built.

Not quite the martyr, huh? How about your father?

Yes, I certainly thought my father was a martyr.

Yet in *The Words* you say, "He loved, he died, a man." Is that enough to define a man?

Yes.

[Our weekly conversations and lunches were postponed for two weeks during December 1970 so that Sartre could serve as the "judge" at the trial of those "really responsible" for an accident that took the lives of six coal miners at Lens, a northeastern mining bastion. It was a "people's trial" wherein anyone who had anything to say could testify, and Sartre's job, until the end, was basically to be simply a coordinator and director, keeping order and making sure everyone had a turn. The "trial" took place in the ceremonial hall of the local town hall, which was controlled by the Socialist Party and the socialist mayor. The hall could seat six hundred people, but seven hundred actually crowded in without a problem. When he returned, Sartre explained.]

Four workers had been accused of manslaughter as the justice department tried to narrow the case to the specific incident. We would have none of that. The "prosecution," which was made up of miners, engineers, wives, in fact anyone who felt involved, broadened the case to the way the mine was run, to the security measures and their cost that the owners installed, to their profits, to the wages miners got, in fact to the whole capitalist mining industry. Everyone, me included, thought that miners earned a very good salary. Wrong. We found out that their average pay was $20,000 a year. Doctors testified on the damage that such work caused to the miners. Wives testified on the side effects that the miners suffered at home. Daughters testified that unless they ran away from home they were stuck as backup labor, servants, or cheap labor in the textile firms nearby. Filmmakers showed up with documentaries. Engineers showed up with blueprints, reports, plans, which were ignored by the owner's engineers. It was like Zola's *Germinal* all over again. At the end it was up to me to make a summary, or a summation if you like, and I said what was obvious to all, that the state was guilty of murder for tolerating such conditions, and specifically the owners of Mine No. 6 (where the deaths occurred), the general director, the engineers who obeyed the bosses by short-changing security. The court—and me in my summation—demanded that the miners who had been careless and were accused of manslaughter be freed and that the owners be arrested. Because most of the press attended the "trial" from beginning to end and gave it a lot of coverage, the miners were indeed freed. But, as you expect, the owners were not arrested. Still, perhaps because the left-wing press published first-person life histories of the miners, wives, and daughters, the owners did pay compensation to the families of the dead. It was the best possible result we could have hoped for in a capitalist state, and it showed to all that a really fair trial must include all the circumstances, the atmosphere, the history of an "incident," and not declare it, as our courts do now, "irrelevant."

So too in the United States, where everything seems to be irrelevant when a poor person is on trial. Let me tell you about one case I'm familiar with. It took place a few of years ago in New York. A black woman was living without a husband or partner in Harlem with two children, one five, one eight. On the day in question, a very hot July Monday, her five-year-old was very sick, and couldn't go to school. So she made lunch for him and asked the eight-year-old to come home during his lunch break and bring him some milk. Then she rushed off to work; she was in a secretarial pool for a Wall Street firm. The subway she was riding broke down, as they often do in New York, and she ended up thirty-five minutes late. When she explained to her boss, he quipped: "*You people* are always stuck in the subway." She had rushed so much that when it came time for lunch she realized she had grabbed a token on her way out but forgot her wallet and had no money. She asked her co-workers for a loan of a couple of dollars, but none would help, one saying: "*You people* never pay your debts." So she didn't have lunch. When it came time to go home she had to beg in the street for a token. Once home, she found her five-year-old crying by an open window. Her eight-year-old had played with his classmates and forgotten to come home with the milk. As the five-year-old cried louder and louder, she suddenly whipped around and hit him with the back of her hand. He lost his balance and fell out the open window, on the fifth floor, and died. She was charged with manslaughter, and when the court-appointed lawyer tried to tell the story of her day and asked the judge, David L. Bazelon, who went on to become an appeals court judge with a very socially minded agenda, perhaps because of this case, if he could subpoena her office mates, and the prosecutor objected as "irrelevant," Bazelon agreed. She was convicted and given five years. Her eight-year-old was put into an orphanage where he was beaten and raped by older boys and eventually escaped, became a drug runner, and was shot by police in a raid. The woman then ripped her clothes into a noose and hanged herself.

Wow, that's some story. But that's capitalist justice: never consider the circumstances.

Of the poor. When the rich are tried for stealing, they come into court all dressed up, with their wives and children in the audience, and beg for mercy on the ground that their children will be this or that, and they promise to pay back the money. The poor, who can't afford fancy suits and ties, and whose families can't take time off from work to waste a whole day in court, get jail time. The statistics are that for every dollar stolen by the poor without the use of violence, the rich steal eighty-seven dollars, and for every year that the poor spend in jail for a nonviolent crime, the rich spend seventeen minutes.

Do the American people know this? Does the press say anything about it?

There's a great book that I used in class called *The Rich Get Richer, the Poor Get Prison,* but no, most people don't know because the mainstream media doesn't want to tell them. They want everyone to think that the real danger in the streets is the black unemployed youth, which, as [Jeffrey H.] Reiman, the book's author, pointed out, is just not true. But to get back to your definition of what is a man, insofar as you said about your father "he suffered, he loved, he was a man," did you feel that when you learned about his death? When did you learn the details of your father's life and death?

I'm not sure. There was a time, I guess I was seven or eight, as I wrote in *The Words,* when I was terrified of dying. Was it because it was then that I learned about my father's death? Neither my mother nor my grandparents ever talked about it, or very little. I learned, then or later, that he was born very far from oceans, in Le Périgord, in the center of France, a place of small mountains and rivers, but not even lakes. How did he become fascinated with the sea? He worked very hard to pass all the exams, Polytechnique and L'Ecole Navale, became a petty officer of some kind, went to sea and got the illness that killed him when I wasn't even one year old. I can't tell you how it affected me, though I often brooded about it. The fact is that he had a goal and died because of it. Was he a martyr? Once I became convinced that the only real value was literature, or the arts in general, was it because I believed that all artists were martyrs, and my father's death made me seek martyrdom? Who knows? And was that martyrdom, which was defined by suffering, solitude, non-recognition, ostracism, and a painful death, because the martyr fought the good fight?

But Zévaco did not suffer . . .

Wait! At eight and nine, when I was writing my "novels" at a ferocious speed (copying a lot of it from the episodes that were serialized in the newspapers, granted), it wasn't Zévaco who was my martyr. Actually, I don't think I had a martyrdom complex yet. In any case, it was Zévaco's hero, Pardaillan, that flamboyant swashbuckler who fought the bad guys alone. And was never recompensed for it.

Pardaillan fought cops, armies, the government, as well as muggers and gangsters. Was that the root of your anarchistic temperament?

Zévaco was certainly an anarchist. But what came first, my aloneness, fighting my classmates for recognition—that was after we moved to La Rochelle—or my aloneness of not having a father? Who knows. But I certainly thought of my father, once I knew of his circumstances and his death, as a martyr. I know that for years my fantasies included me defending a poor girl sought by the nasty tutor, or the missionary, non-religious, mind you, who is sent to America in the 1860s to pacify the imperialists—of course, I didn't use those words yet, but I meant the whites who were violent against the non-whites—and the good guy who keeps getting beaten up himself. None of my fantasies had an end, by the way. I always thought I would have to end them in a "novel."

And gain immortality on the shelf.

Exactly. That's what made a book immortal: the shelf, the book on my grandfather's shelf. That's where I saw the Chateaubriands and the Victor Hugos. Chateaubriand was a perfect example for me of the martyr, disgraced, so sick he had to be transported in a chair, suffering, and there, on the shelf, were his books. As for Hugo, he had a great influence on me. By today's terms, a real anti-fascist, exile, proscribed, but earning a lot of money in the process, adored by his wonderful Juliette with whom he stayed until she died, but always unfaithful, sleeping with the wives of others, with maids, even peeking through the keyhole at the young ones.

Doesn't sound like much of a martyr to me.

Ha, well, no, right, but still, always in trouble, saved by the revolution of '48, then by Napoleon III's coup d'état, then ignored, then up on the shelf. In a way, like Charles. I was sorry for him that he didn't write. But, you know, he was handsome, big, admired by a lot of the female students at the school of Hautes Etudes, and by the men too, all of which he hid from me, and I think from himself as well, his miserable existence, a professor, which is what I was to become, which I considered a misery, and when I finally became one at Le Havre, was indeed a misery.

Why? I don't get it. Charles loved teaching. He screwed half his students, he was admired by the guys. And so were you at Le Havre. Your penchant for violence got you to box with your students, and despite your size you apparently held your own quite well. And despite your eyes, you seduced the female students you wanted. Where's the misery in all that?

I wanted to be a great writer, like Hugo, on the shelf, and I think that secretly so did Charles.

Would you characterize it as an obsession?

I think so. But not the kind of obsession that shrinks talk about. The kind that says simply, no matter what, I will write. Like your father: no matter what, I will paint, which is why we were so close, I think. We had that commitment in common. And you had it when I came to America in 1945, I remember. Your father, however, wouldn't take it seriously, then.

I was fourteen.

So? I remember you had written a couple of short stories you wanted me to read, and Fernando stopped you, saying stop bothering him, remember?

Sure. He did that when [Maurice] Merleau-Ponty visited us too.

And do you remember that argument about earning money, when Fernando yelled at Stépha: "I don't care if you starve. I don't care if Tito starves, first I paint."

Stépha claims that I made that up when I broke with my father at sixteen.

I was there. You didn't make it up. And do you remember that letter when he went to Spain?

Of course. [This is the letter mentioned earlier in which Fernando wrote that she should forget him because he had killed a man in battle.] Stépha kept that letter. She cherished it. I've seen it many times. Why did that letter so upset you?

You have to understand our obsession, mine and what was, I thought, your father's, and it certainly was when he insisted that "first I paint." We were committed to our art. To me that meant that it came before politics. Or, to put it in context, politics was part of our art—that is, we would incorporate it . . .

In a painting?

In what the painting could mean in a deeper sense, freedom. That's the difference between *les pompiers* [literally, "firemen," a French slang term for those in the arts who in effect work for the establishment by making art that is expected] and the real artists. Genuine art is an expression of freedom. What the bourgeois critics call the soul. What Heidegger called the entrails. That's certainly how I would have defined my writing and your father's art, which is certainly one reason we were so close.

Indeed, you never really go out of your way to meet someone if it means interrupting your schedule, but you did for Fernando, you rushed down to Biarritz when he came across from Spain for a break in 1937.

That's right, as does Mathieu to see Gomez in *The Roads*. I wanted to show the genuine bond that existed.

But you were not only writing literature then. You had finished *Nausea*, yes, but you were polishing up your theory of emotions and working on your theory of perception. You obviously thought of yourself by then as a philosopher. Two obsessions?

Yes, but into one. That is, I always considered my novels and later my plays as a personalized expression of my philosophy. Or my philosophy as a way to work out in theory what my novels and plays established in individual situations. In other words, I saw no real distinction.

And you couldn't fit the political into that?

Not then, I guess. It took the war for me to understand that it's all one. My captivity [in a German prisoner of war camp for nine months beginning in 1940]. As I wrote, to have to live cheek by jowl[2] [with the other prisoners in the camp], I became aware that the political is personal and the personal is political, as Che Guevara once said.

But in 1937 you were still totally divorced from politics. What attracted you to Fernando was your old bond, not his martyrdom, in the sense that you had formulated in La Rochelle about every artist.

I wasn't totally divorced, but . . .

Hey, while Fernando was fighting the fascists in Spain, you and Castor went off to fascist Italy, and you wrote not about Mussolini but about the succulent mortadella that you ate.

Boy, it's a good thing most journalists who do interviews are not so prickly or else don't read. But it's true, the bond I had with your father was basically through our obsession, and that letter he wrote to Stépha proves it. He was the artist at war. No nice, pleasant pacifist farmer would have written it. Only an artist who felt he had sacrificed his freedom, that is, the freedom he recognizes in everyone else, an act that breaks his solitude.

Are you saying that all artists are condemned to be alone?

Not alone, in solitude. Only an artist understands that he or she is condemned to be free, and understands that it means be condemned to live in solitude. By fighting for a cause that is temporary—because, let's face it, fascism is here now, and maybe for another two hundred years, but it's a phase—an artist gives up his solitude to join with others, and thereby violates the others' freedom, which hence violates his own, his immortality not as a human being but as art, which is absolute freedom.

Aren't we back to religion now?

Come on. You want to accuse me of mysticism, OK. But religion? There's no praying, no god, no salvation in being free, it's the state of man, hence a universal.

Aha, we're going back to the fight between universals and particulars? You want to be Occam? I'll be Abelard.

Be serious. I am simply saying that man is free. To deny it is bad faith.

OK. Tell me, why does being free mean being alone? Ah, sorry—to be in solitude?

Because freedom is totalizing.

So your excuse for not being political, in Berlin in 1933 or when your best friend goes off to fight fascists in Spain, is because as a free entity, which is eternal, you cannot be brought down to the particular, which is temporary?

That's one way of putting it. More accurately would be to say fascism, wars, are temporary incidents, while the act of writing is universal, in the sense that it denies any other power. The writer denies the existence of gods, even if he claims to write for god—or better, that his hand is guided by god.

In practical terms then, he who is not part of your writing world is insignificant, correct? That must greatly limit your social world, no?

That's right. And it's true. You know that Castor and I rarely go outside our circle anymore.

What Castor calls "the family"?

Actually, it's been like that for a long time now. It started with [Jacques-Laurent] Bost and Olga, when he was my student and she was Castor's.[3] We would see one, then the other, each of us separately—well, Bost sometimes we see together.

Why? Because they argue or talk too much to each other, what?

No, no. It's just that, though they are excellent friends, when they're together, they present a different world. We want to stick to our established world.

And what is that?

The world of our writing.

And together they impose on you their own world, which clashes with yours? Forgive me Sartre, but that sounds selfish.

Maybe. But when we go out of our writing, well, you'll have to ask Cas-

tor if she feels the same, but when I do, it is simply to be nice or to be helpful, whatever, it's . . .

Not the real you?

It is, but not the me-writer. Anyway, in order not to lose that too much, I limit my visits, I mean I see my people, my family if you wish, separately. Like I see Wanda once a week, the same day at the same time.⁴ Arlette [Elkaïm-Sartre] twice a week,⁵ Michelle two mornings a week,⁶ and Castor four evenings. There was a time when we all led a café existence; that was because during the war, none of our apartments had heat, but the cafés did. And sometimes we still meet in cafés, but now it's political. Besides, all those women now own their apartments—well, Olga and Bost together, but Michelle and Wanda alone, and of course Castor.

I've seen them all now, and Castor wins, by far.

Yes, hers is lovely, and very convenient for me.⁷

But the *Temps Modernes* staff meetings are still in cafés, no?

No, usually at the office.

But I remember, when I came after the war, actually in 1954, we all met at the Flagstaff, which was on rue Montparnasse, just off the boulevard.

That was because everyone wanted to meet you again, "le petit Tito," because everyone remembered you as a six-year-old.

But I remember, there was a lot of political talk. Someone would say did you see Mauriac's attack in *Le Figaro* or Rousset's in *Ce Soir?* Castor would say, We should answer it. Then you would ask [Francis] Jeanson [a longtime aide to Sartre and an editor at *Les Temps Modernes*] or whoever to do it. And so on.

Of course, the family was there, and the family was now a political entity, assembled to our magazine, but normally we met at the office. It was because of you that we met at a café. Your parents, of course, were or had been and would have been family. And you got back in then. Do you know why?

I haven't the foggiest.

Because of your criticism of me. Yep. You don't remember. [Jean] Poullion or Bost or some other *Temps Modernes* editor, I forget who, asked you what you were doing, and you said you were writing a dissertation for a Ph.D. on my philosophy, or some part of it. Somebody asked you to explain it more, and it became clear that you were thinking about *Being and Nothingness*. Someone interrupted you and told you that I was now trying to reconcile

Marxism with Existentialism. You asked me to explain. Question after question.

That I remember. I was stunned by how carefully and fully you were willing to explain stuff to a twenty-three-year-old punk like me.

Your questions were excellent. I felt I had to convince you. And I didn't. What happened?

To the amazement of all assembled, you ended up saying: Impossible, you cannot link Marxism with the Existentialist notion of project, and went on to explain why. You were right. I never did.

Yeah, I remember now, but is that how I ended up part of the family?

Well, that, and your description of America, the economic reasons for the Marshall Plan and the Cold War, which we all appreciated very much, and which is why I always asked you after that to fill me in on what was happening in America. I told Castor that I trusted your explanation more than anyone else's.

Nineteen fifty-four. That was the year of all the breakups, politically I mean?

Yes. I had written *The Communists and Peace* and come to the conclusion that if there were to be a Third World War it was because America would start it. I didn't like the Soviet system one bit, but I knew Russia would never start World War III. It couldn't militarily or nuclearly or economically. So I said that we have to back the communists. Merleau agreed but could not support either the USSR or the communists in public, and he left *Les Temps Modernes*. It was hard times for us then, but I think we were right. America was using the Cold War as an excuse for its ruling class to make fortunes off the arms race, and Russia had no choice but to go along.

But it went too far, so you switched in 1956 and wrote *The Ghost of Stalin* after the USSR invaded Czechoslovakia.

It wasn't a switch. I was always more of an anarchist than a Marxist, but in the context of 1954, with the United States imposing its will on Europe with its phony NATO, which was and still is a way of dominating Europe, and General [Matthew B.] Ridgway who was telling the French, and all Europeans, how to behave, and its bases in every country, we had to take a stand against all that. But when Soviet tanks actually rolled into Prague and good leftists were killed because they wanted to be independent of Russia, and everyone else, we had to denounce the invasion.

But it didn't reconcile you with Merleau? Castor never apologized for her attack on him, did she?

No, but he understood that it was not a personal attack. We remained respectful of each other until the end.

He had always been much less of an anarchist than you, right?

You have to understand that my anarchism, as you call it, was really an expression of freedom, the freedom I described earlier, the freedom of a writer.

And which in fact was engendered by your solitude, by your ostracism in La Rochelle.

Perhaps. But when I came back to Paris to go to Henri IV and then Louis-le-Grand, I was also reading bourgeois literature. Well, all sorts. I kept reading Zévaco and Ponson du Terrail, both good anarchists, but also Abel Hermant, who hated the Jacobins, and Jules Romains. But I also read and reread *Les Misérables*, a really great book, beautifully written. And I also started writing operettas. One was called *Horatius Cocles*, some Roman dude who defended a bridge against a whole army, and another was *Mucius Scevola*, about a warrior who wanted to talk to Caesar and when he was turned down said he would hold his hand over a fire until Caesar agreed.

Whatever you wrote, it always had a violent aspect? Did any of that early writing, or your so-called novels, survive?

No. Too bad. But it's true, I was always attracted to violence. When I was eight or nine, because I was small or wanted attention, who knows. But I fought in the streets like the rest of the kids. At Henri IV or Louis-le-Grand we didn't fight in the streets, but I wrote about violence. At L'Ecole Normale, our violence was political in the sense that Nizan, who was very much like me though not small, and I would go to the roof and fill condoms with urine and drop them on the right-wingers below, those we knew were in favor of France's colonial policy, especially in Indochina in those days. And in Le Havre, I learned how to box. I had a weird colleague there, a professor like me, who is now teaching in Madagascar, who was so good at it that he had been chosen to be one of France's boxing reps at the Olympics, but he got sick just before. He taught me how to box, and I got to be pretty good.

So I heard from one of your students, a big guy too, whom you floored. Did the fact that you were ugly somehow exacerbate your sense of violence?

A bit, I'm sure. But not in the actual use of violence. It certainly made

me aware that it was a hurdle I had to overcome. And I think it helped in one way at least, because I noticed that those who thought of themselves as handsome always became satisfied with the world. At best reformists. For me with women, it meant I had to be more involved, I mean I had to talk well, be a good intellectual, so to speak, and be charming. But that created good and bad consequences. The good was that when I succeeded, the ensuing relationship was never superficial. It was solid. The bad was that to break such a relationship took much more time and effort, unless I wanted to be just a selfish cad, which I didn't. I remember with Simone Jolivet, you know, the "Camille" we talked about who became Dullin's mistress, she once said, like that, not to wound me, but in passing, that I was ugly. I immediately asked how that affected her, and she responded that it made me talk better and she liked that.

Do you think that the combination, your eyes, your ugliness, your smallness, contributed to your revolts?

Hold on! I have never revolted. Against anyone! I went from whatever I was to a revolutionary after long, disciplined meditations on the principles espoused by the bourgeoisie. Humanist principles.

And history? The French Revolution?

No, history bored me. And I now know why: history was then taught by positivists. They never tried to explain, to find the reasons. They simply described. And if I or anyone asked why, they would answer that no one would ever know the causes. But I knew that there were reasons. *Les Misérables* made that very clear. And then I started reading [Fyodor] Dostoyevsky and [Leo] Tolstoy, and I began to understand the Russian Revolution through their characters and the conditions and situations in which they lived. I became a revolutionary because I understood that it is not someone against whom we must rebel, but a state, a system, which must be overthrown.

January 1971

GERASSI: You told me at lunch last week that all your judgments were always wrong. Why?

SARTRE: Hey, not all. I mentioned my mother. But partly because she was such a prude. She would never talk about anything that had sexual connotations. So I sort of dismissed her. Yet, you know, I could discuss Dostoyevsky with her. I did when I was twenty. Before, I thought she was like my sister—remember that before she remarried, we shared a room. She would even read Heidegger, or at least one thing, "What Is Metaphysics?" She also got hold of *Bifur*, the review that Nizan was editing when we were still students and in which I published "The Legend of Truth."

Was that your first publication?

Actually, no. I had written a small piece, insignificant, for some law journal or review about rights.

But about your mother, you misjudged her because she was so puritan, correct? What about the kids, especially at La Rochelle?

Fortunately my mother lived long enough so that I ended up having some pretty good talks with her. She read everything I wrote, even *Being and Nothingness*, and understood it—well, more or less. What I misjudged about my classmates in La Rochelle is more to your point, as I detect it. Yes, true, whenever they gathered after class, I sort of roamed around them, a bit off, saying nothing, until finally they said, Well, are you going to join us? I always did that, and you know, they always ended up saying come on. I never felt wanted enough to just approach the group naturally. I had to be asked.

Did you feel inferior or just not liked?

Never inferior. On the contrary, I always felt superior but never showed it because, one might say thank god, I was always conscious of being ugly and small. I wanted to be wanted.

But so far no class consciousness?

Well, it began then, in La Rochelle, because there was always some kind of protest or strike or job action at my stepfather's factory. Apparently—I don't remember—I used to tell my classmates that my stepfather's workers were exploited, and it got back to him, and we did have some discussion about that. Arguments, I'm told. But he never raised his voice. He was very gentle and polite. A good bourgeois. But he jokingly said one day that I was the secretary general of the Communist Party, and that had the effect of making me want to learn what the communists were for, what was their program. But that was later. We got along superficially very well. He tried to maintain the good bourgeois "family life." On Sundays and Thursdays we used to go to the theater in the afternoon.[1] We saw comic operas. That was my culture. Or stroll along Le Mail, that was the main drag, along the sea, full of flowers and merchants. Mancy's factory had a car and driver at his disposal, so he would pack us in it and order long drives into the countryside. I found that boring, but never complained. I realized already then that I was a city spirit. Like you, as you told me, nature never moved you very much.

Don't forget I left home when I was sixteen, and never had enough money except to hang out with the poor kids on the stoop of our buildings. I think I became a city slicker out of political commitment.

For me, I think it was the reverse. But don't forget we were at war. The nation comes first. So all united. But after the war, in Paris, a lot of my classmates belonged to the SFIO [the Socialist Party] and tried to get me to join. But you know, to tell you the truth, I had a certain esthetic disdain for their party. The SFIO was the big party at the time. There were no communists in my circle, at least that I knew. Until Nizan joined the CP [Communist Party] and tried to convince me to follow suit. At Henri IV and Louis-le-Grand the kids were rough and tough. Their fathers were at the front and their mothers had to work, so there was no one to discipline them, and they never listened to their mother when she got home.

Mancy never faced the draft?

He was too old, almost fifty in 1914—let's see, forty-six. Besides, he was very useful to the war effort. He had graduated from Polytechnique as a naval engineer, then went to work for Delaunay-Belleville, which was making cars and trucks, then I think tanks.

When the old man died and his son took over, a dandy who just wasted the factory's resources to party, Mancy was sent to La Rochelle to save the boat-building part of the factory, but didn't, and after I went back to Paris, he switched to some outfit in Saint-Etienne, and eventually ended up at L'Electricité de France in Paris. He took good care of my mother, and left her enough money so she could live fairly comfortably until her death, three years ago. Also he figured that I would be able to take care of her if he died early, since by then I was a professor. And I did, as you know, for the next twenty-two years after he died. But in 1918, I did not return to live with him and my mother. In fact, I wasn't with my grandfather either; I had become a boarder at Henri IV where I found my old buddy Nizan, and our friendship became intensely close. He was also a boarder, semi-boarder. I would go home Wednesday and Saturday nights, first with my grandparents, then after Mancy and my mother returned to Paris, with them. The boarders, both in première and in philo, slept in a long dormitory room. Nizan and I were next to each other, way at the end. And though we both studied hard, we also played hard. I was elected "S.O.," Satyre Officiel, which meant that I was top dog in insults, tricks, et cetera, but not enough to stop me from getting first prize in excellence in both classes. But I was still a novice when it came time to read good literature. Nizan and some other advanced students were reading [Jean] Giraudoux, the Surrealists, even some writers I never heard of, like Valery Larbaud, while I was still stuck on bourgeois writers, like Pierre Loti. Nizan made me read Giraudoux, [Joseph] Conrad, then he insisted that we read [Marcel] Proust together, which we did. He interpreted, I realized much later, the significance of Dostoyevsky, of Flaubert, of Proust, much better than I did. We also went on long walks, on Thursdays and Sundays, I mean from the Latin Quarter to Montmartre, climbing La Butte, discovering every nook and cranny of Paris. I loved it and I loved Paris. It became my city, the place where I wanted to live forever—that is until the Germans ruined it all. Paris under the occupation changed radically. The Germans took over the fancy hotels and houses, draped the disgusting swastika over the sculptured outer walls, placed barricades in the center of our romantic plazas. I never completely recovered, in the sense that I then felt, after the Liberation, that I could live in any city, Paris no longer being the one.

Were you engaged politically back then, with Nizan?

No, I wasn't at his level in politics either. He was very political. First on the extreme right, in Action Française. I think because in the summer before I returned he had been the tutor to the sons of some count, and with the sons he had gone around pasting posters demanding a revolution of sorts. It was that, the revolution, which attracted him. He was disgusted with the political state of France and wanted a radical overhaul. That lasted a year. Then he converted to Protestantism because his mother was very Catholic, but that didn't last either.[2]

Did you two stay together all the way through Normale?

Yes and no. When I switched to Louis-le-Grand for khâgne, he stayed at Henri IV as full boarder. His father, a civil engineer, was named some kind of boss for the French National Railway, at Strasbourg, so the family moved but wanted Nizan to finish at a good lycée.

What did you talk about on your long walks—never politics?

No. Mostly about Paris. When we went up to the Sacré-Coeur and tried to figure out all the important spots below. We also talked about literature and philosophy. In lit, we talked as if the characters in Proust were alive. You know, like, So what happened to Verdurain, to Swann? Stuff like that. And in philosophy we tried to concoct a very strict rationalism, especially after 1923 when Castor joined us.

But never politics, huh? Yet Nizan must have been ruminating deeply during this time, before he joined the CP, no? Or had he already joined its youth group?

I can't remember exactly. He was very tight-lipped about his search then. Very secretive.

And what was this rationalism you two concocted?

We three, because Castor was part of our discussions then.

So it was in 1929?

Let's see . . . In 1928, I failed my agrégation, yes, so it was in 1929, the same year that Castor and I passed. And Nizan, if I remember correctly, we started talking about a very strict rationalism, that is, one that said a cat is a cat, period, right, in opposition to what was then prevalent, which was to go beyond the given, like some fashionable author used to write "it was more than love," nonsense, love is love, we said, period. We rejected all idealisms.

We were very strict Cartesians. Like he had said, "I think, therefore I am." Simple truths.

How did you and especially Nizan, who was already obsessed with the social, fail to see the idealism in [René] Descartes?

What idealism?

The tabula rasa, that is, going from a clean slate to the *cogito,* because in order to say I think *therefore* I am, one needs to understand, to conceive what is meant by that connective "therefore," which demands years of experience. When one comes to that table capable of making that connection, one brings to the table a whole pile of life suitcases, hence the table is never clean.

Certainly Descartes was no dialectician. But no one was yet. He offered us a respectable weapon with which to combat the idealists.

Is that when you started your little book of selected texts by Descartes?

Yes, but I didn't publish it until 1939. To earn money, then we did translations.

[Karl] Jaspers?

Right. No, there was a guy at Normale named Kastler, an Alsatian who spoke perfect German but sort of fundamental French. So he translated—it was Jaspers's *Treatise on Psychopathology*—and Nizan and I put it into good French.

Were you influenced by Jaspers?

Not at all. Well, I did retain one thing—speaking of dialectics—his distinction between intellection and comprehension. The former is like a mathematical formula, there, accepted. While comprehension is an act, a dialectical movement of thought. Yes, that came from Jaspers, not Husserl or Heidegger, neither of whom deal with it. It ended up being the basis of my *Critique of Dialectical Reason.* And I started brooding about such concepts then, in '28. In fact, I began to write it. You should ask Castor to show you that early work, which I never published. It was in three parts, the legend of truth, the legend of the probable, and the legend of a man alone. I never finished the third.[3] The first was basically the scientific, the evident, absolute certitude. The probable was a sort of exposé of truth according to the elites, an attack on the philosophy that was then currently taught in schools, that of [Léon] Brunschvicg [a then fashionable hack philosopher] especially. The third is what interested me the most, the solitary individual who was not influenced by either the first or the second, who saw the scientific as work carried out in common, with

others, and the probable as the truth of the common. The solitary truth was to be that of the one who emerged from the mass, from the common, and faced a world, the given, with no escapes, no help, and no explanations. I was also working out my concept of contingency, which then appeared in *Nausea*.

Was your solitary man a bit like [Friedrich] Nietzsche's Zarathustra?

No, not in the sense that he was a superior man. He was like Roquentin in *Nausea*, a product not of something mystical, but of the social contradictions of his world. We were all trying to devise a code of conduct then, an ethical norm for that world, perhaps even an actual ethics.

And you've always stuck to that, trying to work out an existential ethics?

And I've always failed. Back then I think I was mostly influenced, or rather mesmerized, by Nizan and his crises. You know, he'd go off sometimes for days at a time, wandering the streets, befriending strangers and talking to them like he never revealed himself to us, terrorized by the idea of death. Then, as you know, he went off to Aden as a tutor and spent a whole year, writing that great little book, *Aden, Arabie,* and eventually moving more and more into social engagement until he finally became a communist. I considered that a form of infidelity to our friendship. But I continued to read all the books he recommended, and then, of course, as he made his choice, we started reading Marx together. But as you know, as I said in *Questions of Method,* I didn't really understand Marx. I mean, Marx's language is easy, but I was much too much entangled in a bourgeois esthetic to fathom the meaning of his confrontations. One must smash stuff in one's head to really understand the depth of the class struggle. I must say that I really began to understand Marx only after the war, or in the war. Class struggle is usually just a term to anyone not in it, in the soup itself, so to speak. Nizan understood it during his trip to Aden. Since I flunked the first time, and he had taken a year off to go to Aden, we ended up taking the agrégation exam together, and with Castor, who was younger. I think we finished one, two, three. No, Maheu, Castor's first lover who's now head of UNESCO, was third. I can't remember about Nizan, but he published his book on Aden. An amazing book, and it shows how deeply he was in the soup. So he viewed man stuck by his condition, hence not free. I was then characterizing man as absolutely free. And so we argued for hours during our long walks through Paris. But our philosophical bases were the same.

You mean your Cartesianism? Were there any other major influences?

Well, there was Alain [pseudonym of Emile Chartier, a poet and worldly thinker]. We were against, of course, but influenced just the same, since he was the main voice of the day. He was Cartesian, Kantian, Hegelian, all at the same time. Very eclectic. He would say such stupidities as "The True Hegel is the Hegel which is true," and everyone thought that was the epitome of profundity. But he had tremendous influence, and in the sociopolitical field, he represented radical socialism, which was a very petit bourgeois but atheist movement. But at least Alain introduced a tiny sliver of Hegel into advanced studies. You know, until then, Hegel was banned from the French university system. Twenty or thirty years earlier, [Jules] Lachelier, who was head of the agrégation program, president of the jury, had said that if anyone introduced a Hegelian thought or mentioned the word Hegel in a dissertation, he would be flunked. In Brunswick's massive three-volume history of philosophy, not one mention in the first two volumes and three or four pages in the third. Hegel was not introduced seriously into French thought until the 1930s, when Alexandre Kojève published his brilliant treatise on master and slave, and after the war by [Jean] Hyppolite's translation of *The Phenomenology of Spirit*. But then, we didn't know much of German philosophers anyway, I mean people like [Johann] Fichte and [Friedrich] Schelling—I still haven't read them well, just a smattering here and there . . .

You mentioned [Arthur] Schopenhauer the other day . . .

Ah, but that had nothing to do with my courses or studies. He became fashionable around 1880. A poet, whom I liked very much, Jules Laforgue, talked a lot about Schopenhauer when I was twenty, so I read him then.

But not Nietzsche?

Oh, yes, a lot. But I hated him. I think his crap about the elite, his übermensch, radicalized us a lot, especially Nizan, especially since at Normale those snobs loved him. When we dropped urine-filled condoms on their heads, when they came back in tuxedos from some fancy social event, we used to shout "Thus pissed Zarathustra!" I always believed that being, the individual, had to be saved whole. And to do so, one had to use violence against those who stopped the process.

You say always, but you considered yourself superior . . .

Not to my fellow beings. Superior as a writer because the writer is immortal through his writing, not as a member of society, not like a Zarathustra who considers himself, and Nietzsche says categorically, superior to his fellow beings because they are unable to achieve his insights.

And Kierkegaard?

I had heard of him, perhaps even read some pages by or about him, before the war. But it was as a prisoner that I got into him. I asked Castor to send me his book on anguish, his *Fear and Trembling*.

How did you react to god ordering Abraham to kill his son?

Not as I was supposed to. To me god was the state ordering its subject to do as told. But that was my reaction before, my anti-pacifism during the Spanish Civil War.

You were in favor of nonintervention?

Not at all! I was in favor of intervention, absolutely. Even official intervention, meaning that France should have sent a few divisions against Franco. After all, we had an elected popular front government in France, just like the Spanish Republic.

Yet while the fighting is going on you go off to Mussolini's Italy and write about eating mortadella, and Mathieu . . .

Stop! Mathieu is not always me. Well, perhaps in 1936, but not by 1937.

And that great conversation when Mathieu goes down to see Gomez when he comes across from the front to buy planes or whatever, and Gomez tells him that the Republic has lost. Mathieu can't understand why, in that case, is Gomez going back to fight. Gomez answers that one doesn't fight fascism because one is going to win, one fights fascism because it is fascist. A great response.

Precisely. That's Mathieu and Gomez, but not Sartre and Fernando at that point. I put those words in Gomez's mouth precisely because I believed them, but of course in the novel Mathieu had not evolved into a man of action yet, as he does in the third volume. But that's me, as much as Gomez, or your father. I was—and am today—absolutely committed to the proposition that one must always fight the fascists, whatever the consequences, which is why I work with La Gauche Prolétarienne, and why, I might add, you are here, blacklisted at home.[4]

OK, so you were for intervention, and you went off to see Mussolini's fascist state?

I was totally and completely for intervention, but on the condition that I didn't go. You got me. That amounts to not being for intervention.

Is that part of your rebellion against everything, because as Jeanson has written[5] and a lot of folks mention, you have a bastard complex?

That's totally absurd. Jeanson is a good writer and on our side, but he's wrong on this point. First, as I told you, I was never rebellious. Second, I was not a bastard but an orphan, or half orphan, which is completely different. As I wrote in *The Words,* I was very comfortable at home, growing up with a sister (my mother) and Moses (my grandfather) who both adored me, or at least, in my grandfather's case, made me believe that he did, very convincingly until the double betrayals.

Weren't you rebellious after those betrayals?

My impulse is to say no, because I did not rebel against either Charles or Mancy and my mother. Yet, the more I saw and learned what bourgeois society did to ordinary people, especially to the poor, the more I became aware of the viciousness and greed of white colonialists and imperialists, the more I moved to the left. The question is, can one become a revolutionary without being rebellious? Isn't the rebel more determined than the revolutionary, in the sense that the revolutionary who is not a rebel makes his stand, is convinced politically, through an intellectual process? A rebel who becomes a revolutionary is in the soup. His inner guts are committed.

And his pride is involved.

Exactly. Does that not mean that the revolutionary, the intellectual revolutionary, who is tortured is more apt to give in to torture, than the rebel-revolutionary, who is not only totally convinced, not only totally committed, but also angry, full of hate for his torturers? Think of Algeria. I was one hundred percent with the FLN [the National Liberation Front, the Algerian fighters for independence from France]. I gave them money, I transported medicine for them, I signed Jeanson's "121" [Declaration on the Right to Insubordination in the War in Algeria, known as the "Manifesto of the 121"].[6] But would I have been able to resist the *picana* [an electric cattle prod used in torturing prisoners, including by the French in Algeria]?

Are you saying that one cannot really be a rebel-revolutionary without hate?

I don't know. One always says more than one does. I have always, well, for the last twenty years, been with the revolutionaries, participating in their demonstrations, in their occupations, in their inflammatory statements, even in their hunger strikes—well, one of them—but I never end up on the front lines anywhere. So if one is what one does, as you and I both insist, then I am not a real revolutionary, only a parlor-type one, hence a reformist.

Like your hero in *The Wall?* A genuine revolutionary would not have talked, I mean, would not have given false information, would just have said nothing, correct?

There's a book by a Czech communist named Fucik who was tortured for days and days, then shot. In between tortures, he somehow managed to write an absolutely amazing book, and what he says basically is that since he knew he would never talk he looked upon his torturers not as humans but as part of a cholera epidemic or part of the plague—that is, a deadly virus—who are totally at a loss whenever they come up against someone whom they know will not talk.

What's the name of that book?

A l'ombre de la potence.[7] **It's impossible to imagine how one would act in similar circumstances. Clearly, Fucik was amazing. Was he so well trained by the party—he became a communist at fifteen and was twenty-three when the Gestapo seized him, in 1943—that he had become a sort of automaton? Or was he so convinced of his faith that, like any religious fanatic, he could sustain any and all punishment that the Gestapo could subject him to? Or was he just so incredibly proud of being a just man that no one who was unjust could defeat his resolve?**

Perhaps all of the above. Pride, faith, conviction, hatred of the enemy . . .

That's very important, hatred. Without it, one often stops too soon. It happened in the French Revolution; I think it happens in every revolution, when those who do not hate the enemy suddenly say, Enough already, and stop short of accomplishing the complete restructuring of society, and the result is that the revolution is betrayed.

But love of those for whom one revolts, too. Like Che Guevara said, "At the risk of sounding ridiculous, the revolutionary is motivated by love." Hate the enemy and love the enemy's enemies. Simultaneously.

If we say that he who revolts out of hatred of the greedy capitalist who exploits our fellow humans, are we then saying that the love of our exploited fellow humans is motivated by pride? Or by intellectual understanding of the reasons and conditions of the exploitation? Do we become revolutionaries out of emotions or reason?

I think both. When I was fifteen (but lied about my age), I went with the Unitarian Service Committee—that's an organization that helps the poor, the disenfranchised, the rejects of capitalist society—to work with a southern poet named Don West to build an interracial camp for needy children in the middle of Talmadge County in Georgia, one of the most racist places in America. Don was a real militant, a Baptist minister who ran against a congressman named Wood, another genuine Southern fascist, who wanted all progressives to lose their jobs, like Senator Joe McCarthy did later. One day as Don was driving our group around the state, we were stopped by the police because a lynching was taking place. There were a score of cops around and hundreds of people watching, and we could do nothing. The hapless black youth who was lynched was about my age. The cops did nothing until the boy was dead. Then one fired his pistol in the air and shouted, "Lynching is illegal!" The crowd laughed and dispersed in a jovial mood, including scores of children. I began to really freak out, but one of my group, a female graduate student from Ohio, cuddled me and held me so tight until we were well away that I couldn't yell. Don's brother-in-law was a communist, in fact a member of the Central Committee of the CPUSA, and he visited us a few days later. I was so upset by what I had seen that I told him I wanted to join the CP. He asked me why, then told me that the party does not want recruits based on emotional conviction. "We want recruits who read, understand, and accept the tenets of the party," he said. A couple of years later he turned and testified on his fellow communists for the government.

Hatred and love. A revolutionary is made by hating injustice and loving his fellow sufferers, like Che said, like Nizan. I agree. One revolts out of hatred, one becomes a revolutionary out of reason. Both simultaneously.

March 1971

GERASSI: We had sort of concluded last time that revolutionaries must also be rebels, the difference being that one rebels out of hatred and one becomes a revolutionary, as Che claimed, out of love. Questions: When one is influenced by a novel, is it emotion or reason?

SARTRE: Are you talking about the novels that influenced you, Dostoyevsky and Tolstoy?

Well, as we discussed at lunch last Sunday, I was influenced especially by Dostoyevsky. Tolstoy I read as history, at least *War and Peace. Anna Karenina* bored me.

One of your colleagues at Vincennes [the University of Paris VIII, where I was teaching] once said to Castor that the difference in our novels was very revealing, because Castor's characters made their decisions very slowly, very contemplatively, while those of Sartre's were very brusque, tempestuous even. That's the difference between Tolstoy and Dostoyevsky as well. But I wasn't bored by Tolstoy, not by *Anna Karenina* or anything else he wrote, and I was especially moved by that short novel, ah . . .

The Death of Ivan Illich, a real gem.

Right. A real masterpiece. But it was Dostoyevsky's heroes who dug into me.

You mean like Ivan and Mishkin and Raskolnikov?

The first two for sure. Raskolnikov is not really a hero, is he—more an anti-hero? But that guy was right. As you can see in *The Age of Reason*, Mathieu makes all his major decisions as a reaction to a crisis, until the third volume, right, when he realizes that the war is over and he doesn't count anymore.

Even when he makes the decision to sleep with the prostitute, it's she that sort of drags him off, right? It's like the first volume of *The Roads to Freedom* is Dostoyevskian in imagination while the third is Tolstoyian in contemplation.

Let's not push this analysis too far; after all, there are all sorts of earth-shattering decisions being made in *War and Peace*.

Sure, in the war, but in human terms, the decisions are really made by Pierre, who is not really alive. He's a construct. The flesh-and-blood character, the existential character, as I once wrote in a paper at Columbia, is André.

So in *The Brothers Karamazov* you must consider Alyosha a construct too.

Absolutely. But there are two existential characters in *The Brothers*: Ivan, of course, as every one says, but also Dmitri, who acts with his gut, but always true to himself.

So Shatov is the construct in *The Possessed*? And who's the existential character?

There are three, in my view, which no one agrees with. Stavrogin, of course. And Kirilov, who commits suicide to prove that he is free. But also the communist. What was his name? I remember Shatov and Kirilov and Stavrogin, but for the life of me, I can't remember the communist, who fascinated me more than all the others.

Because he is the man of action, right? You judge novels politically.

I was seventeen and not very political when I read *The Possessed*, and it possessed me.

You were a political creature from day one. With a father who ranged from being [the first president of Israel, Chaim] Weizmann's bodyguard, a subminister of culture in the two-day Munich Soviet, a general and the last defender of Barcelona in Spain, to an OSS spy during World War II—how could you not be political, whether you rebelled against your father or not? Which is why you never had the patience to read Proust.

You're going to maintain that I didn't like Proust because I was political? I mean, Christ, seventeen pages to describe *les aubépines:* I don't see how that didn't bore the shit out of you.

But the writing is superb, that's what fascinated me, the writing. Even for the *aubépines,* though I grant you that didn't move me particularly. His description of the bourgeois world, the salons, the feasts.

Are you going to say that about [Flaubert's] *Salammbô* too?

Boy, you're really after me today. No, *Salammbô* is a piece of shit, agreed. But *Madame Bovary*! The way Flaubert described his crowd told me a lot about the morality of the times, and mind you, you can use his perspicacity to dissect the same society today.

Politically?

I wasn't very hip politically then. But I learned from them [Flaubert's books] that anyone can write. That writing is having the patience to write. The will. The stamina. That's the basis. The rest comes from reading, reading, and reading.

So if you have the stamina and the will, but read nothing but Proust and Flaubert, you too will end up in the entrails of the bourgeois world.

That's why you have to read everything you can. I read the Russians, the English—and they're a hell of a lot worse, from your point of view, that is, than Proust or Flaubert—and [Paul] Valéry, whom I also read at that time. But, you know, they were in the world in which I lived. Mancy, my stepfather, a typical bourgeois, a director but salaried, always trying to get ahead. Typical.

Your grandfather wasn't like that.

Oh yes, he was part of that world. True, he was a Republican, a radical-socialist, meaning a secular defender of freedom for all, but bourgeois nonetheless. To him, a novel should not take sides, so to speak, I mean it should not advocate. Yet still, a good novel should evoke a humanism, should provoke a sense of wanting to serve.

So what did you read that made you begin to serve, to get out of that other world, in your head at least?

Well, as I told you, the Russians and then the Americans. That was later, of course, but [John] Dos Passos! Oh, Dos Passos, the power of that man!

Do you know that he is almost unknown in America today? My students came out of high school never even having heard of him.

It doesn't surprise me. The education system is a tool of the government.

Not completely. Our education system is left to the states, cities, and communities. It's not centralized as it is here.

But our ministers of education must operate within the context, the tradition, the history, even the myths of France, and that means our social revolutions, 1848, the Paris Commune. No minister would or could eliminate Zola, say, or [Mikhail] Bakunin from the curriculum. But you haven't had your social revolution yet; every educator thinks America has the greatest freedom in the world, and your press supports your government no matter what it does, no?

Yes, but not because of government censorship. Because of money. You see, we do not have a free press. We have a *free-enterprise* press. Advertisers dictate the policy of our press. Oh, not on every issue. But overall. Like the Red-baiting laws that we got. For example, the Taft-Hartley and McCarran laws said that no communist could be in leadership positions of a union, but it never occurred to anyone to make it equally illegal for a Nazi or fascist to be head of a company.

You think our press is better?

Sure, because you have a political press. The right-wing or socialist paper worries that if it doesn't report some outrage, the communist paper will, or if *Le Figaro* doesn't, *Le Monde* will, so they tend to be much more careful about lying. So when did you fall on Dos Passos?

During the Great Depression, I think. Anyway, much later—after Normale.

I know he had a great influence on you. But what? The style, the subject?

Both. Reread my story "The Youth of a Chief" [in *The Wall*]. I think it's pure Dos Passos.

The Wall was published after *Nausea,* but written before, correct, at least that story, yes, but it was not the first piece of fiction that you had written?

Oh no, there were the stories we published in our ill-fated review.

La Revue Sans Titre [The Review Without a Title], which you co-edited with Nizan, dates back to 1923 when you were still in khâgne.

Actually, the director, the administrator, was neither Nizan nor I, but a guy named Charles Fraval, who became a communist I think, and then I don't know what happened to him, but Nizan and I were just contributors, and we

sort of wrote everything, giving different names to the stuff that was not our main contribution. But aside from my short story, I published in it the beginning of a novel I wrote during the vacation, in other words, between khâgne and hypo-khâgne, in which I talk about "the old friend," which means that Nizan and I already had broken up.

Over politics?

No. I never criticized his political choices, even when he was flirting with the fascist Action Française group. I mean, we discussed politics, but I was into trying to define, or characterize, freedom, which did not yet involve politics in my head. No, I think we broke up over the *Review*. It only had two numbers, January and February 1923 . . . well, that doesn't add up, does it? If only we could find them. I couldn't have written the novel, started it, during the vacation of '23 then, it had to be '22, and we had reconciled by '23, in the fall, when we went into Normale.

Why did you break up then?

I do think it was about the *Review*. Something about it. My novel after all was about two fantastically close friends who break up because of a review. But it couldn't be just that, because after all it was Fraval who decided what ran in it and what did not, and we had no power over him; he was a real dictator, I mean, he'd listen to our views, but he would decide, and that was that. So there had to be other reasons.

Were you jealous of Nizan?

Maybe. After his trip to Aden, and his book, which was very well received, perhaps. I do know that when we were back together at Normale I was much happier. Well, not just to be friends with him, but to be in a group, because there were some ten of us that ran around together, that caused trouble to the snobs. The great thing about group activity is that it deculpable-izes you. You are part of the decisions, but the decision-making process is generalized to the group. So when we decided to take over a bar and that led to confrontations, whatever, yes, each of us was responsible, but it was a common act. Of course, there were some individual disasters, too. Well, not disaster, I'm exaggerating, but like when we decided to experiment with drugs. I ended up having a nervous breakdown.

You mean the crabs?

Yeah, after I took the mescaline I started seeing crabs around me all the time, I mean they followed me in the streets, into class.

How could you study, then?

I got used to them. I would wake up in the morning and say, "Good morning, my little ones, how did you sleep?" I would talk to them all the time, or I would say, "OK guys, we're going into class now, so we have to be still and quiet," and they would be there, around my desk, absolutely still, until the bell rang.

A lot of them?

Actually, no, just three or four.

But you knew they were imaginary?

Oh yes, from the beginning. As long as I was at Normale, they didn't bother me. But after I finished school, actually a whole year later, I began to think I was going crazy, so I went to see a shrink, a young guy then with whom I have been good friends ever since, Jacques Lacan. In fact he became a psychoanalyst and once, much later, he tried to psychoanalyze me.

With what result?

Nothing that I or he valued very much, except with the crabs, we sort of concluded that it was fear of becoming alone, or to put it more in context, fear of losing the camaraderie of the group. You know, as soon as I got my *agrèg* my life changed radically from being one of a group of ten or so, a group that included peasants and workers as well as bourgeois intellectuals, to being just me and Castor.

Peasants? Workers?

Sure. Remember Pierre Guille? The son of peasants.[1] And the guy we called Blondie, because he was the darkest of us all. He was the son of a coal miner. Remember that education was free, and if one passed the tests, and had no money, the state gave you a stipend for living expenses. That was the law. Still is. Travel expenses too. If you passed well enough to be able to choose your advanced school but lived too far to take a Métro to it—like Frantz Fanon, remember? The government had to pay his plane rides from Guadeloupe every year until he was hired by the government as a psychiatrist in a government mental hospital.

Did you all have nicknames? What was yours?

"The Little Man." Not very original. And we kept to them. It was Maheu—I can't remember his—who gave Castor hers, and when Stépha joined the group, she became "la baba," which led to your father being called "le boubou." You know, now as I think back, being part of a group, a collective if you wish, solves a lot of psychological hang-ups. I always got along fine in collectives. I never felt I had to rule and I never objected to being told what to do if all agreed. I've always been somewhat anxious, not too seriously, but with feelings of an orphan, living with someone who thought himself to be Moses, being ugly, small, a stranger, betrayed by my mother and Moses, rejected by my first great love [Simone Jolivet]. I adapted very well to collective life. In the army. As a prisoner. The feeling of being equal is extremely important, but I didn't realize it until the war, until I became a prisoner with other prisoners.

What about women at Normale?

There were no female students then.

I know that, I mean sexually? I'm curious how the group reacted, if there were jealousies, fights, et cetera?

No, not at all. We would pick some up at a bar, bring them up. It was forbidden, of course, but the concierge was a nice guy, and he would look the other way as we snuck them in. The women very quickly adapted, or liked, the situation. After a while, they'd sleep around, and no one felt cheated, or said so anyway. There was one guy, Larroutis was his name, who was a virgin and insisted he would stay that way until he got married because of his strict Catholicism. But he would get drunk with us, and horse around, and he was very funny, so we never felt that he was not part of the group.

And you were all on the same wavelength, philosophically?

Politically no, in terms of what party or movement we favored, but we all agreed that the government stank, that the system was for the rich to get richer. We were all rebels. Philosophically, we were all rationalists. We all said a cat is a cat, a jerk is a jerk. But Nizan and I were the only two who were preparing the agrégation in philosophy. Peron, the guy who died in the resistance, was studying English. There was a couple doing German. And most of the others were in literature. But of course we all studied everything, it seems.

Did you want to become a philosophy teacher?

Not really. At Normale the philosopher of the moment was [Henri] Bergson, who claimed that philosophy begins from an initial intuition of the world. It may be a vague intuition, but it was the absolute beginning, and if one did not have that intuition, one could not philosophize. The intuition was like a gift [un don]. Well, I didn't have it. I was a rationalist; I obviously didn't fit. But, I figured, I had to earn a living, and once I got my agrégation I was guaranteed a job teaching, so the best deal, I thought, was to teach philosophy. I never wanted to be a philosopher, but I knew that to be seriously committed to write novels, I would have to understand as much as possible, and philosophy would serve me in that. So to write, I concluded, the best job was to teach philosophy, because it meant reading and learning what everyone else thought and being able to make my own intellectual decisions based on an ever widening knowledge.

But Castor told me that when you two became friends, you wanted to be a philosopher and she scoffed at the idea.

Scoffed is a bit strong. She simply said that it was crazy to get bogged down in that when I could write. I know that your reason for giving up philosophy was because you thought it was, as you said, mental masturbation. But Castor didn't go that far.

Yet you didn't take her advice.

Well, I did in the sense that I stopped thinking of myself as a philosopher. But remember, we were both preparing the agrèg in philosophy.

And you were studying together, right? At the Cité Universitaire.[2]

After I flunked my first try, I checked into an apartment there, and met Castor, who was preparing hers at the Sorbonne. But we were introduced more formally by Maheu, whom she met at the National Library and who became her first lover. Castor then brought into our group her best friend, your mother, whom she also met at the library. Stépha then brought in Fernando, and I, Nizan. That became our circle, although Stépha was not preparing an agrèg, and Fernando was painting. But she was adorable and he was funny.

Was it true that you wanted to have an affair with Stépha but she turned you down?

Ha-ha ha! Did your mother tell you that?

Oh no! Stépha would never talk about such things, to me anyway. No, it was Castor who ratted on you.

Ha-ha-ha! Well, it's true. Stépha was an adorable bundle of energy, sexual too, and incredibly beautiful, and a tease, and . . .

Castor said you were in love with her . . .

Yes, maybe. But she turned me down, as you said, but softly, nicely. Your father slept with every woman in Montparnasse, including Castor and her sister, Poupette. But Stépha, nope, faithful to the end.

Do you know the story of Noiditch?

Her Ukrainian boyfriend?

They had met in Berlin. He was also a refugee and a very nice guy. I met him later in America. A charmer. But nothing happened because she came to Paris. Well, one day, when Fernando and she are living together, and he's screwing every model who poses for him, and she knows it but doesn't seem to care, which makes Fernando feel guilty, Noiditch shows up in Paris, broke, absolutely penniless. So Fernando encourages Stépha to go out with him, to show her a really good time, and he gives Noiditch enough money to really entertain her, and for a hotel room. They have a great time all right, but when it came time to go to the hotel, she said, No thanks. And he then spilled the beans to her, which made her laugh her head off, but decided to go along with it in the sense that she stayed with Noiditch—platonically— that night and made him promise to keep up the pretense to Fernando. When he asked why, she answered, So he can stop feeling guilty about all his one-nighters.

I knew that story. I love it. I wanted you to tell it to see if it jibed with what Castor had told me. Great, isn't it? How can one not love a woman like that.

I guess that's why she's the model for your Sarah in *The Age of Reason?* But why did you make her Jewish?

For various reasons. First of all, Fernando was the most un-Jewish Jew I have ever met, even if he was once Weizmann's bodyguard. He's a real Spaniard, with all the machismo and bravado and ridiculous face-savingness of any Spaniard. Since he was right in front of me, in my head that is, when I wrote about Gomez, I couldn't make Gomez Jewish. Second, because Stépha was a typical Jewish mother. Oh I know, not to you perhaps, a typical Jewish mother would not abandon her son to go fight in somebody else's civil war, but to everyone else, to all her friends, to any bum in the street, she was always ready to help.

You even wrote in the novel that she could kill with kindness.

Right. And third, it was important in those days of victories by the anti-Semitic Nazi hordes, to find a way to bring up that issue, and it wouldn't have fit in Spain—I mean, as nasty as were Gomez's political enemies, the Stalinists, I couldn't possibly imply that the Comintern agents or the Russian advisers were anti-Semites, especially since in real life they were all Jews. The Russian ambassador, Marcel Rosenberg, whom everyone adored, was a Jew, and if André Marty was secretly anti-Semitic, saying so would not have been believed in those days.

You said a while ago that you brought in Nizan. But he was not really part of the group, was he?

Well, yes and no. He was often extremely depressed, about death mostly, his anxiety about dying. In those moments he would go out and get drunk by himself.

But you guys got drunk all the time too, no?

No, let's not exaggerate. Once every two weeks, but not out of depression. I mean we'd get completely drunk, rolling on the floor, but in a kind of group purification, emptying ourselves of all problems, worldly thoughts, something like your sessions with pot—except we ended up with headaches and you didn't. We, I'm talking now about the Normale group, we never got drunk out of depression. Nizan did. Alone. His decision to teach the kids of that rich man who took him to Aden was part of that depression. He wanted to pierce through the normal, to go beyond it, and I mean both what is standard and the school. And when he came back, or soon after, he got married. I was his best man, and that tightened the bond between us. Do you know that the very day he got married he suffered a ferocious appendicitis, very bad one, which laid him up for three months. But he came around again after he recouped, and we studied together and we passed at the same time. We celebrated together, with Castor and Rirette, his wife. She sort of stuck in. With Maheu and Guille, then.

Merleau-Ponty?

Merleau was a year younger. We knew each other and liked each other, I guess, but we didn't become close until the resistance.

Aron?

He was also at Normale with us and he was part of the group, but he was an extern. He never went on our binges with us. We kept up our friendship, but not with the kind of intensity that I had with Nizan. When Nizan was named at Bourg [-en-Bresse, a city in central upper France] and we didn't see each other for two years, It was Guille who replaced him as my closest friend. We stayed close for fifty years. He became the analytic chief at Parliament. You know, the one who analyzes every day what the deputies say and what they mean and why, et cetera. Parliament keeps a transcript, but they pay some individual to reduce the goings-on to their essentials and publish it every day. That's what Guille did, and he still does it, as does [Jean] Pouillon by the way. But Guille and I broke up a few years ago.

Because of politics?

No. One of those things, you know, you see someone every day almost for ten, twenty years, then one day you don't call and neither does he. But not because of politics. I had other nonpolitical friends, like Maheu. You interviewed him, so you know that he can be charming, gregarious, warm. Everyone at UNESCO considers him a scumbag, imperial, mean, conniving, just

plain nasty, but with me he's charming, and we have never broken up over his right-wing politics—well, his centrist politics.

But with Camus . . .

That's a whole other matter. Complicated, too. We became good friends during the resistance, when he was editing *Combat* and asked me to write for it. Then he published *The Stranger,* and I reviewed it in *Les Cahiers du Sud,* very favorably. It is an excellent novel. But, you know, he's a *pied-noir* [slang for whites who settled in Algeria, whom the Algerians consider colonists], and he could never really come down solidly in favor of the FLN.

As you know, after I gave up trying to do my dissertation at Columbia on your esthetics, before I switched to political science, I had planned to do it on your feud with Camus. In my project, in the page or two that we had to present to explain why we chose such a subject, I had said that Camus himself was actually proud of never making up his mind about any contemporary issue, that he claimed the only position he could wholeheartedly maintain was to have been for the Republic during the Spanish Civil War. Jeanson got it right. But I could never get a doctorate in the United States by criticizing Camus.

Jeanson was a good comrade, and we worked together a lot during the Algerian revolution. But when *The Rebel* came out, I immediately realized I would have trouble if I wrote the review in *Les Temps Modernes,* so at the staff meeting I asked Jeanson if he had read it—he hadn't; I had gotten an advanced copy—and if he had any bias pro or con Camus. I knew that they had met a few times, but just superficially, at social gatherings. So I asked him to review it and did not edit a single word in his copy. Well, Camus reacted with fury that someone dared to criticize him, and wrote that bitter response, an extremely disingenuous response, since he addressed it not to Jeanson but to "Monsieur le directeur des *Temps Modernes* [Mr. Director of *Modern Times*]." So I had to answer, and that destroyed our friendship.

It was a first-rate response. It made the point so well, without saying it, that we are determined by what we do. Camus, by not taking sides on the Algerian question, was therefore, in my mind, pro–French Algeria, opposed to independence. And I wrote that in what I thought was an extremely well argued preliminary paper to my dissertation, a thirty-odd-page analysis of your feud, which of course my committee at Columbia didn't like. That was the drop in the bucket that made me quit Columbia.

The Algerian question broke up many friendships here. You remember

Mme Morel? Castor tells in her memoirs how often we went to her country estate, how we had picnics with her and her child, and friends. Castor and I used to take Guille and Maheu there, and Nizan too, although Guille and Maheu didn't like Nizan, whom they thought was too stiff, too obsessed. Anyway, I was a very close friend with her until the day that she said "Je suis Algérie française" [a slogan that originated in a speech by François Mitterrand when he was minister of justice, and was then yelled by right-wing French, or beeped with their car horns, meaning Algeria is a French province]. That did it.

Yet at Normale, politics never disturbed your relationships?

No. My group had a kind of political makeup, since we all hated the rich kids, but not because they were rich but because they were snobs.

Aron wasn't rich?

He came from a bourgeois background, but so did I. But he fooled around with us. He didn't get drunk when we did, but he was an extern and so wasn't around in the evening very much. You know, we had a very tight schedule. Up fairly early, coffee, then studying until lunch. After lunch, which was leisurely, a couple of hours, back to studying until nine, except when we had to attend a lecture, and then at night, unless we were too exhausted, we relaxed one way or another.

Sounds like you went to few lectures. Weren't there any profs that inspired you?

There was a historian of philosophy at the Sorbonne whom I liked, and I did go to hear him, especially on the Stoics. But otherwise, I almost never went to the Sorbonne lectures. And, at Normale, oh no, all the profs were pedants and really incredibly stupid. So, I studied alone, in my box, next to Nizan in his. And when we stopped we always discussed what we had read, unless we went to get drunk.

You couldn't study the Germans and you hated Bergson. What did you like?

The ancient Greeks. Especially the Stoics. Descartes, of course. He never bored me. I was a Cartesian through and through . . .

You still are.

In a way, yes, I guess. I liked Spinoza a lot, and the English, Hume for example, though I preferred [Immanuel] Kant. But I often went off to write my "novels," or to read, like Stendhal, who I thought was the greatest of all French writers. But don't forget we had all sorts of other subjects to master, like Greek and Latin, because we would be grilled in those philosophers' original language. In fact, Castor almost came out first when I made a terrible error in Greek, which cost me six points. I had a better grade than she at the written though, and I did better in French and Latin.

Were you competing?

No, not at all. We actually looked forward to becoming professors then, and we knew that those who finished best would get the top choices, so we wanted to be up there.

So you chose Le Havre, "Bouville"?

No—well, yes, the choices were very limited in '29. But I got transferred to Paris after I was released from the stalag.

I thought you didn't want to be a professor?

Oh, when I got my agrèg, I did. You know, for four years I had my tuition, room and board, even spending money, not very much, but still, all paid for by the state, so I felt I owed the state the ten years of the contract.

Ten years? I thought it was more.

No, just ten years, and one could always pay it off, as I did. In part. But no, I liked being a prof since it did give me enough time to write, and first of all, I wanted to write.

And yet you had total contempt for your professors at both Normale and the Sorbonne.

At Normale, yes, though I loved the life there, and everything paid for, even spending money. Not much, mind you—as I told you, I couldn't afford to go to Toulouse to see Simone very often, but still, enough to get drunk and have a good time every other week. The Sorbonne was different. There were young teachers there, giving lectures on all sorts of subjects, and we had the right to attend any one. As I think I told you, there was one guy who would give very interesting lectures on the history of philosophy. So we all went to hear him, Maheu, Nizan, and I, our whole group.

And Castor, right? Was Stépha also there?

Castor yes, every session. Stépha, no. She had decided by then not to get a degree. She spent a lot of time at the National Library, which is where she and Castor became close, mainly because she taught Castor, as she reveals in her memoirs, how to dress and make up to pick up boys, all those Hungarians, remember? But she stopped going to class once she got involved with Fernando. She too had lived at the Cité Universitaire, but once she moved in with him, she had to earn money so he could paint.

Nice guy!

Well, it was her choice. He was not going to earn a living. He used to do quick odd jobs when he had no money for food and could not exchange a painting for a meal. You know, that was very common then. The owner of La Coupole, just to name one, was great that way. He used to feed, maybe as often as once a week, all of Fernando's pals, Mané Kats, Giacometti, Utrillo, Soutine, Masson, Chagall, Modigliani, all those Montparnasse artists, and eventually made a fortune with the paintings or drawings he got for the food. But like them, Fernando refused to work full time, so Stépha had to work.[3] Castor told me once that she thought Stépha was a genuine saint, despite the fact that she never believed in saints.

But when Stépha dropped out of the Sorbonne, did she stay close friends with Castor, was she still part of the group?

Yes, but that was later, in 1927. The year before I spoke to Castor.

Why not? You attended the same lectures.

She was Maheu's girl, I mean Maheu and she were an item, and he wouldn't share her. He refused to introduce us, either to me or Nizan or anyone else of our group.

But you were in the same class, listening to the same lecturer, you didn't need to be introduced? You couldn't go up to her and say, What did you think of [Gottfried] Leibniz? I mention Leibniz because you apparently drew him "in bed with the monads" and gave it to her. Didn't she thank you? Didn't that start a conversation?

She thanked me and walked on. In France in those days a man and a woman couldn't just start talking, unless it was in a bar, where the women were different. I mean, the class distinctions were rigid, and it wasn't money, as I was poor by then, despite my rich stepfather, and Castor's family had lost their investments—it was a class thing. Someone introduced Maheu to Castor, and unless he introduced us to her, we didn't really commune. If I remember correctly, it was Stépha who did it. Castor had gotten her a job as a tutor to Zaza [Elisabeth Lacoin], her childhood friend who was madly in love with Merleau-Ponty, and Stépha, who disregarded all class habits, introduced everyone she liked.

What happened to the Zaza-Merleau couple?

A real tragedy. When they found out about the couple, her parents got some investigator to probe into his background, and they came up with the fact that his mother had been unfaithful to her husband, with a long affair with some engineer named François, making it almost certain that this

François was really the father of both Merleau and his sister. The parents then wrote to Merleau telling him that they would oppose their marriage, and Merleau then broke with Zaza, who, as you know, we all assumed died of a broken heart—in fact, [she died] of a bad illness.[4] Castor hated Merleau until she found out the truth. So did Stépha. So during that period, when Merleau was also at Normale, but a year behind us, we never became friends. Not until during the occupation.

In 1946, when he came to the United States, Stépha treated him very nicely. I showed him New York by day (my parents did by night), took him shopping for his wife, and arranged for him to speak to my school's philosophy class, which allowed me to sit in even though I was a year younger than the students. I didn't like him.

He wasn't very funny, was he? But he was a very good man, and an excellent philosopher. His *Humanism and Terror, Sens et non-sens,* and *Adventures of the Dialectic* are all first-rate works. He was an important phenomenologist.[5]

And not a rationalist, like you?

Not quite. He was too much of a Marxist to believe that we are all absolutely free.

Indeed, how could you, can you, believe that all men are free?

As you know, that's a philosophical position. I mean, I certainly don't believe that the dissenter in jail is free, or even that he who is dependent on his boss to live is free, or that anyone who has no feeling of security is free. Politically, which means of course economically, freedom is a bourgeois reality. The worker is not free precisely because he is insecure.

But isn't the bourgeois who constantly worries about his financial future equally insecure? If he's a vice president, he wants to be president. If he's an assistant professor, he wants to be a full professor.

Let me be precise. Philosophically, we are all free to accept what we are.

Which is what you meant when you made that statement that got you so much criticism for saying that during the occupation, the French were absolutely free.

Exactly, what I meant was that we had no real choice. Or put this way: we could be collaborationists or we could be resisters. If resisters, that position entailed determined actions and reactions. It illustrated my point that individual freedom is to accept being what one does.

I once gave this example when I tried to explain *Being and Nothingness* to my students. If we had every scientific data on Joe's makeup so that we could predict exactly what he would do, and Joe knew it, he would still feel free. For example, he decides one night to go to the movies. He sees the choices: a comedy, a thriller, or a porno. Scientifically we know he will choose the porno. So does he. And he does. But when he comes out of the theater he complains: What a bore, I should have gone to the thriller. *Should have!* He holds himself, not science and all the data, responsible, even though he knows he was totally determined. Joe's sense of freedom, I explained, was his sense of himself as a human being. I think, therefore I am free. But that's not the way most people talk about freedom.

Of course not. Politically, they say freedom is being able to do what they want. Economically, it is they are secure. That's how Nizan saw it.

He didn't think humans were free?

Nope. To him, the concept of freedom was absurd. Like Kirilov [in Dostoyesky's *The Possessed*], he would say we don't chose to be born and we don't chose to die. We can't fly and swim at the same time. I'm ugly as hell, he would say, and you're not, so you get a better deal. As a good communist, he would insist that no one who has to work for a living, no one who worries if he's going to be fired or have enough money to send his kid to Normale, is free. And in that sense he was right, of course. Economic freedom is limited to a small sector of the bourgeois class.

You had that, didn't you? Did he?

Despite my theft in order to buy the affection, or acceptance rather, of my La Rochelle classmates, I never worried about money. I always assumed that I would have enough. If I had more, I spent it. Castor too. When we had money in those early days, we'd go to a decent restaurant. In the late 1920s I think we managed to have lunch at La Coupole once every two weeks. Nizan would accuse us of being petit bourgeois with a ruling class mentality. In a way, that's true. Why do we still have lunch at La Coupole? For privacy. We sit, as you know, in a particular section where the waiters and headwaiters make sure no one disturbs us.

They're absolutely amazing. They have an incredible intuition about who to let approach you and who not, like when I come to join you, they know somehow that you were expecting me . . .

They'd seen you with us so often.

Yes, but when you told me to invite [Herbert] Marcuse when he came through Paris last year, remember, he had never been here before, and he was late, so we were all sitting there when he looked for us. They knew. They actually pointed where we were without him asking.

Hey, don't make heroes out of our poor waiters. The maître d' knew we were waiting for someone and he took one look at Marcuse's lost demeanor and . . .

OK. Tell me, you and Castor never worried about money?

Never. If we didn't have enough to go on vacation, we'd spend it at the library. Right now I'm close to being broke. *Flaubert* **[Sartre's three-volume study titled** *The Family Idiot***] has not yet appeared, and I don't think it'll make much. But I'm still getting royalties from** *Nausea,* **thirty years later—weird, especially since I don't make a connection in my mind. Like writing and money have nothing in common. While a worker's job and his salary are two sides of the same coin. To the worker anyway.**

I read somewhere that you feel guilty about having money.

Naw! Perhaps in the sense that I never understood why working, say, on a novel for a year should then bring the author enough money to live for twenty. Doesn't make sense. Enough money for him to spend another year or two or even five writing another novel, OK. But a fortune?

It said that your incredible generosity is the result of that guilt?

Maybe. That's up to the psychoanalysts. I don't consider myself especially generous, just if I have more money than I need, why not give it to those who need?

Somehow, it all fits into the question you often asked yourself, namely what is the role of the intellectual in a revolutionary society? Castor says that this question got you to read Trotsky intensively.

She exaggerates. First of all, I was not a revolutionary when I read him, so I was just curious. Second, I didn't think he said anything brilliant on the subject. But it's true that it is a serious question. In bourgeois society, the intellectual is privileged both in terms of prestige and financially, if he makes it, that is. I mean why should an actor earn millions, more for one film than a worker makes his whole life? Same with a best seller. Or an artist. [Chaim] Soutine sold one of his paintings for a meal. The restaurant owner who bought it can sell it today and live happily on the Riviera the rest of his life without working. In a revolutionary society, Trotsky would put the artists on salary, workers for the state. Fine, but which artists? The avant-garde painter or sculptor or writer whom no one admires? And who decides? It's a tough question. Why should Fernando not be able to sell his paintings today for mil-

lions, when Picasso thought he was as good as he was, as a colorist at least? Every art dealer wants a Picasso, but they discount his opinion about art? None of that makes sense. And history has shown that it is never those who are "ahead of their time" who are recompensed, but those who mimic their times, who invent nothing new, who are feted with fame and money. Those "ahead of their time" usually have to die first.

Did you solve the question?

You mean of the role of the intellectual in society? No, but I did toy with the idea of creating collectives of intellectuals, something like all the writers who are obsessed with the use of power, say, getting together, choosing their peers, and dividing up the money that any one gets among all according to their need. Something like that.

My need is to get drunk every night. Otherwise I can't write in the morning. So I need more money than the one who never drinks. Fair?

The collective would decide.

How about the writer who murders his wife and is writing in jail; does he still get his share?

Hey, it was just an idea, but its meaning is that the way society now gloats and recompenses its intellectuals is not fair.

Another reason to tear it down.

Agreed. But there are a lot of better reasons.

April 1971

GERASSI: Aha, I see *The Sun Also Rises* on your desk. Are you reading Hemingway these days?

SARTRE: I read them all a long time ago; I'm just rereading this one. I read an article that said Hemingway was an anti-Semite and fought with all his Jewish friends over this book, because the only Jew in it is bad. Our intelligentsia pretends that there's an unwritten rule that says if the villain is the only black man or Jew or whatever in the novel, then the author is saying that all blacks or Jews or whatever are bad. Your father had a fight with him, didn't he?

Not over that book. Over *For Whom the Bell Tolls*. Apparently Hemingway changed the word "fascist" to "nationalist" in order to please the film-version producers who did not want to insult our good ally Franco, or something like that. Fernando called him a filthy opportunist. So I was told, as I was not present for that fight. But I'm sure their fight had much deeper causes. Maybe Martha Gellhorn, Hemingway's third wife and a great reporter. My father adored her. Probably slept with her.

Wasn't the general who sends Jordan to join the guerrillas [in *For Whom the Bell Tolls*] modeled after your father?

I don't think so. I remember once during the war when Hemingway came to dinner early and Fernando had not arrived yet, he asked me if I had read the novel. When I said no, he said, You should, it's a lot about your father. But both Fernando and Stépha said baloney. I was eleven or twelve then. Anyway, when they had that fight, I never heard anything about anti-Semitism. Have you finished rereading *The Sun*? What is your conclusion?

Totally trivial debate. What it shows to me is that the left cannot just fight the right, it always has to fight other leftists as well, which is why, I fear, we will never achieve—or you, because I'm too old now—ever achieve a decent revolution.

Still an optimist, hey? When did you become so depressed, I mean politically?

In 1958 when de Gaulle made his coup. I was fifty-three then, and it dawned on me that I would live the rest of my life under that ridiculous sample of anachronism.

Your trip to Cuba didn't recharge you at all?

Yes, when we were there. Our talks with Fidel and especially Che were great, and very inspirational. But it didn't last long. The repression to hide the inefficiency became so pervasive. Revolutionaries inevitably become guilty of the same crimes as those they overthrow, and that's more depressing even than de Gaulle.

Boy, you sure hated him, didn't you? You never gave him credit for creating Europe, did you? OK, OK, let's not get into that one again. But you never blamed the United States for the repression in Cuba? The inefficiencies you mentioned were caused by the enormous exodus of all the trained, and hence rich, Cubans to Miami. Even so, until 1967, there was almost no repression. The euphoria, the excitement of the revolution, especially during OSPAAL and OLAS [large conferences of world and Latin American revolutionary leaders that took place in 1966 and 1967 in Havana], was mind-blowing.[1] It's true that there were great inefficiencies. I remember an enormous amount of boxes of oranges rotting on the docks, and Che took me to a depot full of imported bicycles without tires ("We don't have rubber," he laughed) and another full of snowplows imported from China, in hot Cuba! But any new revolutionary country would make such mistakes. You said so yourself in your preface to Frantz Fanon's *Wretched of the Earth*.

Of course. That's all very normal. But you don't arrest and jail those who disagree with you and charge them with being responsible for such beginner's mistakes, as Cuba did. Or arrest its intelligentsia because they criticize the government, great writers and poets, like [Heberto] Padilla, for example.[2]

But that's not what depressed you, or made you a pessimist. What did? De Gaulle?

Certainly de Gaulle. As I told you, I just could not stomach that charlatan yapping about the greatness of France. But true, it started earlier, much earlier. I think my first depression started when I graduated from Normale. Suddenly I realized I had to be a normal cog in the system. It's not that I didn't like teaching. It's that I was now determined and defined as a teacher. Pigeonholed, classified, situated. Where was the freedom I claimed we all had, the freedom to accept one's fate? Something wrong with that. I had meant it as a moral tenet, in the sense that we must accept what we do insofar as we are responsible for it. In other words, my world had become serious. The year in Germany was a hiatus to that. But just a hiatus. Then came the prisoner-of-war camp. Suddenly everything changed. I became a social being, not a writer, not a philosopher, not a teacher, even if I wrote during my time in the stalag. I had become just one of a group, one of a collective, not worse or better than anyone else, no matter how different we each were. It's there that I understood what the word "humanity" really meant, why your father went to Spain, why he was going to go back even when he was sure his side would lose. But, I was discharged. I became a solitary being again. Yes, I joined the resistance, in a way, by writing, since with my eyes I could not do otherwise. But I was still an individual. Sitting in a café, writing. Yes, with Castor at the other table. And soon we developed what she called a family. But each of us were individuals. We thought. Terrible thing, thinking. Hemingway knew that. Don't think. Go swimming, fishing, hunting, anything to avoid thinking. Thinking leads to folly.

A new Cartesianism: I think, therefore I'm crazy.

Very good. Seriously though, thinking, I mean real thinking, what one does alone, at the table, is the opposite of passion, commitment, being alive.

What you then termed "being in the soup"?

Exactly.

And that's why you prefer to be with women.

Exactly. Men always want to discuss ideas, to tell you how they interpret something. Women tell you what they feel, what they felt. Think about ideas at your table and leave me alone. Tell me your experiences, how you felt about them, and I learn something new, every time. Very rare for a man. Your father was like that; that's why I could spend hours talking with him. You're like that too. Calder is like that. But most men are a royal bore. Like Malraux. He'll tell

you why two juxtaposed colors work beautifully, but never what he feels when he looks at those two colors.

But all your work is made up of ideas.

Which is why I must test them in concrete situations, hence my plays and novels.

So I don't need to read *Being and Nothingness* if I read or go see *No Exit*?

In a way that's true. Your Catherine never read the former and she claimed she never understood my philosophy, but she did too, because she read *No Exit*, and *The Flies* and whatever else you scheduled in your class when she was your student.

Yeah, but I spent hours explaining them, re-creating the essence in concrete situations . . .

Ah, concrete situations! That's it! You personalized my philosophy by making it collective, because each concrete situation you created applied to all.

Perhaps, but why does that make you depressed? And what do the crabs have to do with your feeling of being isolated?

The crabs really began when my adolescence ended—that is, when I graduated from Normale to be professor, a cog in the system. At first, at Le Havre, I avoided them by writing about them—in effect, by defining life as nausea, but then as soon as I tried to objectify it, the crabs appeared. A sort of psychosis, hallucinations . . .

Like the woman in "The Room"? [One of the short stories in *The Wall*.]

Exactly. At first I just imagined that I heard things. I remember the first time, at the Coupole. Castor and I were having lunch when suddenly I started hearing "Napoléon, the little one, the big one . . ." Castor did not hear it, so we immediately assumed I was hallucinating. It turned out that there were a bunch of people behind the screen—the Coupole never had such things— who were talking about Napoleon. Castor never heard it, but she remembers how troubled I became. And then those crabs appeared whenever I walked someplace. Not at home. Not when I was writing, just when I was walking, going someplace. Especially, when I went strolling on vacation. The first time I discussed it with Castor, when they appeared one day as we were strolling in the Midi, is when we concluded that I was going through a depression, based on my fear that I was doomed the rest of my life to be a professor. Not that I hated to teach. But defined. Classified. Serious. That was the worst part, to have to be serious about life. The crabs stayed with me until the day I simply decided that they bored me and that I just wouldn't pay attention to them. You know, I used to talk to them when I walked alone and they strolled alongside. Then I started ignoring them, and little by little they left me. And then the war came, the stalag, the resistance, and the big political battles after the war.

When you tried to launch the so-called Third Force, anti–United States and anti-communist?

Exactly. But it didn't work. It attracted too many reactionaries who may have been against U.S. domination but for the wrong reason, out of some ridiculous morality, or anachronistic monarchism, or religious fervor, or god-knows-what. And soon we understood, we had to choose. The basic question: who was ready, willing even, to launch an attack on the other, to lead us into a new war that would devastate the planet? Obviously it was the United States. So we had to abandon the Third Force and ally ourselves, as reluctantly as it was, with Russia.

That cost you the support, admiration, and following of almost all Anglo-Saxon intellectuals. Yet we now know that you were right, that the United States had a first-strike policy while the USSR did not—well, until Gorbachev . . .

He did?

Apparently, when he heard that the United States had one, so many years later, he asked his generals to prepare one also, and make sure it leaked to the CIA, as a sort of deterrent. But Russia had the deterrent all along. In the late '50s, I think, when the Cold War was getting really bad, the Pentagon or CIA or NSA [National Security Agency], someone in government, ordered a feasibility study, and it concluded that a first strike would wipe out all but 6 percent of Russian missile silos. But that was enough to hit many U.S. cities, so they did a study on Denver—why Denver, we never learned—and concluded that if just one Soviet nuclear missile made a direct hit on Denver, 200,000 people would be killed at once and another 5 million within a year, from the radiation. So it was the Soviet deterrent that has kept us all alive, not the other way around.

I wish I knew that when I had all those debates with [David] Rousset.[3]

So during that period, no crabs? No depression?

Not until 1958. We had work to do. Intensive. To push France out of NATO, to refuse U.S. bases, to stop selling our resources to U.S. conglomerates. There were rallies, demonstrations, marches, almost every day. And our magazine had to lead the way. Then that old man seized power and suddenly

it dawned on me that my life would be totally absurd, that my generation was doomed to exist under his pathetic and ridiculous assurances of "la grandeur de la France."

And yet he did some of those things you campaigned for, like closing U.S. bases, like keeping Britain, the U.S. puppet, out of the European Community, like telling the world that no country is free if it has foreign bases on its territory.

Yeah, yeah, but he didn't get us out of NATO, or pick a successor who would continue to keep England out of the European Union,⁴ or nationalize the U.S. conglomerates that still run our lives.

Unlike your previous depression, which was personal, about the meaning of your life, that depression was social, meaning no crabs, right?

I would have liked my crabs to come back. My new depression was much worse. The crabs were mine. I had gotten used to them. They kept reminding me that my life was absurd, yes, nauseating, but without challenging my immortality. Despite their mocking, my crabs never said that my books would not be on the shelf, or that if they were, so what? You have to realize that my psychosis was literature. I was poured into a world where there was certain immortality, and it took fifty years to put all that into question, to go not from an ivory tower, but still, from a privileged state of the intellectual, to the contrary, challenging the role, the use, the justification of the intellectual. I did that by writing *The Words,* by rereading Marx, by approaching the Communist Party, and by realizing that I had been simply protecting myself, telling me that the miseries of others were not my affairs, except of course as I might write about them, but as outside me. Like Fernando had said before he went to fight in Spain, I don't care if the world starves, I paint, I write. It was a way of eliminating all passion from my life, which meant all real fears, all ambiguities. I was protected. Whatever happened, my books would be on the shelf, hence I was immortal. For all my anti-religiousness at the time, I was almost like a Christian who thinks that if he's a nice guy he may end up next to god.

And your social depression got rid of all that?

Indeed. It threw me into the soup, the soup of mankind, alienated, exploited, insecure, terrified—in one word, in nausea. But now it wasn't Roquentin's [the hero of his novel *Nausea*], it was mine, all of us, and made me realize that my struggle is yours and vice versa, that there is no escape for any of us, except that we find our fulfillment, so to speak, fighting together. Without ever thinking that this is a meaning, only an act. Meaning has to be created by each of us, but since we are meaningless, how can we create meaning?

Yet that was the message, so to speak, of all the works you wrote when you were in the grips of your personal depression, that is, when you thought of yourself as privileged but therefore alone, followed by crabs. Like *No Exit, The Flies, Dirty Hands,* your novels, and then your great play *The Devil and the Good Lord.*

Yes, without my being in it. Nothing I wrote then contradicts what I am today—quite the contrary. The difference is that, instead of describing, perhaps more, activating characters who are in the soup, I was a chef, cooking it, tasting it occasionally, but serving it to others. With *The Words* and with my relationship to the Gauche Prolétarienne, I ended up in the soup.

So that was great. Why blame de Gaulle? Praise him.

His anachronistic monarchism made me realize not only how we are all absurd, but also that necessity and absurdity are two aspects of the same coin. So while I became an activist, I also realized that personally, as all beings, I was neither privileged nor meaningful. My activism gave me a sense of purpose, true. But my depression, caused by my awareness that my existence, like all of ours, was totally absurd, made me realize that I, we, are doomed to nauseating insignificance. My crabs had considered me important, or else why bother me? De Gaulle, admired by the French, the ridiculousness of the Cold War and America's drive to conquer and control, all that made me realize that I was not, and never would be, significant, nor would anyone else.

That kind of depression, as you call it—I would term it enlightenment, rather—often leads to some kind of mystical search for salvation.

Like Fernando? When I met him, despite his statement that first he paints no matter what, he was very active politically. He was involved in Artists and Writers Against Fascism, and was always trying to drag me in, and he often went to fight the fascists in the streets. Then of course that incredible commitment to go fight in Spain. Yet, and I didn't realize it then, he always had that mystical trait, did he?

Like when he tells you, and you make Gomez tell Richie in *The Roads,* "Mondrian does not ask difficult questions." What does that mean in art?

Exactly, that's a mystical statement. But he was always searching for something, which we never discussed. Like he read the Bhagavad Gita, and [Jakob] Böhme and [Meister] Eckhart, Thomas à Kempis, even [Ignatius of]

Loyola,[5] stuff like that, and if I asked him why, he would pass it off as widening his knowledge or whatever.

I once asked him why he stopped a particular series of his paintings. You know, he would start a type of painting and keep doing more and more of them until he made one that he thought was the best of the series, and it always was, and then he stopped, and started another series. Why stop, I asked him. "Dead end," he answered. But Stépha once gave me a better explanation: "Your father tries to find god through his paintings. When he realizes that a particular visual concept he's pushing will not get him there, he stops and tries a new concept." So one day I asked him if he believed in god, or at least did he think he could ever find god. He answered, No, of course not, then added, I remember very clearly, "There is no god but the purpose of life is to find him."

Yes, that was Fernando all right, the last time I saw him, when we went to that exhibit in New York in 1946.

It's like him, and Gomez, saying one doesn't fight fascism because one is going to win, one fights fascism because it is fascist.

You know, I still have problems understanding your father. No one explained art to me better than he did. When we went to the Prado together, and he started explaining his beloved Velázquez, he was amazing. He made Velázquez come alive before us. Castor and I could see him painting before our eyes, telling his models, Turn that way, no that way, and feeling why that was the best pose. But I see him also skiing with his buddy Heidegger, then walking out on him and his master, the great Husserl, never to return. But most important, I think, and that comes through in _The Age of Reason_ [the first volume of _The Roads to Freedom_ trilogy] very well, I'm told, the influence that your father, Gomez, had on me, Mathieu or at times Brunet, in forming in me my first awareness of why capitalism leads to fascism, why we must be anti-capitalists, why we must be revolutionaries. And yet, of course, my doing nothing about it for thirty years.

But in volume four of your _Roads,_ which you never published, you make Brunet become a communist resister.

Yes, but without being sure of what he would do with his commitment after the war.

Which is why you have him killed?

Precisely.

And why you sort of drop Gomez in miserable exile in America?

I guess I didn't know what to do with Gomez either. No one has had more of an effect on me than your father. I remember how, when his parents showed up in Paris impoverished after [Kemal] Atatürk [first president of the Republic of Turkey] expropriated their wealth [in the late 1920s], and he had to support them. Castor and I often visited him in Madrid and then Barcelona, where he worked to make a living—a good living because he quickly became boss of some Hungarian electrical appliance firm—and when all Spaniards took their siesta, painting like mad in his studio. That encouraged me a lot, as I too had to make a living while all I wanted to do was write. And that was true about him when I visited you all in 1946. Fernando had just started to paint again after ten years—right, the Spanish war, then his stint as a spy during the war [World War II], and you all had no money. You lived in a slum and your parents were not allowed to work.[6] So Fernando spent hours translating things for some official he hated, while your mother gave facial massages to her friends. But he painted. Furiously. Perhaps only three hours in bad light. No café life this time. No one to exchange art for food. And he kept it up. He still does, I gather.

Very much so.[7]

He's no longer political, I gather.

He's become a kind of pacifist, but certainly in favor of the Vietnamese. He remains full of contradictions. Like, he loves his Vermont hills, which he calls "my Pyrenees," but despises America's conceit and especially its ultra patriotism. He still can never understand how people accept having to listen to the national anthem whenever they get together, like at every ball game, at races . . .

Races? You mean you have to listen to the anthem before you can bet on the horses?

Oh yes, at baseball games, football, every public gathering almost, and men have to take off their hats and everyone has to place their hands on the left of their chest, signifying their heart. Do you know that every time one of our politicians makes a speech, especially presidents, he must end it with the phase "God bless America."

No wonder you think you have a right to dominate the world. And yet your culture, your novelists, your artists, your musicians, especially jazz, are among the best in the world.

And you are perfectly right to herald them in France.

Boy, what contradictions. But tell me, Stépha still teaches at that school? What does she teach?

The Putney School, a boarding high school [in Putney, Vermont]. Very expensive for the rich, totally free for the poor. Very progressive but very hip too, with great music and art. And self-sufficient, meaning the kids take care of the farm, milk the cows, clean the shit in the stables—and that included the Kennedy girls, since they were there when I used to go. I even taught history for a semester once when the regular historian got very sick. Stépha teaches almost anything they need. Russian, French, Spanish, German, ancient history, Greek, Latin, whatever. She loves it, and they love her.

But Fernando never made it as an artist, did he? Why? He's a great artist, fantastic colorist . . . Did it sour him? Is he bitter?

Not at all. For a while I felt guilty about it, because I had been art critic for *Time* and then *Newsweek* magazines, and I thought I should do more for him. But he wouldn't come down from Vermont to ass-lick the gallery owners, and although he was an abstract expressionist, at least by the mid-'6os, he was not a tachiste, a spontanist. He composed his abstractions very carefully and hence did not fit into any vogue or school prevalent at any time.

I take it he lost all interest in philosophy? When I stayed with you all in New York those few days before my trip,[8] I did try to discuss Heidegger with him, but he wouldn't talk about him, except to pass him off as an anti-Semite responsible for the blackballing of their mentor Husserl. And in all the letters since, there has never been a mention of my work. I don't think he read it.

I think you're right. He never talks to me about philosophy either. As for the letters, I have them—they're between Castor and Stépha. You two men never wrote to each other. Why?

First of all, I never write to men, ever—except business, of course, like publishers. I write only to women, love letters—ha-ha. But besides, Fernando and I got into some problem, I think I can't remember.[9]

In 1964 you refused to go see him.

I was writing. I don't interrupt that even for Castor.

Come on, Sartre, I've seen you interrupt *Flaubert* for the kids of the GP [La Gauche Prolétarienne].

Well, now, yes, and I would do it for Fernando and Stépha too. But now I'm a political animal, as you say.

And in 1964 you were in the thick of social depression, remember?

True. I guess I was too involved, too lazy or something then. But, well, too many years had passed. And I was in the midst of trying to write an ethics. As you know, that was what I wanted to write most.

Even when you were writing *Being and Nothingness*? You started that during the war, didn't you?

During the Phony War.[10] I got obsessed, writing as fast as my hand could move. Then, in prisoner-of-war camp there were a bunch of priests who wanted to know what Husserl and Heidegger were all about, so I gave a few lectures, and in the process realized that what I really wanted to write was an ethics. But first I had to place man in the world, understand the human condition, and so I returned to *Being and Nothingness*. In doing that—I had two thousand pages of notes by then—I had to understand man's emotions, his behavior. Anyway, out of all that came my small books on emotions and the psyche. I lost most of that, all the notes, some of the drafts. I resented the war terribly at the time. Not later, of course, when I understood the political significance of commonness. But then, I was all in favor of fighting the Nazis —just not me.

Had you not been part of the Popular Front in '36?

No, not really. Castor and I didn't even vote. We were all for it, in a sense, like, when they paraded down Montparnasse, we cheered and were happy there were so many of them, but we didn't join in.

And you weren't part of the Artists and Writers Against Fascism.

No. It was only for those who were well known, and I was still a nobody. Your father kept trying to get me in . . .

He wasn't well known either then, was he?

Oh, yes, he had exhibited since 1931 at the Salon de Surindépendants. And in '35 I think, at a major show of Spanish painters, with Picasso, Miró, and others. Anyway, he was always trying to get me to join, but . . . and mind you I didn't resent his pressure. On the contrary, I kept asking him what went on at the meetings, and I was seeing him all the time then, literally every day. But he failed. And I was still apolitical, in the true sense of the word, at the stalag. All I wanted was to write. And I figured if I could establish man in the world, then I could write my ethics. But it would have to wait until I wrote the *Critique of Dialectical Reason,* which places man in society. And that I wrote in totally different conditions.

In what way?

Being and Nothingness I wrote in great part as a prisoner and then in

Paris cafés during the occupation. The *Critique* I wrote mostly here [in his apartment], full of corydrane [an amphetamine], all the way through.

I heard you had prepared a rigid plan, chapter by chapter.

Yes, but I never stuck to it. I'd wander off. Actually I often had no idea what I was going to write until I started writing it, so it became fun, exciting.

May 1971

GERASSI: I reread Castor's memoirs during the break [I was then teaching at the University of Paris VIII] and came across her statement that during the Popular Front "we were voyeurs rather than participants." How do you justify that?

SARTRE: It's hard. The rallies, the marches, the demonstrations were all actions we agreed with, but it wasn't our thing; I mean, the Popular Front was a kind of rising by workers, and while we completely sympathized with workers, we weren't workers, so if we participated in their thing, it would be as strangers. Workers seized their factories. What was I supposed to do, seize my office? Which is just my desk.

Ah, come on, Sartre, you've been going to every leftist demonstration since Ridgway popped up![1]

But that was after the war. By then I was much more political. I was trying to explain how I justified our inaction in 1936, with my political consciousness of '36.

Yet Castor wrote that you were anti-Blum [Léon Blum, France's Popular Front leader and prime minister when the Spanish Civil War began in 1936] for closing the frontier,[2] and that "for the next two and a half years, our lives were the Spanish Civil War." Yet you did not participate in any demonstration supporting the [Spanish] Republic.

The other day, one of the kids from the GP told me that "since you are so well known, just a little bit of participation goes a long way, because the press, the world pays attention to what you do. But for those of us who are unknown, we have to go all the way." In 1936 I was not known at all. Neither *Nausea* **nor** *The Wall* **had been published. I would have been just another body, nothing else.**

Like the rest of us.

I understand that now. But in '36 . . .

Yet your two best friends were in Spain, Fernando, and Nizan as a correspondent for the communist daily *Ce Soir?* And in August you travel to Scandinavia with your stepfather and mother.

Weird, huh? And I argued with him all the way about Spain.

But you never broke with him?

Never. To the end. I told you I was never a rebel. But, I know, arguments are not acts. If I am what I do, then at least, you could rightfully say that I was not political.

And in your classes, you and Castor?

We were certainly to the far left of most of our students, but we kept such opinions mostly to ourselves.

What about Colette Audry [one of Beauvoir's students and later a well-known novelist and screenwriter]? She was already by then a militant Trotskyist, no?

Not in class. You know, today, a teacher can voice his opinion, even a subversive one, in the classroom, and no one says anything or complains. But in those days, we had to be careful. We had to be "objective" or the administration could bring up sanctions against us. As militant as Audry was out of class, she had to be very careful in class.

Somewhat like in the United States now. We have a status called tenure, which sort of guarantees our freedom of expression, once we get it, which takes a long time. But even so, a teacher cannot criticize Israel too much, or the administrations get angry.

Are all administrators anti-Palestinian?

Generally, yes, but often because of money. Most financial gifts to colleges tend to come from wealthy Jews, and most Jews in America, like in France for that matter, are so anti-Palestinian that they could be accused of racism, but you can't say that publicly either. Was Israel's treatment of Palestinians a problem in your third-way party? What was its real name?

RDR, Rassemblement Démocratique Révolutionnaire [Democratic Revolutionary Gathering]. No—we broke up too soon.

Are you still in contact with your co-organizers?

No. As you know, I had public debates with Rousset when we broke up. You've seen the little book we published, *Entretiens sur la politique* [Conversations on Politics]. You should interview him. A militant Trotskyist turned Gaullist. He's not important today, but he can give you an idea of what postwar politics was like in France. He tried to move the RDR into the forefront by guiding it to the right, which is why I broke it up.

You did, personally?

You didn't know. Yes, I scheduled a convention of all members, a general call to discuss all issues. The board, which Rousset and a mild socialist named [Gérard] Rosenthal controlled, was against it, so it refused to fund the convention, so I did, with my own money, and from the platform called for its dissolution, explaining why a third force was no longer possible in the intensity of the Cold War, calling on all adherents of the RDR to join the left, without specifying which [party], but pointing out that we must all be aware now that America wants to control us all, economically at least.

Were Jeanson and Lanzmann with you then?[3]

Lanzmann was already too occupied with his Jewishness. Jeanson was extremely militant, long to the left of us, until the Algerian War, when he recruited us into his seditionist network. He was an incredible man, a heavy drinker, a great womanizer, at least until he got married to one who agreed with him completely, but always an extremely courageous militant. He lives in Calon near Bordeaux now; you should go see him, interview him.[4]

During this period, from the end of the war until de Gaulle's coup d'état in 1958, you were haunted by neither crabs nor depression?

We keep calling them crabs because of my play [*The Condemned of Altona*], but they were really lobsters.[5]

Even Castor occasionally refers to them as your crabs. Anyway, they were gone then?

Oh, yes, they left me during the war. You know, I've never said this before, but sometimes I miss them—when I'm lonely, or rather, when I'm alone. When I go to a movie that ends up boring, or not very gripping, and I remember how they used to sit there on my leg. Of course I always knew that they weren't there, that they didn't exist, but they served an important purpose. They were a warning that I wasn't thinking correctly or focusing on what was important or that I was heading up the wrong track, all the while telling me that my life was not right, not what it should be. Well, no one tells me that anymore. Castor tells me what's wrong with what I write. In fact, speaking of *The Condemned,* she told me that my original ending was awful, and made me rewrite it five times.

But during the Spanish Civil War, the crabs, the lobsters, were still with you?

Less and less. As I told you, I was beginning to get fed up, so I would simply say beat it, and they did, for a while anyway. I think what was happening was that my depression, which was a personal depression, caused, I insist, by the fact that I was dreading my life as a teacher, writing in off hours, like sneaking to write, was suddenly being put into a wider context, one in which I would be facing fascism, we all would. In 1937 I was given a choice: Lyon or Laon. I guess everyone in their right mind would have chosen Lyon, a great city with fantastic foods. But Laon was near Paris, and Castor had gotten a khâgne in Paris and I wanted to be near her, so I chose Laon. Only one year! In 1937 I was offered Lycée Pasteur, and stayed there until I got drafted. So I should have been much happier. Well, I was, on a personal level: I was in Paris, saw Castor every day, lived in a charming little hotel at the avenue du Maine, at the end of La Gaîté, had my breakfast at La Liberté, and wrote there too. What more could I ask for? But France was becoming fascist. The Popular Front had failed. When it became clear that the Spanish Republic was going to lose, at first I thought, Well, it's a tragedy, but it is just Spain, it won't come to us. Then little by little I couldn't ignore my eyes and ears anymore. There were the Croix de Feu and the Action Française, the Nazi punks running wild, the stupid speeches by the politicians, and then of course the Sudetenland and Munich. I became absolutely certain that war had become inevitable. Castor and Olga were on vacation, that summer of '38, taking long walks through the Midi. I sent them a telegram saying: War inevitable. And my depression was no longer personal.

Except for your communist friends, Nizan . . .

No, no! That came later, when the Soviets signed the Nonaggression Pact with the Nazis. I didn't object to that in itself—after all, at Munich, the Western powers had abandoned Russia. There could be no doubt that Hitler would next go after Poland. He got Austria without firing a shot. He got the Sudetenland without a shot. Clearly he wanted Poland next, and Stalin was perfectly justified to think that the West would let him take it. So he had to prepare for it. No, what was terrible about the French communists was that they applauded the pact. That Stalin had to do it, fine. But no French communist should approve it for France. Instead, when the war started, they called it a capitalist war, and refused to back France and England. That's what was disgusting. French communists were more Stalinist than Stalin. But not Nizan. He refused to adhere to the French communist pacifist line, joined the army and sent his party card to his party boss, Maurice Thorez. Once Hitler attacked Russia everything changed, of course. Suddenly the communists were the great resistance fighters, and we were all good allies. In my group, with the communists, were all sorts of former anti-communists like Camus, and the Catholic writer Mauriac.

And that's what volume four of *The Roads to Freedom* was all about, the resistance. Why did you give it up?

Because of volume three.

That's the one I liked best.

Frankly, I did too. So did Castor and *la famille*. But the critics did not. The reviews were all negative, some horrendous. It seems no one liked to read about French officers abandoning their troops and running like mad to escape the enemy. Yet I saw that myself. My officers all fled. Fernando told me the same happened on his front.[6] So I abandoned the project of volume four.

October 1971

SARTRE: Welcome back. How's Fernando?

GERASSI: He was operated on for cancer of the esophagus. A tough one. He's OK now, but the doctor told me it can't last.

Et la petite [Catherine Yelloz]? She went with you?

Yes. She was great. We were at the hospital almost all the time, but she was very helpful, especially to Stépha, who can't really see or hear very well anymore.

Like me, huh?

Worse. And she can't walk without terrific pain. Do you know that she is so fond of her garden, and she knows her flowers and vegetables so well by touch, that every day she crawls to the garden and can feel which are weeds and which not. And mind you, her hands hurt her so much from arthritis that when she plays the piano she can't hold back the tears.

But she plays anyway?

Whenever she gets depressed. She says that only music works.

Isn't she too deaf to hear it?

She claims she hears it through her fingers.

How about you, did your Vincennes classes start yet?

Yep. And how was your summer?

During the summer, nothing. In July everyone prepares for August, and

in August everyone is away. France comes to a dead stop in the summer, as you know. But since the return, all hell has let loose.[1] [Interior Minister Raymond] Marcellin has been going apeshit since the return, arresting anyone he can. So the GP has been escalating its occupations, its confrontations, and it'll get worse.

And I hear you have been participating in some of their actions, like occupations of empty buildings, with the intention of letting the homeless live there.

The GP kept doing that, and Marcellin's goons kept arresting them, and beating them up, so some of us decided to join them, to see if they would beat us up too—you know, famous people like [Michel] Foucault and Claude Mauriac and I, and of course the cops didn't attack until we left at night—well, I had left, feeling guilty, I admit, but as you know I can't see very well, and I have trouble walking. There were no chairs, and I have trouble staying on my feet for too long. Anyway, Foucault and Mauriac stayed, and the event got great coverage in the press. And I must say, no one condemned me for leaving, not even _Le Figaro_.

Of course not, since everyone, or at least the students, and the media, knows very well that it was your _Critique_ which really set the stage for the intellectual justification of the May events. In that work, you explained by using examples ranging from the French Revolution to, as I would describe it, people waiting for a bus on Third Avenue during rush hour, that revolutions spring forth out of a group united by the combination of a dream and a purpose. The bus line, a long one of folks waiting after a bad day's alienating and basically meaningless office work. A bus rolls by packed to the rafters, with no more room, hence refusing to open its doors. Then another bus, equally packed, rolls by, ignoring the folks waiting bitterly. Incredibly, an empty bus with sign reading "out of service" comes by next and is stopped in front of the line because of the traffic. Everyone stares longingly. Suddenly, one of the people in line pushes his hand through the front door's rubber door-guard and forces the doors open. The driver yells that he's off duty. Where are you going? asks the assailant. To the garage, answers the driver. Knowing that he lives on the way, the rebel says, Well, you can drop me off on the way. Then everyone else waiting in line piles in. A group-in-fusion is formed. Where do you live? OK, stop on Forty-seventh Street. And you? OK, stop on Sixtieth. And you? On Ninety-sixth, but four blocks east; I have to get a transfer for another bus because I cannot walk with my old legs. Hey driver, on Ninety-sixth, make a detour, go east four blocks. But I'll get in trouble. No you won't, we'll give you a statement. And someone proceeds to write on a piece of paper that they all are responsible for commandeering the bus and ordering the driver to go out of his way a bit for old folks, poor folks, needy folks. They all sign. And they all start talking to each other. Where do you work? What do you do? You have kids? By the time the bus dropped off the illegal passengers, a whole new conception of life was born. A revolution? Yes, but very small. Spontaneous. And extremely moral. Every passenger's life is changed. So is the driver's. By the end he too, like the rest, was laughing and singing and wishing everyone well. So, tell me, Sartre, are you merely supporting the maos [the Maoists, which is what the left dubbed the GP] or have you joined them—are you now a Maoist?

First of all, thanks for making my points so lucid, so clear. That was beautiful. As for the maos, understand, they do not advocate terror—quite on the contrary. They believe that people must make all decisions that affect their lives.

Right out of the Cultural Revolution. But that means massive decentralization? How is that possible in our modern world?

Look how well it worked at Lens. There you saw that a constitutional government's traditional "rule of law" just does not apply to the conditions, needs, the reality of ordinary folks. Laws in France, as in all Western "democracies," especially in America as I understand, are made to defend the status quo, to defend the sacredness of private property. Hence they ignore the feelings, the hopes, the needs of ordinary folk. Just like you showed me with that story about that poor woman who accidentally killed her young son . . .

The case that eventually destroyed Judge Bazelon's faith in the American justice system?

Exactly. Only popular justice can deal with such cases, and popular justice is one where all the people in the neighborhood or factory or mine, and their families, can participate. And of course the only way such trials, but also decisions of every kind, like where to build a hotel, or a road, or a market, or a church, can take place is by limiting the decision-making process to those directly affected by them, to what your students call "AG"s [assemblées générales, general assemblies, where policies of the University of Paris VIII, Vincennes, were decided].[2]

And that can only happen if all property is communally held?

Not necessarily. That is the ultimate goal, to be sure. But in Lens, the

mines were not expropriated. A decision on new safety regulations was made, and the owners put them into effect. They were condemned to pay sums to the victims, and they did. None of which was ordered by a state court. Just a vote by the people of that community.

How did the Lens trial get started?

First came the demonstrations, protesting the arrest of some of the surviving miners for negligence. Then the cry changed to demanding that the owners be put on trial. Then the mayor of Lens, a socialist, was asked to offer his city hall. Then somehow it got organized a bit by the GP, who asked me to come down and be the "judge"—that is, the sort of master of ceremonies. Except for the summation, all I did was point to someone who wanted to say something, then to the next one. In a way, one can say that the whole thing sprung forth spontaneously.

And that's the key, isn't it? That's what defines the GP as Maoists, their reverence, so to speak, for the spontaneous demands of ordinary folk?

That's part. The other part, perhaps as important, is their morality. Maoism as it is now defined in France, because of the GP, is moral Marxism. Think of the GP's recent actions. Occupations of empty buildings, giving them to the homeless, and staying there to fight the cops ordered to evict the homeless. Or Fauchon [the fanciest and most expensive gourmet food store in Paris, right on the Champs-Elysées; the GP seized it one day, then distributed the food to the poor Africans living nearby in the 18th arrondissement]. Or what they did the other day at the Goutte d'Or [a neighborhood in Paris populated mostly by poor Algerian immigrants]. They started yelling at the cop directing traffic in the center of the main crossroads, taunting him, Why do you work for the repressing forces? You also belong to the working class, why do you fight your fellow class members, et cetera? They were stationed all around him, and as some of their comrades stopped all traffic, at the moment when there was the biggest crowd, some from each direction started advancing on him. Finally they reached him and quickly disarmed him. Then they yelled to him and the crowd: "Now you are like all of us, exploited, dominated, a member of the underclass, demeaned like the rest of us. This thing," they said holding up his gun, "is part of your bosses' domination. Without it you are part of us." And before more cops could arrive, they gave back his gun (having taken out the ammunition) and disappeared. All moral gestures. And as you know, they created Secours Rouge [Red Aid, a free health and legal-aid service offered to all, run by doctors, nurses, and lawyers], with vans equipped for emergencies, which dash to the slums whenever they hear of a fire or an accident there. They end up having to turn over their patients to regular paramedics or officials, of course, but they always arrive first, and they have doctors who can administer lifesaving measures immediately. Since they are not sanctioned by the government, they are illegal. But revolutionary morality cannot but be illegal.

And do you adhere to their decisions?

Absolutely. When Cornell invited me to give a series of lectures there, I said no, not as long as America is involved in its war of aggression on the people of Vietnam. So, as you know, I never went.

Do you condone all their actions?

Most. We do have arguments. I keep insisting that they should be a party that never lies. When they make mistakes, they should reveal them, analyze them, and explain them, openly, like in an article in *La Cause du Peuple*. [The People's Cause, a free weekly newspaper published by the GP from 1968 to 1972. It quickly gained a huge circulation among young people, making Marcellin livid. He banned it, and ordered its "responsible editor" arrested. So Sartre was listed as responsible editor, causing de Gaulle to shout before he died, "France does not arrest its Voltaires." This may have sounded great to him, but it was wrong, since Voltaire had indeed been arrested by the French government.]

You're ending up a real romantic, Sartre.

Ha-hah. You know, when I asked Fidel why he gave up his good life to make the revolution, he answered, "Because I'm a romantic!" A romantic! I exclaimed. "Of course. I believe in justice. But there is no justice in the world. So I'm a romantic."

So when are you going to put it all on paper, I mean, your long-desired ethics?

I started many times, as you know, and I really got it going in preparing for my talk at Cornell. I had entitled it *History and Politics* [now titled *Ethics and History*]. My main point was going to be that there can never be an ethical code of action unless there's total freedom first, which meant that morality is determined by man's fight against those who limit man's freedom. History, hence, determines ethics. And, conversely, ethics changes history.

In a revolution then, the ethical justification for killing someone changes at each stage?

Precisely. Every revolution that I have studied has always stopped short of executing its worst enemies, like the top echelon of the previous repressive regime, because that layer always adapts. Those who are executed are the torturers, but they were mere cogs acting under orders; they were also victims of the repressive apparatus and hence could have been reeducated and salvaged.

They did execute the top Nazis after the war.

Yes, but that was vengeance of the winners. Those who commit crimes against humanity certainly deserve the death penalty. But history has shown that only such criminals are executed if they lose all their power. Do you think that the leaders of your country who committed crimes against humanity in Vietnam, and on all levels mind you, torturing, murdering innocents, poisoning livestock and foodstuffs, all as grave and disgusting as any savagery by the Gestapo, will ever be charged, much less executed, for crimes against humanity?

Of course not, just as they weren't charged for such crimes in the Philippines, or against Native Americans, or for murdering thousands of noncombatants at Hiroshima and Nagasaki, or for the million children under the age of eleven who die every year in Latin America because American mining corporations pollute their drinking water, or the British for their fire-bombing of noncombatants at Dresden. But they are the weak, who do not have the power to apply the laws of crime against humanity, justified in seeking vengeance? Is revanchism ethically justifiable?

As revolutionary justice, yes.

Would that not lead to vigilantism?

Perhaps, if that is a communal decision, maybe. We have a serious problem here. Laws are enacted to protect the rich, the powerful, the elites. No law exists primarily to help the poor, except insofar as it applies also to them, but enacted originally for the elites. Agreed. So the laws defining crimes against humanity are laws meant to justify the power of the powerful. The culprits may very well have violated those laws, like the Nazis. But they were ultimately executed not for having violated them, but because their executions reinforce the system whereby the powerful have the right to impose them.

But, let me bring up a concrete example, which worries me. Cuba, 1960. Fidel puts on trial the Batista torturers. Almost a people's trial, insofar as anyone could testify, and indeed hundreds of folks who were tortured, or who saw their loved ones tortured to death, did testify. The evidence is overwhelming. Not even *Time* magazine challenged that. Indeed, it claimed that the trials were a catharsis, saving the country from a wild bloodbath of vengeance. At the same time, the media concluded that because the torturers were executed, 365 of them, it showed that Castro was not just a bourgeois reformer, as *Time* and the United States hoped, but a genuine revolutionary, and so decided to condemn him. Now my question: should the torturers have been executed, when we all knew, and Castro knew, that the real culprits were the top echelon of Batista's government, specifically the bosses of his regime, namely the owners of United Fruit, IT&T, and the other American corporations for whom Batista and his henchmen exploited the people of Cuba?

I agree that, under an ideal situation, the torturers could have been rehabilitated. But I also agree with Fidel, that at that moment a bloodbath had to be avoided, and these torturers were scum, after all, so if executing them for their proven crimes, even if the president of IT&T is ultimately responsible, will avoid that bloodbath, then ethically their execution was justified—as you showed so well in your play [*The Cell*].³ But had the trials taken place a year later and with no bloodbath to avoid, then no, their executions would not have been justified.

And had Fidel caught the owner of IT&T?

In 1960, yes. In 1965? . . . What's your view?

I am so totally opposed to capital punishment that it creates a problem. I was, as you read, completely in accord with the executions in 1960. In 1965? I would have rather condemned the IT&T president to twenty years of cleaning latrines with a toothbrush.

So you see the problem.

How do you situate the Red Army Faction in this?

You mean the Baader-Meinhof group? In context, they were totally justified. Remember that context. The shah [of Iran] comes to Berlin and the students protest peacefully. They are severely beaten by the shah's security goons and the German police who shoot and kill one student, Benno Ohnesorg. The pro-U.S. press then yells that the real responsible one was Rudi Dutschke [leader of the student protesters] and he is shot in the head. From a moral and revolutionary point of view, the group's rampage and murders of German industrialists are absolutely justified. But . . . you see my problem— all ethics depend on circumstances.

I guess that's why you haven't written yours yet . . .

At one time, after I wrote out the notes for Cornell, I had planned to write my political testament. I did discuss it with some of the guys from the GP. But I concluded that it made no sense. A political testament is a criticism of realpolitik. But for a revolutionary that makes no sense, since all realpolitik is rejected. Still, I keep toying with the idea of a revolutionary morality. I tried in Italy, you know, when I was invited at the Gramsci Institute to explain my position. The materialists, the so-called straight Marxists who refuse to consider any ethical questions in their historical vision of the class struggle, were really outclassed then by all the participants from the Soviet states, especially the Czechs, who attacked the communist structure through its bureaucracy, which was clearly the immorality of bureaucracies. I decided I would write about it all in volume two of my *Critique* some day.

Meanwhile, what happened to your trial? It was for defamation of the police?

The one about [the newspaper] *Tout?*[4] [As the "responsible editor" for the paper, Sartre had been charged with defamation of the police for claiming that they systematically beat up gays whenever they caught them.] Nothing. Dropped. The one about the suitcases? [The supporters of the "Manifesto of the 121" were dubbed "suitcase carriers" by the press for their advocacy of carrying money, medicine, and arms to the Algerian revolutionaries.] Also dropped.

No, I mean the most recent one, charging you and *La Cause du Peuple* with defamation for claiming that the police systematically resort to torture.

The trial itself, if it takes place, is nothing. But it brought out some nice little contradictions. Like, for example, the GP says, Everything from the workers. OK. That means they don't need intellectuals, or that intellectuals are workers and no better and no worse than any other worker. Fine, we all agree. But then, *La Cause du Peuple* is seized by the authorities and an order forbidding its publication is issued by the government. So the GP publishes a new issue denouncing the cops, the government, the edict, everything, and in the process accuses the police of widespread corruption. So all the violations, ignoring a government order, defamation of the police, et cetera, are put aside so that the responsible editor, me, can be arrested. But after de Gaulle, and Pompidou, too—you know, he said that France will not arrest Sartre—they're stuck. Meanwhile, Castor and I and a few of our well-known friends are distributing the paper very publicly. The press takes our pictures and plasters them on their front pages. There's Sartre and Castor and some actresses hawking *La Cause du Peuple*. What can the government do now? Well, they decide to ignore the public demonstration and instead focus on the defamation. But they don't want a trial. The cops do, the minister of the interior also, but not Pompidou. So what's next? The GP claims that they don't use or even court famous people, right? Everyone is equal. Intellectuals are no better than workers. All true. But their paper is saved because they got intellectuals to hawk it. If [Jean-Pierre] Le Dantec [a well-known adherent of the GP] had been the responsible editor and had been distributing the paper in the street, he would have been arrested, jailed, probably beaten, and the papers, the press, all materials seized and destroyed. So as long as we live in a bourgeois state, we end up at times profiting from their laws. Right? The people want freedom, the bourgeoisie wants the law. Yes, but it's not that simple, at least until the revolution.

Yet when a revolution says that intellectuals must be part of the people, you object, like the Padilla case.

Revolutionary Cuba does not treat its intellectuals as workers. They have special status. Look who's Fidel's ambassador here [Alejo Carpentier, a Cuban novelist who was then ambassador to France]. And until a revolution can change by education the habits of its militants, it will continue to give its intellectuals special status. But to single out Padilla because of "anti-revolutionary attitude" is something else again. Just what is a counterrevolutionary attitude, do you know?

In the case of Padilla it was smoking pot and saying I don't care about the law. He implied that poets are exempt from such laws. I think the law is terrible. I've smoked pot since the Korean War. But I won't smoke it in Cuba. Not because I think they're right to ban it. But because it's a young revolutionary country, trying its best against massive interference and sabotage by the richest and most powerful nation on earth.

But you agree that all laws in a revolutionary country should not be laws but agreements discussed and agreed upon by popular assemblies, not by a dictate from some entity sitting above the people?

Yes, theoretically. But we have to live in the situation as it is. No socialism can succeed without some repressive measures as long as the United States dominates the world, since it will resort to almost anything, even, eventually, I am convinced, phony causes to justify invasions and war, to crush a socialist, or even neutralist, state. You yourself warned us that America was willing to launch World War III to save laissez-faire capitalism, and you were right. We are alive today only because Soviet Russia had a deterrent. Marx warned us well, when he said that the first country to go socialist had to be the one with the most developed proletariat, hence the richest country. How can we expect Cuba to resist this terrible bully without all sorts of nonrevolutionary measures, like a strong army, an extremely aware intelligence service, and, unfortunately, yes, repression. Look what the United States tried to do at the Bay of Pigs. Not just an invasion, but one done with the help of one of the worst bastard dictators in the world [Anastasio Somoza of Nicaragua]. It has overthrown every decent government in Latin America it considers "neutralist" enemies. Any country that wants to sell its goods to the highest bidder and buy its needs from the lowest bidder is an "enemy of democracy," according to the United States. Considering all that, I think the Cuban regime has been unbelievably mild in its repression.

I completely agree with you in the politico-economic context. But to condemn an "attitude"?

Aren't we now back to where we started today? Morality! Isn't your whole point that the political is moral and the moral is political?

Indeed. But for that, the revolution must be waged from below, like May '68, not by a small band of iron-willed ideologues.

Sartre, if we wait for the empty bus to roll by and for a bunch of strangers to seize it, we're going to wait for one hell of a long time. And then, what happened? The next day, everyone on that bus was back at work, serialized as before, with only a wonderful memory that they once jointly were a "group-in-fusion," as you say, that they once jointly ran the bus.

In history, fifty years is nothing. The Cultural Revolution will not be forgotten. Forget its excesses. Focus on what it meant, on what it said, namely that people decide policies, administrators carry them out. The GP kids are convinced of that. They genuinely believe that we are all equal, that if you have an IQ of 125 and I have one of 25, our experiences are equal, your suffering is equal to mine, your hopes just as valid as mine, and that a human society must treat you and me on that basis. That message is ingrained somewhere, and will surge again someday.

You're treading on psychology there. Is that the reason for your break with [Bernard] Pingaud, [Jean-Bertrand] Pontalis, and others?

It's related. In fact there were two crucial issues. One was waged by [André] Gorz [chief editor for _Les Temps Modernes_]. He claimed that the universities had become such important stepping-stones for the elitist system,

such a propaganda tool of that system, that they should be boycotted, and people's universities set up, like you tried in New York, I gather.[5] The other issue was the *Temps Modernes* article "The Man with the Tape Recorder." That was the piece in which a patient of a typical shrink, who tape-recorded his sessions, brought in his own tape recorder. The shrink strenuously objected, telling his patient that he was unduly aggressive and paranoid, and eventually refused to "treat" him. Our magazine took the position that the patient was totally justified, that the only way to "treat" a patient is to be "in the soup" with the patient, that if the former takes a chance to reveal himself, he has the right to have his "helper" reveal himself as well, that ultimately no one can be "cured" of anything unless both the shrink and the patient are committed to the task. That got Pingaud, [Henri] Lefebvre, and Pontalis to distance themselves from our group. They didn't become opponents, just distant. Pingaud had always been more to the right than any of us. Pontalis, who was a shrink, felt uncomfortable in our challenge to his methodology. But what was at the heart of the matter was, as we were talking, the privileged position of the intellectual.

You showed that very well in my interview with you for the *New York Times*.

The *Times* understood that, didn't it? I mean, you didn't call your piece "The Responsibility of Intellectuals"—they did. And you originally didn't do it for the *Times*, did you?

No, I was asked to do it for *Ramparts,* the left-wing peacenik California monthly for which I was then Paris editor. But the editorial staff I had originally signed up with had quit by then, and the new editor-in-chief was a doctrinaire Trotskyist named David Horowitz, whom I never liked or trusted. When he took over *Ramparts,* he rejected the interview on the grounds that it did not fit his ideological agenda, which was that intellectuals should produce the framework for his agenda and not, as you said in that interview, be responsible members of the group fighting oppression. So I handed it to my literary agent and it got reproduced in lots of places, like the *London Guardian* and the *New York Times Magazine.* Of course, Horowitz was merely an extreme opportunist, but most American intellectuals have trouble understanding your position on commitment. They usually assume it means saying I'm with you, and not putting their body on the line. And you have a bit of trouble there too, with your obsession on Flaubert.

True. I can't get that family idiot out of my mind. But I compromise. In

the morning, I'm with the GP. Whatever is decided in the assemblies. March. Demonstrate. Picket. Write for *La Cause*. Distribute it in the streets. Whatever. After lunch, I revert to my bourgeois existence and write about that ultimate bourgeois writer. I have some excuses, though: I am too old to stay on my feet all day, or stand on a soapbox in front of Renault workers,[6] and certainly too old to sit down or lie down in unoccupied buildings waiting for the homeless, who are usually too scared at first, until they are told that the police are not going to charge them because some fancy intellectuals they never heard of, like Foucault and Mauriac and me, are there to protect them. I can't even get up from the floor without help.

And the contradiction continues, since the reason the cops aren't going to charge the homeless is precisely because the big names might get hurt, right? When did you understand that you weren't and should not be privileged?

During the war. During my captivity. It was very strange. It began because some of the prisoners kept buttering up the Germans, and some priest prisoners, chaplains, asked me to help convince them that they should stick with us, not the Germans. They had been humiliated in defeat, and they blamed democracy, and also, now they could not screw, that in their humiliation they didn't even want or long for sexual contacts. So they became fascists of sorts, trying to mimic the Germans, who actually didn't give a damn, as long as there was no trouble. Not that we created trouble. It was that we created committees for everything imaginable. It was a form of engagement. Yes, words, not actions. But we created a communal entente. A committee for collecting clothing for those who lacked some. Another for getting writing paper. Another for music. A couple of priests and I started a lecture series, where anyone could talk about what he thought was important. And then of course there was the theater. That's where I worked hardest. And I wrote *Bariona,* which we then put on. But it wasn't like, here's a play by Sartre; rather, we all presented the play, and because it was about religion, that is, as far as the Germans were concerned, it was OK, yet the priests knew very well that the message was just because you are a prisoner doesn't mean you are not free, which was a call to commitment; weird, of course, a commitment of conscience, since our bodies were obviously not free. I think it was then that I understood the difference between conscience and bad faith.[7] And I saw how working together for each other's well-being did create that well-being in others and in oneself. In other words, how socialism really is a humanism. The

Germans were the elite. The fascistoid prisoners were the enforcers of the elite. And the rest of us, the exploited who could only surpass the feeling of exploitation by bonding together.

Yet your commitment to that class struggle disappeared the day you walked out of the stalag.

The walking out was a fluke. I saw an opening and started walking. Then I went to the army center and got myself demobilized.

But you signed a loyalty oath.

That had no meaning. Castor had signed it and got a job teaching. So I did too, and got the lycée at Laon, then in Paris. Signing meant nothing, a piece of paper in order to earn a living. But I sought out the resistance movement and started writing according to the common concept of why we should resist.

It wasn't just to oppose the Germans?

No. By 1943, we knew the Germans would lose the war. And we knew that the Americans would arrive. So our task, what we jointly decided in the resistance, in my group anyway, which was in charge of propaganda, I guess, since we were publishing newspapers and leaflets—and mind you, Camus, who ran the newspaper *Combat,* agreed—was to create an understanding among all the French that yes, we would be liberated by an American army, but under the German occupation we had formed our own fighters, our own resisters, and that these resisters are perfectly capable of leading France into a stable democracy after our liberation. In other words, we were already conscious that the United States hoped to control "liberated France" as a sort of satellite after the war, that we would end up with another series of gauleiters.

You used the word "democracy." The communists were the main force in your group; they used that term?

Oh yes, they knew very well that Stalin had no intention of telling the CP to seize power in France. They knew that it would lead to a massacre and that the United States would then never leave. No, they understood perfectly that France should resort to its old form of government, parliamentary democracy, inefficient, corrupt, ridiculed, but capitalist democracy nonetheless.[8]

So you wanted to do what de Gaulle in effect did do, give France enough prestige to keep U.S. domination aloof.

You won't give up on de Gaulle, will you, Gerassi? Everything he did was for his place in history. OK, he was a nationalist, fine, and he wanted France to be politically independent of America, agreed. But not economi-

cally, and as you very well know, that is the way the modern world is dominated. America doesn't want to station troops where they are not needed. Oh,
yes, it wants bases everywhere, just in case. You showed that well in your
book on Latin America. It uses its secret services to rule with money, and will
overthrow any government that does not do what it tells them. It buys governments, police forces, local armies. What was the name of that CIA man
you wrote about, the one who went around teaching Latin American police
forces how to torture?

Dan Mitrione.[9]

**Right. That was Uruguay. There were no U.S. troops there. They didn't
need them. They send in their troops only when their stooges lose control,
like in the Dominican Republic in 1965. But it's economic domination that
America seeks. And de Gaulle never resisted that. So please stop harassing
me with that monster.**

OK, OK, Sartre, relax; it's just that my government so hated de Gaulle
that I figured he must have done something good. In any case, during the resistance, you guys were trying to convince the French people that the resistance leaders were perfectly capable of taking over a liberated France, because, I presume, as you showed in your novels, the whole French prewar
political leadership, and the army's officer corps, were corrupt cowards.

Well, not all. There was [Pierre] Mendès-France, and Léon Blum, and . . .

Both Jews. But you showed in the novel [*The Roads to Freedom*] how the
officers fled, leaving the ordinary soldiers to fend for themselves. And Fernando told me, the same in his outfit. He even told me he planned to shoot
two of his lieutenants, but when he realized that they were all running, he
just guided all the Jews to the Swiss border and told everyone else to go home.

**That's precisely the stories we wanted to offset. The resistance was
real. In that, I must admit, de Gaulle's people were serious. Jean Moulin [an
important leader in the French resistance] was great, no question about it.
But our goal was not to make heroes out of our resistance fighters, rather it
was to tell the world, and of course, especially our people, that we were perfectly capable of establishing a free and independent and honorable country
after our liberation. The point really being, let's not let the Americans turn us
into a protectorate, as they later did all over Asia.**

But in your unpublished volume four, you advocated more. You
seemed to say that violence is a liberating move.

That's right. When Mathieu escapes and joins the resistance, he finds

his freedom, like Fanon would later write—in the act of violence for the liberation of others one finds one's own liberation.

Now while you're writing stuff for the resistance, which is headed by
the communists . . .

Camus was the head of *Combat*, not the communists.

But you were cooperating with them, weren't you?

**Of course, they were the main force of the resistance. Even Jean Moulin
was working with them before he was captured [by the Gestapo].**[10]

Yet while you were with them you were writing their condemnation.

You mean the part about Schneider in volume three?

Schneider is a communist and you're talking about creating after the
war a "Socialism and Liberty" movement and . . .

**Hold on. He was a communist. His real story is in volume four, which I
did not finish and has not been published, except for the part that deals with
his friendship with Brunet, who is a communist.**[11] **Captured again, Brunet is
told by his fellow communists that Schneider left the party because of the
Russo-German pact, as did Nizan in real life, and is therefore a traitor. In fact
they beat him very severely, so Brunet decides to escape with Schneider. In
the attempt, a German guard fires his machine gun, killing Schneider, and
stopping Brunet. I was then going to write that Brunet escapes again and
when he goes to confront the communist hierarchy in Paris about Schneider,
he's told, No problem, Russia is now at war with Germany, so all is cool, we're
all in the same boat now. Brunet then becomes like Schneider in effect.**

The theme of your play *Dirty Hands*.[12]

**Exactly. That play caused the communists to break with me completely.
From 1945 to 1952 they did everything to smear me. There were all sorts of disgusting articles in *Action*, their newspaper. They even had someone eaves-
drop on Castor and me at Les Deux Magots [the main café in Saint-Germain
where the so-called existentialist crowd hung out] and report on our conversation, making up a lot of it.**

And it all changed with the "Ridgway Go Home" campaign?

**That and the Henri Martin affair. The Ridgway stuff galvanized the
whole left, not just the communists. Even bourgeois liberals. After all, no one
wanted that general, who had commanded not only U.S. troops but also the
fascist forces of the [South Korean] dictator Syngman Rhee, to be head of
NATO, and in France to boot. No, for the CP the Henri Martin affair was more
serious. You remember that, don't you? The communist sailor who refused to**

board his ship because it was going to Indochina, as part of France's imperialist war there. He was arrested and all sorts of demonstrations and strikes ensued. So the CP then asked me to head a delegation to go see President [Vincent] Auriol. But the old politician refused—well, he said that out of courtesy I will see Monsieur Sartre but not a delegation. So I asked the responsible commie, a gynecologist named Dalsace if I remember correctly, whether I should go. He checked with his bosses, then said yes, and when it led to nothing, the CP denounced me. Henri Martin was eventually freed. But for me, it was the Ridgway affair that made me an ally of the CP. The fact that NATO had become an aggressive arm of the United States against Russia, one in which England, Italy, et cetera, and we of course, especially we, were to play an important role, that the United States was now clearly the aggressor, that it even perhaps wanted a war with Russia, changed all of our views, either approvingly or against. The Ridgway affair convinced me that our little group, the Third Force, as we were called, was useless in trying to save the world. So I became a fellow traveler, so to speak. I didn't like it, but to be active politically means to live schizophrenically.

Which you had done during the occupation as well, no?

And how! On the one hand I was working with the communists. On the other I was writing stuff for *Combat*, headed by Camus, who hated the communists. In the third place I had to ask the German censors to approve my plays, two of them, *No Exit* and *The Flies*, which I hoped would communicate to their audiences that honor and integrity demand resistance to the Germans, no matter what the consequences.

Do you think that came across?

The German critics certainly got it. The *Pariser Zeitung*, which was published in Paris in German for the occupying forces, said that *The Flies* was a good play but obviously entirely against us. The French critics, however, were horrendous, and Dullin had to pull the play after fifty performances. They of course refused to stress the fact that Orestes represents the resistance, that even if he ends up feeling guilty of killing the rulers, in this case his mother and her lover, but clearly meant to be the Germans, he must do it. The real issue at the end, which no one mentioned then, but the Germans did in 1946 when they put on the play in Berlin, was why did Orestes leave? Why did he not then rule? After all, he was now king, having eliminated his royal parents. The post-Nazi German critics understood that I was making a moral point, namely that someone guilty of murder cannot rule . . .

Not feeling guilty, but being guilty, correct?

Correct. Orestes takes the flies with him. It is his decision. Hence he is not, as the German critics pointed out, a revolutionary.

When the play was put on after the war, did the French critics not make the same point?

No. The play flopped almost everywhere.

How did your family react? You were then teaching in Paris, right? First at Pasteur, then at Condorcet, so you saw your father-in-law and your mother often I take it. Did they see the play?

Yes, and they liked it. Mancy was a Gaullist, through and through. A patriot. He refused to even consider a class struggle, but he was absolutely willing to uphold the anti-Nazi struggle as best he could. I'm sure he would have hidden our resistance fighters if asked, even at the risk of his life But it never occurred to me ask him to hide our stuff, the pamphlets, the Roneo [mimeograph] machine, papers.

And Castor says you were all extremely careless.

And how. Bost going around Paris with the Roneo under his arm, the leaflets in my briefcase when I stopped at the café and sat there for a long time. Waiting for Merleau to show up, incredible mistakes like that. Which sometimes cost lives, like Merleau's girlfriend who was caught with leaflets and deported. She never came back.

You were friends with Merleau then?

No. He was part of our group, but we were not really friends. Castor would barely talk to him. Don't forget, we didn't know the truth about why he broke up with Zaza yet. We discussed philosophy a lot. He was about to publish his *Phenomenology of Perception,* and wanted me to take out some points he had made that I had incorporated into *Being and Nothingness,* because it looked like mine was going to come out first.

Did you take them out?

Nope.

But he stayed in your group?

Yep. Though not very friendly.

Was Camus in your group?

No. I met Camus at the opening of *The Flies.* I had written a review of *The Stranger* that said it was a very important book, but "of the moment." He was a bit upset by that. So we talked. What I meant was that it made a lot of sense in the circumstances, the war, the occupation, our incapacity of making

sense of our everyday situation. Anyway, we got along. He couldn't stomach the communists, and although he was part of the writers union, the CNE [National Writers Committee], as I was, and it was basically run by communists, like [Louis] Aragon and others, he would write for their clandestine newspaper, *Lettres Françaises*. That's where I was writing then.

Not in *Combat?*

No. Camus started that about then, 1943 I think, but I did not write for it until much later. But we got along fine. In fact, I got the idea, and Dullin agreed, that he could play Garcin in *No Exit*, which we were beginning to cast. Olga was supposed to play Inès, and her sister Wanda, Estelle. But Olga got sick,[13] and somehow everything changed. But Camus and I became pretty solid friends then. He liked *No Exit*, although when I thought about it years later, it said, in effect, that he was very much like Garcin, don't you think?

Insofar as Garcin pretends to be against the dictator, which then meant the Germans, but judges himself not by what he does but by what he says. That applies to Camus during the Algerian War, but not then, during the occupation. Camus was very active then, especially after launching *Combat*.

You're right. Anyway, we stayed friends a long time.

Until *The Rebel?*

No, actually, we had a minor cooling off when Merleau published *Humanism and Terror,* in which he states that to be opposed to a revolutionary government is to be a traitor, by turning the phrase around, that traitors are those who oppose revolutionary governments. There was a party at Boris Vian's, and a minor argument began.[14] First between Merleau and Vian, who was an anarchist and a great human being, really a fantastic guy, then between Merleau and Camus, who interpreted Merleau's statement as a personal attack on him. It got heated, and Camus stomped out of the party. I ran after him and tried to cool him down, but he wouldn't come back. So the fight was not with me, except insofar as Camus could pretend that my views were the same as Merleau's, which I guess they were. Anyway, we stayed a bit offish for a while, then our friendship resumed until, as you say, *The Rebel*. But during that period, we did see each other frequently. Camus even asked me to sign all sorts of petitions, to grant amnesty to this one, to release that one, petitions usually concocted by Malraux, who was by then a fanatic Gaullist. But I signed. Yet when I asked him to sign the petition to free Henri Martin, the sailor jailed for refusing to fight in France's colonial war in Indochina, Camus refused, on the grounds that Martin was a communist. And of course, he wouldn't join us in the "Ridgway Go Home" campaign, nor later denounce France's war in Algeria. But you're right, it was Jeanson's review of *The Rebel,* his [Camus'] ridiculous letter addressed to me as "Monsieur le directeur des *Temps Modernes,*" and my answer, which broke us for good.

And you never wrote for *Combat,* only for the CNE's newspaper *Lettres Françaises* after that?

I think I wrote a piece here and there, maybe, but not as part of the *Combat* team. I went to their meetings though. After the war, when *Combat* became a legal newspaper, and the Americans invited Camus, or one of his people, to go to America and travel around, he asked me if I wanted to go, and I agreed. That's when I came a few days early so as to stay with you all, and renew my old friendship with Fernando and Stépha.

And go see the exhibition of Mondrian at the Museum of Modern Art, now immortalized in volume three of your *Roads to Freedom.*

Nice of you to put it that way, but today that conversation doesn't really have much meaning.

Sure it does. The whole notion that art can ask important questions . . .

. . . has no meaning for the masses. The real question is for whom do we produce art?

In a hierarchical class society, I guess, we write and paint to convince the bourgeois to oppose the worst measures of the ruling class. *The Flies* is going to be produced at La Cartoucherie. What will be its audience? The masses don't go to the theater.

That's true, but the petit bourgeois, who do, have more contact with the masses than the regular bourgeoisie. And then there's the tracts, the leaflets . . .

The masses don't read those either.

Some do. We distribute them where they work. Also *La Cause du Peuple,* which carries their stories, their experiences, their harassments at work. The GP kids go to the factories, to the shops, to the bus and subway exits, and tell them what's inside. That was the purpose of the newspaper, as [Alain] Geismar wanted. [Geismar was one of the organizers of the 1968 student rebellion, which soon came to be known as the 22 of March Movement, for the catalyzing protest that took place on that date.] At the beginning of 1969, when he brought some of his 22 March people to me so we could start the paper, and I agreed then to be part of it, the idea was to compile all the news that affects the masses, so that when a worker is upset at a new ruling in one factory, he can learn that they're trying to impose the same rule in other factories, and when they decide to sequester the boss in one place to press for their demands, they can get an uplift knowing that that other boss was also sequestered at that other joint. And it works. Look at what happened at Contrexeville. The workers there had not staged a strike for thirty years when they finally decided, after a lot of talk with the GP, to strike for one hour, just one hour, on a particular day the following week. But by the time they struck, their cause was well known thanks to an emergency issue of *La Cause*. Other workers came to cheer them on. Before you know it they voted to stay on strike until their demands were met. It lasted three weeks, and they won. Not because some union boss sitting in Paris gave the order for such a strike, but because they learned about worker power. Rank-and-file power. The job of the GP was not to teach—intellectuals cannot teach the working class—but to inform. To tell them what others have done and why. And that is the principal job of *La Cause*.

Widely distributed revolutionary films would do more of a job, no?

That involves a lot of money, to make such films and then to distribute them. Sometimes it works. Like with *Salt of the Earth*, and *The Battle of Algiers*. Even with *Queimada*, although that was too highbrow, really aimed at the intellectual world, wasn't it?[15]

True, but it's a fantastic tool to be used in class. A great film that makes students understand how exploitation of the Third World is achieved by exploiters preaching democracy and liberty.

The British then, the Americans now. I tried to give that dimension in my adaptation of Arthur Miller's *Crucible*.

In 1953, when Miller wrote it, he was fighting McCarthyism. When you did your adaptation four years later, you focused on the class struggle between the poor folks of Salem and their rich exploiters. But essentially it was the same struggle, since Senator [Joseph] McCarthy was merely a pawn for that sector of the American ruling class that was trying to stop the success of the eastern establishment. The main question, however, is serious: Can art be revolutionary? You seem to say so in "What Is Literature?"

Well, not quite. I said that a good writer cannot be a reactionary. Or specifically, a collaborationist.

That gets us back to our lunch conversation about Dos Passos.

Indeed. Did he start writing shit because he turned right-wing, or did his almost fascist politics turn him into a shit writer?

What do we do about [Louis-Ferdinand] Céline? Or Saul Bellow? Or in art, Nicolas de Staël, that police informer?

We have to put our discussion in context. When art was a bourgeois experience, most writers did not concern themselves with politics, at least until something exploded. Like Dostoyevsky facing an execution squad made him religious. Tolstoy reacted to the invasion by Napoleon. In any case, they had no illusion about for whom they were writing, since the masses not only didn't read but couldn't read. Look at what happened to Victor Hugo. A great writer, of songs, one could say, a charlatan until the coup of 1848. Then he becomes a socialist and writes plays challenging the state, plays that herald man's freedom.

Which, nevertheless, are read or attended only by the bourgeoisie.

But in a period when only that class, the petite bourgeoisie anyway, can stir things up, can demand and make changes. But that all has changed. Today, the masses are the motors for change, so a writer's commitment must be in that context.

Yet who will read your *Flaubert*? And what changes can your *Flaubert* generate?

Indeed, that's my contradiction. Though Flaubert did show how repugnant was the upper bourgeoisie and . . .

Could you ever imagine a worker reading *The Family Idiot*?

No, true, but my audience really changed in 1968; the whole world changed then. Until then a left-wing writer wrote for the left wing of the bourgeoisie, hoping to stimulate reforms. After '68, he had to choose, do I just advocate reforms or do I want a total restructuring of society? If I choose the latter, it means I recognize that the world is in the midst of an all-pervasive class war, and though I am by my birth, by my education, by my skill, by my trade a bourgeois, I must join those fighting that class.

Like Amílcar Cabral?[16]

Which of course is very hard, since we come to the struggle with all sorts of baggage we take for granted. You know, when my play *The Respectful Prostitute* was staged in Russia, in a popular hall, the end shocked the workers who attended. They couldn't understand why the prostitute ends on the side of the cops. What happened to her social conscience, they asked. And in '46, when I walked around Harlem with Richard Wright, folks who came up to talk to us, knowing who he was, always took the attitude that I was rich because I was white while Wright was poor because he was black, when in fact his best-selling novel *Native Son* had made him much richer than I. So one must never ignore the context. I am now a contradiction within the bourgeoisie. I write books that only the bourgeoisie reads, but I also edit a newspaper that is aimed at the masses and which, to an amazing extent, the masses do read.

But that's because you are well known. What does a new young politically hip writer do?

Tough question. He or she would have to find a new style, which somehow puts not only the writing but also the writer in the soup, as we say.

And the soup keeps changing.

Indeed. Look, for example, at *The Flies*. I wrote it to convince the French that, yes, to murder a German is to be guilty of murder, but morally it is the right thing to do, though he who does commit the murder will find no moral solace in the act. OK, in 1946, it's put on in Berlin by a group of German resisters, or friends and family members of those who had been executed by the Nazis for distributing tracts and stuff. Boy, was the audience critical. Why does Orestes go off alone? Why did he not act as the liberating king? What is this message of a hero murdering the town's dictators then going off by himself, telling the town, OK you manage now? A ridiculous romantic solitary hero. Well, they were right. When I wrote *The Flies* there was no possibility of the resistance taking over, being the new rulers. In any case, it was thought by all during the war that the resistance did not want power. That's how Camus saw it. So did Mauriac. Even Malraux, although I suspect he was already conniving to get into the Gaullist inner circle so as to be part of a future de Gaulle government. And we were all wrong. As soon as the war was over, the various resistance groups—well, not all, but most—began jockeying for power.

I hear you wanted Malraux to join you in *Les Temps Modernes*?

I did ask him. I went to see him in the South in 1943. I showed him the plan for socialism that I had devised . . .

Oh, you actually wrote out a plan? A program?

Yep. But he wasn't interested. He was already then thinking of joining up with de Gaulle. And I lost the program in the train, when I came back.

So in 1943, your contradictions were already flourishing, so to speak?

Well, no—I mean, socialism is perfectly acceptable to the petite bourgeoisie, no? I was still an individualist. The effect of my experience of commonality in the stalag had not led to a drastic reworking of my views. After all, in *Being and Nothingness* I wrote that to be a Lenin or to get royally drunk is all the same, an individual act, which belongs to the individual. Of course, if the Germans had gotten drunk and left us alone, we would all be much happier, but in terms of one's individual act, one is responsible for it equally. An act has no moral character. What does is the effect of that act. That's 1943.

And Castor says that you personified that into your admiration of the works of [the artist Alberto] Giacometti, whom you were seeing often then.

What I saw in his work was an essential thought, so to speak, a self-containment of society in one individual. But not society's contradictions. Here we were, invaded by Germans, occupied by Germans, who told us what we could do and what we couldn't. We hated the Germans, or the Nazis, and we wondered what was going to happen next. Like *The Plague*, right? That's Camus' novel. We were occupied, some opposed, some died. Voilà. It was absolutely wrong, and Camus was wrong. We were all wrong: the Germans weren't the plague, and we were occupied not by the plague but by human beings, who did what they did because of the kind of society that human beings had created, there, here, everywhere. But none of us thought that way in '43. It was these nasty Nazis who were telling us what to do, and some of us who didn't like it reacting by killing them. Camus was dead wrong: not a plague that no one could understand, but an invasion by humans who came out of a society that we must understand, occupying another society that we also had to understand.

And when did you understand all that?

Slowly. After the war. But we degenerated so fast, it was hard to balance it all. I had worked with communists during the resistance, but now they attacked me vehemently in their paper, *Action*. Mainly because we tried a Third Force. That didn't work, of course. So, to tell you the truth, I stayed out of politics after the Third Force collapsed. Well, we kept the journal going, and we gained a lot of respect because of our independence. Our group became more and more solid. There was Bost and his buddy, Jean Pouillon, who also had been one of my students and with whom I stayed friends all my life, still am. We saw a lot of Vian, and his wife, Michelle, who as you know loved to dance. And I worked with Dullin and others to put on my plays. Movies, too; I wrote a few scripts, like *Les jeux sont faits*, which was made. This was a period when we spent a lot of time having fun, going to clubs, taking walking trips in mountains, going abroad.

Apparently, whenever you did so, you did with Castor, just Castor.

Not always. Sometimes Lanzmann would join us. But it's true that im-

portant trips—that is, trips we considered a learning political experience—
we did together. Like when we went to Egypt to meet [Gamal Abdel] Nasser or
later to meet Fidel [Castro] or to Russia, though I went there alone too.

Is that still true?

More or less. Except when we went to Israel with Pierre.

You mean Bloch, that is, Pierre Victor, the head of the GP? [Pierre Victor and Pierre Bloch were pseudonyms used by the political activist and philosopher Benny Lévy.][17] I hear from some of my students who are in the GP that he is sort of a Stalinist, yes?

I guess so. I don't want to be part of the GP, just a member of their newspaper's editorial staff, and I am the official responsible editor. But I don't want to get involved in the GP itself. If they ask me to go talk somewhere or join a picket, things like that, I do. But I stay clear of their internal discussions. Pierre is unquestionably brilliant. He wants the GP to be a party that listens to the masses, specifically the big enterprise workers, but small ones too, and responds only to their needs. He's very dogmatic about that. He seems to have allowed no secondary cadre to be created. He says that his goal is to develop a party of full-time militants, totally transparent, open only to workers. We'll see.

You're also the responsible editor of *Vive la Révolution,* which is basically Trotskyist, isn't it?

Not really. Since '68, those labels have faded. But unlike *La Cause,* where I actually participate, I mean, I go to the editorial meetings, and look over each article, and—well, when I can. But for *Révolution* I just gave my name when the cops started arresting its editor, and now I'm in trouble with that leaflet . . .

The one about the cops distributing heroin to the inmates?

Exactly, someone put that in the paper, somewhere. I never saw it, and the lycée kids took it out of context and printed up a leaflet saying that, and it can cause me a lot of trouble as I would end up being responsible for the leaflet as well as the paper, and it's not true.

And *Révolution* is not the same kind of paper, is it?

***La Cause* was—is—meant to be an organizing tool. We expect it to be totally banned soon, hopefully not before a few months, time to create centers all over France based around it—that's the object. The paper will eventually be an underground publication, like *Lettres Françaises* and *Combat* during the German occupation. It would carry news about workers and**

peasants from all over France, but for that, these centers have to be set up by the workers and peasants themselves, operating clandestinely and semi-independently, so that if one group is arrested, it does not stop the paper from coming out. That's the plan, and they are hard at work on it now. The other papers, I presume you've seen them all—*Révolution, Tout, Vive La Révolution, La Parole du Peuple*—just use my name right now because the government is not arresting me. But if it gets heavy, they'll issue a new law that will make anyone affiliated with it, not just "the responsible editor," liable for arrest. But things are already changing, since I am now charged with defamation. It'll cost me a fairly heavy fine, but it will also lead to the banning of *Révolution*.

Tout has already died, though they're trying to raise money to bring it out again.

They'll all die, because they aren't trying to establish roots in factories and farms. They run basically like bourgeois papers. You can see that when you compare their language. *Révolution* and *Tout* aren't written like *L'Humanité* or *Ce Soir,* the Communist Party dailies, but they sort of honor the classic composition and layout of the traditional print media. But compare that to *La Cause.* The language is completely different. It is brutal, violent even, direct, simple, you could say simplistic, deliberately. It is in fact written in the language that protesting workers speak among themselves. Just by the language it is already illegal.

But once illegal, all sorts of new problems arise, like where to print, distribution, et cetera. Will each group put out its own version?

No, you know, we're used to illegal publications in France. We did it without problem during the occupation, and even recently, during the Algerian War, all sorts of pro-FLN papers flourished. Jeanson even put out a printed, fairly glossy, magazine, totally illegal since it called for active resistance to the French government, pure sedition.

Yes, but the government didn't go after the magazine's participants, as the Germans would have. Like Jeanson used his own name, not a war name, and that famous interview with you said who you were.

True. But once banned, *La Cause* would be liable to seizures wherever it was being distributed, in the factories, in cafés, in supermarkets, and our people have to be prepared for that, and for the possibility that any worker seen reading it could get fired.

How do you prepare for that?

Remember our "fiestas" during the occupation? Because of the curfew, which lasted until six or even seven in the morning, we often partied until then so none of us would get caught sneaking home during the night. That became a habit. Soon we started having those fiestas, as we called them, just to have fun, not in conjunction with some illegal editorial meeting or whatever. Well that's what we're trying to set up now, in factory towns, in farming centers. Bonding to publish and distribute *La Cause du Peuple*, and having fun in the process.

Reminds me of my meeting with Ho Chi Minh and Pham Van Dong, the North Vietnamese prime minister, in 1966. They already knew a lot of what we were doing in the United States against the war, but Pham asked for some details, and as I told them, I saw Ho sort of nodding in a way that I interpreted as him thinking, "Not very tough stuff." So I started exaggerating a bit, and when he made the gesture again, I really exaggerated. Then he interrupted me. "When do you have fun?" he asked, adding, "A revolutionary who doesn't have fun burns out too fast." To which Pham said: "A good revolutionary must love life."

Fantastic! That's why they're going to win! I'll remember that. Great. And so true!

Wait. There's a problem. For example, what happens to your fiesta if you hear that the other group having a fiesta all got rounded up and tortured and then executed? Can you continue to have yours? I'm not saying that will happen if French cops round up the group, say, in Saint-Etienne, but if the group is declared illegal, they'll certainly get beaten fairly severely—after all, there does not exist a police force in the world that doesn't enjoy beating up its prey. What happens when groups become afraid?

It actually happened during the occupation. Not my group, or the groups I was familiar with. But it happened. And of course it affected us. I remember once when we heard that a group that transported medicine and ammunition got caught, we spent our whole so-called fiesta time talking about them, explaining who each one was to those who didn't know them. There was no fiesta. But there's something special about illegality. It establishes an equality, a bonding, among all, whether you know them or not, that says for the sake of all, keep going. And instinctively we felt that to keep going meant to continue our fiesta as well. We obviously were not as intelligent or experienced as Ho and Pham, but we must have felt what they told you. And I think the guys from *La Cause* feel it too. I sensed that in our discussions. And you

know, even those who came to the fiestas but were not part of the reason why we were having them felt that. Like the writer Georges Bataille. He agreed with us but didn't participate. Or Castor, for that matter; she didn't write or help distribute our paper, but she was with us, and came to our fiestas. So too with Picasso.

He was a regular?

No, no. But when the Communist writer Michel Leiris staged that little Picasso play, he was there, and we kept it up all night, most of us actually playing roles in it, with Camus the lead. But it didn't start like that. Our fiestas came in '42, perhaps a bit in '41, but really '42 and '43. Before that we were stuck in our morass. In 1939, 1940, we were terrified of dying, suffering, for a cause that disgusted us. That is, for a disgusting France, corrupt, inefficient, racist, anti-Semite, run by the rich for the rich—no one wanted to die for that, until, well, until we understood that the Nazis were worse.

You don't sound like you liked the French very much.

Nasty, selfish, petty, arrogant, and many stayed that way during the occupation, collaborating, turning in Jews in order to get their houses or furniture, whatever. Castor has told the story of [Jean-Pierre] Bourla, that marvelous Jewish painter we all adored, whose Jewish girlfriend was turned in by another woman who wanted him, with the unexpected result, for her, that he, not his lover, was picked up, deported, and killed. That happened over and over again. No, we couldn't possibly defend France. But most of our intellectuals did, mind you, because Nazism was worse. True, some collaborated. But by and large, those who did acted out of ideological conviction. Like [Pierre] Drieu la Rochelle and [Robert] Brasillach—though they campaigned in favor of exterminating all Jews, they didn't do it to gain a few francs from the dead.[18] But most of our intellectuals were either active resisters or passive ones. But we didn't become resisters because we loved France, or its cause, only because we hated Nazism more. In fact, I was actually jealous of your father. He loved life. He was constantly joyous, constantly celebrating something. And he went to his probable death, consciously, believing in his cause. Proud of it, not just anti-Franco, anti-bigots, anti-fascist. But pro the Republic, pro-socialist, pro-life.

So what do you do with [Charles] Maurras, Drieu, and Brasillach in your theory that a good writer cannot be reactionary?

That's now. Today. Those writers became extreme right-wingers because they were totally disappointed with their country's idea of democracy.

They saw the corruption, the stupidity, and mind you, the lack of freedom that existed anyway. Today, even if the United States does not allow the freedom it claims exists, even if every democracy is plagued by its McCarthys, its House Un-American Committees, its FBIs and secret polices, its Deuxième Bureaus and Barbouzes,[19] no one in their right mind can claim that the right is more humane than the left. It is impossible today to hide from oneself the most revealing facts.

You think so? Look at America! The great majority believed that its invasion and systematic destruction of Vietnam was justified, to stop the communist dominoes.

America's propaganda works, no doubt about that, with ordinary folks who don't read and don't listen. But not with the intellectuals. Or, if they let themselves be convinced, it's because of money or fame or wanting your disgusting press to adore them. But, as we discussed the other day, they now write shit, like Steinbeck.

We have a lot of good intellectuals, good writers, who are very liberal, but not leftists, writers like [Bernard] Malamud, [E. L.] Doctorow, [Kurt] Vonnegut, [Norman] Mailer . . .

Hold on. I've read [Doctorow's] *The Book of Daniel* and [Vonnegut's] *Slaughterhouse-Five*. Those authors are with us, Gerassi, whatever they or their critics say. Perhaps they haven't experienced decision making by a collective, a true collective where they are totally equal to all. But they're there. You do them an injustice. Reread *The Naked and the Dead*. That's the real Mailer. Your friend, your father's friend.[20] America has not suffered an invasion, a foreign occupation, a bloody dictatorship. So it's hard for its intellectuals to expect and want total structural change. They're all stuck on reforms. That's normal. But when the revolution comes, they'll be on its side.

In a hundred years.

We started hundreds of years before, remember, and we're only beginning to understand now. Our great revolutionaries, and I don't mean Robespierre, but . . .

Orestes, Goetz, Hoederer . . .

Exactly, were also reformers.

And subjectivists, individualists, and moralists.

That's right. They never understood that change is collective. It cannot be done from above. It has to spring from below, and that means collectively. Morality cannot be imposed from above. In fact, morality is not possible in a world of individuals. That's why I could never write my ethics. And that's why I wrote the *Critique of Dialectical Reason,* to explain that man's fulfillment is collective. *Being and Nothingness* was an individual exercise. The *Critique* is the basis for an ethics.

Are you still working on it?

It's hard. I keep trying. It's very hard.[21]

December 1971

GERASSI: Let's get back to the war. I reread the two articles ["Paris Under the Occupation" (1944) and "The Liberation of Paris" (1945), reproduced in *Situations,* vol. 3 (1949)] in which you dealt, indirectly mind you, with fear of death and torture: the first, which everyone knows, is where you wrote that you were never as free as during the occupation; the second, which you wrote for English readers, in which you claim that all the French suffered because of the resistance.

SARTRE: Hold on. Let's put them in perspective. The first is philosophically perfectly clear, right? During the occupation, we had two choices: collaborate or resist. You couldn't be neutral if the Germans picked you up in a raid at a café just because you happened to be there and some Gestapo investigator claimed that an underground group met at that café—you ended up tortured like everyone else. Didn't matter what you did or who you were. Unless you were a collaborator, hence had a special ID that the Germans recognized, you went to jail, got tortured and most probably shot. So every French person had the free choice to be part of the resistance, in their heads anyway, even if they actually did nothing, or be an enemy. But that kind of a free choice had implications. In your head you were a resister. Meaning that if an actual resistance fighter asked you to hide him out, you would. You were consciously a resister. Now the second article I wrote to explain to the British how that free choice affected our daily life. We were terrified, every day, what-ever we were doing, wherever we were, that suddenly, out of nowhere, a Ger-man detachment would invade our street, our block, our building, whatever, seal all the exits or escapes and round up everyone inside their net. That hap-pened all the time, especially after the underground started shooting German officers systematically. Remember the German policy: ten French for every officer killed, then it became fifty and finally a hundred. No discussion, no ex-cuse. You were in the wrong place at the wrong time, too bad. Good-bye. That's a terrifying way to live, isn't it? The arbitrariness of life under the Nazis, like the arbitrariness of life under god. Yet every one of us, whether we ever even knew a resister, accepted that possibility, insofar as we freely had de-cided not to be a collaborator, which meant in effect to be a resister. And being shot was not the worst. It was torture that terrorized us most. If it turned out that I knew something, perhaps just the name of one or two actual re-sisters, or not even, the name of someone who had said that we would even-tually win the war, how long could I hold out, what was my limit? Terrifying.

Those who came to your "fiestas" were not all active resisters, were they?

No, they were precisely the kind that believed, like de Gaulle said, that France had lost a battle but not the war. Like [Armand] Salacrou.[1]

He was a resister?

No, but he was anti-German. And he was absolutely petrified of being tortured. Until one is actually tortured, he would say, no one can know what are one's limits.

And yet he risked his life by joining you all in those fiestas.

No, he risked his life by not being a collabo. He knew it, and we knew it. That's what I tried to communicate to the British, who had no respect for us. They suffered bombs and V-2s and constant casualties. They saw that we lived fairly comfortably, mostly in the cafés. They could not understand our anguish, our terror, especially when, after the war, journals described our fies-tas, which were precisely the consequence of our terror. That's what I tried to explain.

During the occupation, though, that's not what you were trying to achieve by those fiestas; it was to give a sense of "France continues," so to speak, no?

A lot of the fighters, those who sacrificed their lives, their family, will be shocked by what I will tell you now, but, well, it's a fact, namely that our resistance was really unimportant. I mean, when you put it in context, what did it accomplish? Did we force Germany to keep forty divisions in our country, like the Yugoslav partisans did? OK, so we blew up a few trains and shot a few officers. In the scheme of the war, it was nothing. Nor, now this is the important point, was it meant to. The purpose of the resistance was to tell all the French that we were united against the Germans. That they may win the war but they will never win the peace, because we are all united against them. That's why the film *The Sorrow and the Pity*—did you see it?—is dead wrong. Sure we had a lot of collabos who were right-wing capitalist fascists afraid of creeping socialism, or bastards who simply wanted the Nazis to win in order to steal the property and belongings of the Jews. French society before the war was absolutely rotten, no question about that. But rotten or not, it was French, run by rotten Frenchmen if you want, for the benefit of rotten French capitalists. But even they, the rotten French capitalists, did not want to be subservient to maybe-not-so-rotten German capitalists. And our job was to tell all the French, we will not be ruled by Germans. That was the job of the resistance, not just a few more trains or bridges blown up here or there. Those acts of sabotage raised our morale, and that's what their real purpose was. No resister really thought we could defeat the Third Reich by blowing up a few trains. And for keeping the flame of France alive, rotten to the core as it may have been, the Germans knew we were dangerous and had to be shot.

Yet, in both of those articles, you seem to be saying that when it came to who was and who was not a collabo, you did not make a class judgment.

Wait, yes and no. Don't forget that one of the first articles I wrote for *Lettres Françaises* was "Socialisme et liberté," where I maintained that genuine freedom, not one hidden in bad faith, could only exist in a collective—that is, under socialism. But, true, I did not claim, in the two articles you are citing, that the capitalist class was necessarily collaborationist. It depended on each capitalist's self-interest.

But you considered the bourgeois class as a class collaborationists?

Again, yes and no. When I walked into the Deux Magots, I greeted the owner as I always did. I knew that his interest was our interest. The small shopkeeper, the second-level cadre, no, we didn't consider them collabos. We may have at the beginning, but we quickly realized that they knew they would never enjoy their usual lifestyle—I'm not talking about money, but the way they lived their days, how they enjoyed talking with friends, whom they greeted when they walked their dogs, that kind of situation was untenable with German occupiers, and they knew it. Add to that this ridiculous senti-ment that we all have despite ourselves, this emotion we call patriotism, which comes from our history, our ordinary frame of reference, our language even, and we end up with resisters. Like my stepfather. He wasn't a resis-tance fighter, he was sixty-five, seventy, but he helped his Jewish friends hide out, things like that. He hated the occupiers simply because it diminished his sense of being French, as vague as that is. And I think that's what made the owner of the Flore or the Deux Magots comrades—well, that's perhaps too strong a word, but with us, without being tested. At Le Dôme it was a bit different. It was the place for "the gray mice" to have breakfast every day.

You mean the German female soldiers?

No, not soldiers, but logistical workers, the secretaries, the attendants, the chauffeurs of noncombatant officers, like your WAFs or WACs, I gather, who were dressed in gray uniforms, and came with their pot of jam to have coffee and bread at the café. Why they chose Le Dôme, I don't know. We stopped going there, not just because of them but also because they had eliminated the Vavin subway station out of economy, so we stuck to Saint-Germain.[2]

So no class consciousness during the resistance?

True, by and large, but it came back fast during the Liberation, as [Gen-eral Philippe] Leclerc's division approached. Many German soldiers had sur-rendered then, to the resistance fighters, and as they were marching them off to Leclerc, all those bourgeois came out to jeer them, to shout insults at them. Those who had fought guarded the Germans; those who had not now called them pigs. And they were the shopkeepers, the merchants at the entrance to their establishments. And so we said, Ha, the dirty bourgeois collabo. But all our judgments were wrong. The worst collaborationists were the cops, those who rounded up the thousands of Jews and herded them into the Vel' d'Hiv [Vélodrome d'Hiver, a huge indoor sports and entertainment stadium] to then be deported to their deaths in the concentration camps. But even blanket judgments on the cops are wrong. Various times, rushing home past the cur-few, I was stopped by a cop who simply asked where I was going and said hurry up. Castor had the same experience. On the other hand, we know of two friends in similar situations who were told by some family to stay in their apartment until the end of the curfew, then were denounced by them to the Germans (and in both cases it was the Germans who said "be careful next time").

What it seems to prove is that one should never judge individuals by their class but judge the class by its historical self-interest.

Exactly, Mr. Marx, exactly. Individually, we are what we do. As a class, we are part of historical forces that determine our fates.

So your ethics, if you ever get to finish it, will deal exclusively with the freedom of the individual to act in good faith?

But in the historical context.

As you tried to show in *Les jeux sont faits* [his play translated into English as *The Chips Are Down*], I presume. But I can well understand how your message there can be construed as a kind of mystical attempt to ignore reality. Of course, it was written in 1943, in the thick of the resistance, when a lot of French were saying OK, the reality is that the Germans are going to win, we will become part of Germany, nothing I can do makes any difference, but I will resist so that, what? History? I refuse to accept reality?

And make the peace intolerable for the Germans.

That's not in the play. In the play, Pierre knows that his friends have been betrayed and that they are going to be wiped out, yet he joins them, knowing he too will die. Period. There's no hope, no coming salvation, nothing but a moral decision that if his friends are doomed, he will be doomed with them. That's mystical, no?

In the same way as your father told me he was going back to fight Franco even though he knew Franco had won.

But you correctly sensed, or at least I read that in the novel, that Fernando was leaving a message for history, namely that one fights fascism not because one is going to win, but because the fascists are fascists. A message for history?

A moral act, but not a Kantian in-itself. A moral act in history, because history is the acts of human beings.

Which means that you are proselytizing.

I don't like that word, it's too loaded. No, what I am ultimately saying is that a person who fights Franco or the Nazis or today the Americans in Vietnam says that it does not matter if I lose, what matters is that my action, all the actions of those who fight for freedom, for self-determination, and ultimately for collective decision making, are part of the historical movement that defines humanity.

But that's not why Pierre does it, or Fernando, or Nizan or Schneider, or Brunet, or Mathieu or Bariona. They do it because they are faithful to their sense of justice or humanity or self-respect, none of which is political. Their act is moral and rejects reality. Philosophically, that would define you as an idealist.

Indeed. But, mind you, these works you cite were all prewar or pre-liberation, or before I quite digested my experience as a German prisoner.

When you were still anti-efficaciousness?

You could say that. In *The Wall*, cooperating with the enemy, even by telling him a lie, leads to disaster. But in [the play] *Men Without Shadows* [Mort sans sépulture, later translated as *The Victors*], Canoris, the communist, argues against his men wanting to be true to their self-image and insists that they must lie, that interior honesty does not save lives, that they must do what is efficient in their struggle, and so what if the militias interpret their lie as having given in, being afraid of torture and death. Their honor, Canoris says, means nothing in the overall struggle.

So then what happens to your ethics? Are you back to efficiency, to realism?

We're on a difficult course here. The problem has always been, for me and for any noncommunist leftists, how to relate to the party, and to good friends who might be in the party . . .

Like Francis Ponge?

Exactly. A wonderful guy. When he edited the literary pages of *Action* and I was attacked by the party, he invited me to answer . . .

I saw that. He sure gave you a lot of space . . .

My history with the party was always confused and confusing. It began with my closest buddy, my classmate, Nizan, with whom I shared everything for all the years at Normale, and who first condemned me, correctly, mind you, as a petit bourgeois, then quit the party over the Stalin-Hitler pact. I didn't know how to deal with the good communist resisters in *The Age of Reason*. It wasn't until the fourth volume that I tried seriously, through the relationship of Schneider who, like Nizan, quits over the pact, and Brunet, a loyal but very honorable party member. After Liberation, I tried to avoid dealing with the issue, as I launched the Third Force movement, which could not succeed precisely because movements have to be for something, not just against, like Camus, which is why he ended up with no political influence in the world . . .

. . . except in the United States.

But that's because he was used by your cold-warriors for their own

ends. OK, so we decide, well most of us, but not David Rousset, the co-chair of our movement, who moves to the far right, to become conscious fellow travelers because the world is then clearly threatened with nuclear devastation by America. So the CP tries to be nice to me, and Ponge, who was a very good friend, unwittingly—he was much too honorable to let himself be a pawn—helps pave the way for a rapprochement. Not only was he a good guy, he wrote two good novels, which were ignored. Camus, who was so anti-communist that he could not go out of his way to praise Ponge's novel, asked me to do it. I did. You should read [Ponge's book] *Le parti-pris des choses* and [Raymond Queneau's] *Zazie dans le métro*. They're really very good. Anyway, with me, Ponge was always a straight shooter.

What about Raymond Queneau?

Same thing, or even worse, in the sense that he was an absolutely first-rate novelist, yet was mostly ignored because of his party affiliation. The whole postwar art of the novel owes its language, its structure, to Queneau. But then, they elected him to the Académie Goncourt, poor guy; that killed him.

Why did he accept?

Specifically, Queneau, I don't know. But in general, people have a need to belong to something that is bigger than them. It explains the success of the church, of clubs, of movements, of political parties. The Communist Party is especially apt at this, you know, by making belonging both an act of charity, that is, helping others, and obedience. It eliminates the anxiety of choice.

Ah yes, the choice, that's the basis of your existential psychoanalysis, and your rejection of Freud.

Not completely. When I was twenty, yes. I refused to believe that infancy or childhood predetermined the behavior of adults. Remember, I substituted Freud's notion of the "unconscious" with my notion of the "lived," meaning the constant anxiety of choosing. But over the years I moderated that point of view. But we were talking about the need to belong. Like Queneau, a communist, accepting his admission to the Goncourt. Why? The prestige and honor? Why join the Communist Party in the first place, or any strictly hierarchical party or movement or club or church? The need to belong, a security blanket, like in one's infancy. And just like parents, or family, can be unfair, vicious even, the offspring longs for its security no matter what. So, once the family unit is gone, where to turn for that security?

In every autobiographical essay you've written, especially in *The Words,* it is quite clear that you had that security. And yet you sought it at Normale, didn't you, where you rarely completely agreed with your classmates, except Nizan, and he, too, was at first sort of fascist, then communist. So obviously, Freud was right is stressing that predetermination . . .

Hold it. First of all, he insisted that the primary upsetting factor in the need for security was the sexual. That it exists, of course. That it is important, sure. But the primary source of action? No. Castor disagreed with me on that point; we often argued about it. She was much more Freudian than I. But I never negated the role of sex . . .

And you certainly focus on your mother as your sister, the significance of sharing the same bedroom, how surprised you were when you saw her underarm hair, et cetera.

True, but I also wrote at length on the god of the family, my bearded, tall, majestic grandfather, and the security I derived from his presence.

Until his double-cross, what you call betrayal. That's a violation of your security, that is, your sense of belonging, so, if you had been Salacrou, you would have joined the CP, and then the Goncourt club.

That's exactly where existential psychoanalysis tells you no, not necessarily. A choice is involved. And every choice is in the lived, in the context of everything that is happening in the world. The harder the choice, the more the anxiety. But that does not mean that the chooser is not free to make the choice.

Garcin wants to be known as brave, a good guy on the good side. But he can't. Why? Because he also wants security, first of all to belong to the class that his environment or his education or background, whatever, respects—that is, "men with their shirtsleeves rolled up." He craves fame. So while he wants to be loved as a resister he also collaborates to survive. Now what in existential psychoanalysis explains why he chose what he thought was the easy way out: to run, a coward?

Existential psychoanalysis does not explain, like a Freudian version would. Nothing in his childhood gives us a clue. It's the soup, right? He's in the soup. We analyze the soup. Every one of us in a capitalist individual-oriented society seeks recognition and security . . .

And if they are in conflict? They often are. Recognition means to feel relevant in an absurd world, right? And security means being nice and safe in a well-ordered world. So? Will you not grant Freud that if Garcin had been happy in his family life, once he transferred that to his newspaper, he had gained his family again.

I guess you could say that's why he did not want to risk losing it. Which in practical terms, in the soup, means not to jeopardize it. But is that why he is a coward? Or is it because despite his terrible matrimonial situation, he likes his life as it is? But the point is: he chooses. He knows the reasons for his choice. It's not because of Inès's attack on his justifications that he ends up admitting his cowardice to himself. Her taunting gets him to say it out loud.

That's your "Hell is each other" bit.

But that's only that side of the coin. The other side, which no one seems to mention, is also "Heaven is each other."

You mean that if those three people cared about each other instead of trying to present themselves as righteous or at least human, they would have overridden their terrible history to create a group with the psychological security we all took for granted, and needed, as children. As you would later put it in the *Critique,* they were serialized. Had they created a group-infusion, their situation would not have changed, but by making it theirs, they would have been able to accept it.

Precisely. Hell is separateness, uncommunicability, self-centeredness, lust for power, for riches, for fame. Heaven, on the other hand, is very simple —and very hard: caring about your fellow beings. And that's possible on a sustained basis only in collectivity.

But Garcin would still have died too soon, as he says, and your message remains that we all die too soon—or too late.

That's part of the human condition, and applies to all. And the verdict, whether one did die too soon or too late, is hell or heaven on earth. Suppose Lenin had continued to live, would not Soviet socialism be different today? Had Céline died right after *Journey,* would he not be hailed by all French today? But he lived on to be pro-German, and has basically disappeared from the pantheon of great writers.[3]

That's true for Dos Passos too. He should have died after *1919.*

And if Malraux had died in Spain he would still be the idol of the world's left.

Yet we both agree with Freud at least on one thing, that there are no accidents in life.

Historically speaking, correct. But in context, in the "lived," Céline died

too late, so did Dos Passos and Malraux, but [Franz] Kafka, and maybe Camus, died too soon. And Hemingway? That awful book about his young mistress in the trees, or something?

You mean *Across the River and into the Trees?* Yes, that was pretty bad, but he got his true form back with his next novel, a really great one, *The Old Man and the Sea.* Hemingway offers so many contradictions. He was at one point the most famous American novelist, yet he became an alcoholic; he was married to fantastic women, and viewed them as rivals so he divorced them. He won the Nobel Prize and got depressed.

And he committed suicide from that depression?

Not sure. He had all sorts of health problems dating back to his wound in World War I, or perhaps hereditary, plus two airplane crashes in Africa, and various other accidents. Absolutely amazingly successful and miserable. Speaking of the absurdity of life . . .

But don't forget that the absurd is an objective description of reality, and who lives accordingly? Look at the occupation. Until Stalingrad and the African landing, we were all convinced that Germany would win the war. That meant that we would be ruled by Nazism. Some were glad, like the fascist groups Action Française and Croix de Feu, or like that aristocrat in *The Sorrow and the Pity* who joins the Waffen-SS to go fight against the Russians. And of course some said, OK, let's adapt and became collaborationists. But the majority, whatever their politics, referred to them as *boches* and would have nothing to do with them, if they could avoid them. And then there were the Maquis, the resistance. You could argue that, in 1943, with the Russians advancing on Germany and the Allies' invasion of Sicily in July and their triple landing in Italy in September, every collabo suddenly became anti-Nazi. In fact, most of the upper class switched just like that. Most, but not all, as we discussed the other day. But in June 1941, as Hitler launched [Operation] Barbarossa, which swept two hundred miles into Russia in just a week, the world probably thought the Third Reich would rule, as Hitler had said, for the next millennium. And yet, the underground grew. More and more young men were willing to fight. Why? Totally absurd. Because subjectively, each of us refuses to live according to the absurd. The majority will deny that it is absurd, just like the majority want to believe in a god who will satisfy all. The difference, of course, is huge, because to believe in god entails at the most a bit of ritual praying and spending a tiny sum of cash, while to believe that the enemy can be crushed is to be willing to sacrifice life.

The dichotomy between objective and subjective conditions reverberates throughout the discussions of the left. I remember once in Cuba, five Latin American committed journalists and I were invited to have lunch with Fidel. As the discussion progressed about where and how to make revolutions throughout the continent, Fidel began to get irritated by such statements as "But in that country, no one thinks it's possible," or "In that one, the majority are too downtrodden." Over and over, we—because I did too—raised the issue of the "objective conditions." Fidel finally exploded. "All it takes is seven revolutionaries willing to die to get a revolution started. Like here!" None of us argued with him directly. But we did point out that Cuba had a long history of struggle against Spain, the United States, dictators, et cetera, and had a very conscientious student body. "That's not what made the revolution! What did are those who believed in it." To which I risked answering, "But that's what the priest is telling his flock, believe and you'll go to heaven." I was expecting a tirade. Instead, Fidel smiled and said: "Of course, he believes in the absurd. So does a revolutionary. The difference is that his absurdity does not help the living. Our absurdity does. And what is the absurdity of the revolutionary? That he believes in something that does not exist on this planet, just like the priest, but for humanity, not some bearded old man playing with saints. The revolutionary believes in justice."

Conclusion? Since "justice" exists nowhere, Fidel is an idealist. He told me the same thing.

But to get back to the post-liberation years, your cooperation with the communist-led journal *Lettres Françaises* continued, didn't it?

For a while, yes, but soon they began to attack me, not in that journal, but in *Action* or *L'Humanité*.

Why? You hadn't written anything against them yet.

I think because the press, the media, talked too much about me and Castor, and "existentialism," which was a word invented by one of them, [Roger] Garaudy, when he was still a communist.[4]

This was before you launched *Les Temps Modernes*?

Indeed. Their criticisms were mild at first. Purely cultural. I had a meeting with three of them, at the apartment of a philosophy professor from L'Ecole Alsacienne. Garaudy was there and some other guy I can't remember. Theoretically, the meeting was meant to work out a common strategy. But it degenerated quickly into mild criticisms, then very antagonistic statements,

insults almost. Then the Russian writer [Alexander] Fadeyev let loose, and that ended it until the Henri Martin affair in 1952.

Fadeyev was that Russian critic who called you a hyena with a pen? So you then decided to form your own journal?

No, no. His attack was not the cause. I mentioned that so you can have a sense of our post-liberation situation. The communists wanted to dominate, or at least set the tone, of France's cultural existence after the war. Many of the best writers and poets were communists, to mention just Aragon and [Paul] Eluard, as were many of the best-known artists, like Picasso. Almost every Frenchman respected them for their role during the resistance, and no one knew about the secret outrages that surfaced later. The CP was the biggest party in France. But Stalin did not want them to take the government, just make trouble for the United States, and one of the ways to do that was to make sure that communist writers, singers, painters, et cetera, stood in the full limelight of the country's cultural activities. And we often agreed with the communists' political maneuvers, so an alliance between the noncommunist left and us was very natural. But they didn't accept that we had quite a following in 1945, which made them feel we were competitors for that limelight. So they tried to ostracize us. Instead we launched *Les Temps Modernes,* which quickly became the primary independent journal on the left.

And it was at first fairly ecumenical, in the sense that founding members included Raymond Aron, a right-wing social democrat, Merleau-Ponty, a very left philosopher, André Malraux, a Gaullist. How did you fit in this crowd?

Badly, and as you know it did not last. Malraux wanted to be part of de Gaulle's government. Aron started writing for the far-right *Figaro.* But Merleau and I saw eye-to-eye for a long time, and we published some extraordinary articles, like the first complete analysis of and attack on imperialism, not just France's, but America's as well. The danger of neocolonialism. The outrage of the French war on the Vietnamese. America's attempt to turn the Caribbean into an American lake . . .

Yes, very true. But as I reread the first issues, I found that there were some grave, indeed major, lacunae, like no class consciousness, no sense of the importance of collective decision making, not even an understanding that politics is everything . . .

Very true. As you can see in *Being and Nothingness,* I believed then that politics was how people talked who wanted to get something for themselves. It took a while for me to understand that politics is everything, and I spelled that out in the *Critique*.

You went, it seemed to me, from one extreme to another. In the first, you reject the importance of the collective, to focus on the significance of the individual's authenticity in defining his or her choices. In the *Critique,* permanent revolution, that is, the creation of groups-in-fusion, you tend to push a kind of voluntarism of the individual, that is to say, that subjective force of a group is caused by an individual, like the guy who seizes the bus, and not collective action.

Did you read Merleau's *Adventures of the Dialectic*? You should. He attacks me precisely along those lines. He says that I am an ultra-Bolshevik voluntarist. I think you're both wrong. Yes, the man who seized the bus acted impetuously without consulting his fellow sufferers. But his decision to do so was precisely because they were in the same soup. He represented the will, the decision of all. Face it, had he been alone waiting for a bus, he would never have dared seize it, right? His individual act was a collective act. I'm quoting Castor there; she answered Merleau in *Les Temps Modernes*.

But that wasn't the reason for the break with Merleau, was it?

No, not at all. Merleau was in a very tough position after the war. He sympathized with almost every action waged by the communists, as I did, mind you, and he accepted the fact that the party represented the workers, hence could not be opposed on that score, as I did. But he wanted to inject into our revolutionary attitude, hence inside the party ideology, a fundamental respect for the formal aspect of bourgeois legality. Just because bourgeois democracy violates its principled laws, just because it deliberately misinterprets in practice its genuinely democratic laws of individual rights, he said, does not mean we can discard the whole bourgeois legal structure. To Merleau, individual freedoms were sacred, yet he did not want to break with the CP just because the party hacks ignored them.

And you did.

Our Third Force, as the press called our movement, that is, our RDR, brought us unbelievably intense criticisms, I mean attacks, by those hacks.

Like from your former student Jean Kanapa?

He was something else! You know, I had gone out of my way to help him as a student. I even took him to a psychiatrist when I thought he was going bananas. But he needed a church, to believe, so he found it in the Communist Party. And when they said prove your loyalty by attacking Sartre, he did.

Not very successfully, I must say; your reply in *Les Temps* totally destroyed him. But he wasn't the only one; there was a whole series in *Action*.

But as I said, I think they were really motivated by our dominance of the cultural field, and not our politics, since after all the RDR had almost no influence in the political arena. And they didn't attack Merleau very much, or when they did, with kid gloves, because he did not threaten them in the streets, so to speak. I mean in plays and novels, like both Castor and I did.

Still, I reread *Humanism and Terror* recently. It decimates the party's lack of human rights. I don't see how they could accept it.

You're absolutely right. They didn't. But Merleau, who had basically become the political editor of *Les Temps Modernes*, didn't affect the CP's rank-and-file. Workers don't have the time or leisure to read novels, go to the theater at night, or to read long philosophical articles. But they do read in the popular press about the scandals caused by that play or the secrets revealed by that novel, they know what is being talked about in the cafés. So that's the enemy on which the party focuses.

So why did the party attack so vehemently the RDR, which was not an important political movement?

Because of us, of our standing, I mean Castor and I and our friends, which included some famous names, even foreign ones, like your writer Richard Wright. Then we began to suspect that Rousset, the RDR co-chair, might be getting CIA money—you know, that was the period when the CIA was spreading money to all anti-communist forces in Europe, and even such respectable reviews as England's *Encounter* and the Congress for Cultural Freedom were taking it. And denying it, of course. We now know that the CIA financed our new workers' confederation, Force Ouvrière, and tried to bribe our leftist but noncommunist CFDT [French Democratic Confederation of Workers]. And Rousset did turn to the right, as did his pals. It was then that the CP staged a massive rally in Paris of the Movement for Peace—you know, the famous one for which Picasso painted that beautiful white dove. The CP tried to make that movement as broad as possible, and invited me to speak, which I did. But then, two or three weeks later, Rousset and his pals tried to sponsor another such rally without the communists and, more important, intimating that America was a sponsor of world peace. That really got us. First we—I mean

Merleau, Wright, and our group—wrote a letter denouncing it. Then I called for a convention of the RDR and paid for it with my own money, because while we had a vast majority in the ranks, Rousset had a majority in the organizing committee and, of course, refused to back the call. That's when I asked the members to vote to dissolve the RDR on one basic issue: which country was willing to start World War III?

And you didn't even know of the U.S.'s first-strike policy then?

No, we concluded that since America had developed the H-bomb, it so wanted to dominate the world, it would risk blowing it up to do it.

Actually, the United States had given up the idea of dominating the world through nuclear power by then. It did [have that idea] for a while, when it thought it could do it without blowing up itself.

Boy! But back then, while we did not know about first strikes, we certainly were aware of America's ambitions. We were well aware that NATO was an American plan to dominate Europe, and we knew that the Soviet Union was using the Warsaw Pact to defend itself, not conquer us. So we decided, I mean the editors of *Les Temps Modernes,* decided that if we had to choose between America and Russia, we had to choose Russia. That was the first point. The second was that, whether we liked it or not, the CP represented the working class. It was a reformist not revolutionary party, but it was systematically against any exploitation of workers, and so were we. And the third point, of course, was that all other important parties or movements, political or cultural, were corrupt, bought by American CIA largesse. So even from a point of view of honor or pride we had to be anti-American, and we still are. But that did not make any of us like the CP.

But your CP friends?

During the war, they were comrades. As comrades, I got along fine with them and enjoyed their company. But once that Stalinist apparatus of trying to control the minds of its adherents took effect, it became very difficult to relate to them. Fundamentally, they were all mentally sick. I mean that about Aragon as much as Garaudy. Take this example: Morgan, one of the intellectuals ordered to convince me to make an alliance with the CP, finally realized how bad the Soviet Union was and reacted to the invasion of Hungary by writing a careful letter to *L'Humanité,* which did not publish it, but instead printed an answer by another of its intellectual robots denouncing Morgan's letter—which no communist could read. And he was expelled. If they didn't do their assigned dirty work, they were themselves dragged in the mud. And their contempt for their allies was unbelievable. That other commie at that meeting sent to woo me, a famous gynecologist, told me: "Fellow travelers travel with us to a point, then they always stop, and we call them traitors." Or Claude Roy, a despicable Pétainist during the war, then quickly converted to the CP to guarantee his future. The whole French CP leadership and its intellectuals were made up of these sickos, from that carpet merchant [Jacques] Duclos down.[5] But we had no choice. In light of the bigger picture, we had to be their patsies. If only our CP was like the Italian.

It obeyed Stalin just as much.

Yes, but individually, Italian communists were so much nicer, so much more affable, so much more intelligent. I would most certainly have joined their party and quit in 1969 with Rossana Rossanda and written for *Il Manifesto* had I been Italian.[6]

Yet in the '50s you really liked America.

Mixed. I loved New York. But I had a great guide.

Dolores [Vanetti]?[7]

A really wonderful woman, and friend, as you know, since you knew her before me. She knew every dive and jazz joint, and the musicians, every opium den (which included cocaine and speed and everything else except opium), every intellectual hangout, just everything, and I got to know a lot of America, really a lot, thanks to her. What I liked most about your country was its petit bourgeois world, people who lived most graphically the contradictions of the country, namely the discrepancy between life and the representation of life. America is so full of myths, it's mind-boggling, myths of happiness, progress, freedom, equality, that everything is possible, making Americans the most optimistic people in the world, yet living under a total dictatorship of public opinion, so naive that they're wonderful, until their ruling class tells them that everyone else is inferior, of course. Officially, they scorn Europe, except for their attachment to their country of origin, but it's all false: with all their wealth, their power, their formidable drive, Americans have an incredibly acute inferiority complex. Fantastic contradictions! I loved it. Especially in such places as Iowa, or Kansas, or Wyoming, where folks had never heard of Stalingrad or Auschwitz or even Churchill. I found an America extremely poor, another in Chicago that was fascist, still another that was open, charming, and generous. I loved its skyscrapers but also its main streets, and I was delighted to find the America of Dos Passos, of Steinbeck, of Faulkner. Whether traveling by train or in a small plane—with a former fighter pilot who delighted in trying to scare us by flying through the Grand Canyon a couple of feet from the cliffs—I relived the novels I had so loved.

You made three trips to the United States, right?

Yes. The first I went as a correspondent, and wrote my impressions in various newspapers. The second was to see Dolores. We traveled then for three months, all over America and Canada, too. I made my living by giving conferences. The third trip, I stayed one month in New York, then went all over Central America and the Caribbean, including Cuba.

What did you do during that month in New York?

Mostly just walked around. Dolores, and your mother, were working, so Fernando, who wasn't, and I just walked through all the neighborhoods during the day, and the four of us got together in the evening.

Did you wander through Harlem then?

The first time I went to Harlem was with Dolores. It was a bad experience. She was frightened. She thought everyone saw her as white, which wasn't true. She wanted to pass as white, and it made things uncomfortable. The next time, I went alone. No problem. People were very nice, friendly, smiling, and of course incredibly poor. The third time I went with Wright and Fernando. Wright took us to nightclubs and restaurants and all sorts of hangouts. That was a great trip.

I thought you had broken with Fernando by then.

No, we never formally broke. It was just, well, sort of estranged, but that was the first trip; when I arrived, the second day, I rushed to see him, but I found him a bit bitter, like he resented the fact that he had had to leave France and live in America, which at that time he hated. He held it against me, I think, that I hadn't gone to Spain, or rather that because he did, he was now stuck in America.

I thought there was something before that, before the war, even.

Well, yes, there was the business with Poupette [who had studied painting under him]. Both Castor and I had been angry that, in 1931, when he was still in Spain and Stépha had come to Paris to get an abortion, but actually, to give birth to you, Poupette went to see him in Barcelona and they had an affair. She had been a virgin, and it wasn't just an affair, he screwed her anywhere, standing up at the door when she walked in, that kind of stuff. It wasn't that she disliked it, but that, after all that, he told her that her paintings were shit. She was devastated, and both Castor and I were very angry. I think I even wrote him a nasty letter.

But you stayed friends, since you came to La Closerie that day when I was born and you were the first nonhospital person to see me alive when Fernando got drunk.

I loved Stépha so much, as did Castor, that we would never think of breaking, but then, in America, when he understood that Dolores and I were lovers, he talked to her very badly, so much that she didn't want to see him with me.

Jealousy?

No, I don't think so, just his bitterness. He was so unhappy then, at being in exile, not painting, that he couldn't stand seeing me happy, I think.

During these three trips you made, did you understand U.S. politics?

No, not until I went to Central America and especially Mexico—no, Cuba was even worse. In those countries it is impossible not to see the damage that American businesses do, impossible not to understand that American capitalists, aided by their government, defended by the American army, just want to exploit the people living there. And by the way, it is impossible not to understand why American businessmen are racists; they justify their exploitation on the ground that the people of those countries are inferior. That alleviates their consciences. After those trips, especially the third one, I came home loving daily life in America and hating its capitalists and its government, which did what the capitalists wanted. My last image of that last trip was Venezuela. I went to Maracaibo to see the oil; all the American executives of the Creole Oil Corporation[8] lived in absolute splendor, while those who did the work, the Venezuelans, lived in hovels with barely enough to feed their family. Then I went to Caracas, where it was even worse. When it came time to have lunch just before I left, my American hosts said there was only one place: the Tamanaco Hotel, the most splendid hotel I had ever seen at the time, where no Venezuelan was allowed unless invited by Americans, or unless they worked there, of course. I had never seen such luxury. Then I came back to France, where America was trying to Americanize my country.

January 1972

GERASSI: Speaking as we were at lunch about your book *What Is Literature?* you agree that you write for the bourgeois to get him or her more committed against the very bourgeois class's selfish self-centeredness, correct? Isn't that the same reason Aragon writes? You don't write for the worker, and neither does he. Workers aren't going to read your *Flaubert,* and workers aren't going to read [Aragon's] *Aurélien* or [his wife, Elsa Triolet's] *Cheval Blanc.*[1]

SARTRE: Hold on. You're mixing different issues there. First of all, novels by communist hacks are sold at communist rallies, meetings, conferences, and conventions by hawkers who imply that buying their books is a communist duty. That's how they wage and win their so-called battle of the books. Workers buy them but don't read them. Now, you mention my *Flaubert.* Not a novel but a thick, difficult book to read, granted. Neither bought nor read by the working class. (Still, by the way, it sold fifteen thousand copies, presumably to people who wanted to and perhaps did read it. A detail.) Now, the main issue. For whom do we really write?

You've said that you write for the oppressed class via the intermediary of the intellectual elite, that is, the petit bourgeois class. You've also said that the writer writes to express his freedom, which is a way of saying that he writes to escape the absurdity of life, to create a world that has meaning, which would be with a beginning, a middle, and an end—in other words, to be god.

No. Well, perhaps. That certainly is why the great writers of the nineteenth century wrote, to give meaning to an absurd world.

In other words, to cheat death.

Correct. But the modern writer does not. Alienated himself in this absurd world, he writes to exalt his freedom, and the freedom of his readers, precisely in this absurd world.

How is that different from a Dostoyevsky? Forget what he claimed were his reasons—what did his novels actually say? That the only really free individuals are those who accept the absurdity, like Stavrogin, like Prince Mishkin, even like the communist terrorist Verkhovensky in *The Possessed,* and not Alyosha or Shatov, or even Kirilov, who commits suicide to prove he is free.

You're right, as we now interpret his novels, but you ask, Why write? Today, the writer writes to change his society, to help his readers—and himself—liberate themselves within, not without, absurdity. And that means commitment. That is, politically conscious that the ruling classes dominate and want to dominate the poor, the helpless, and the lost.

He names, and to name is to change, yes?

Well, I'm not so sure. For our generation, yes. But Flaubert . . . He was full of ill will when he wrote *Madame Bovary*. He wrote it to demoralize. He was extremely reactionary; he believed that the bourgeois class was a universal class. He was still young when he wrote that, yet . . .

So what happens to your theory that only a man committed to the poor, the unfortunate, the exploited, can be a good writer?

I wrote that in 1946, '47, still full of the resistance. I'll have to reconsider. There are writers with bad faith, certainly, like Hemingway, whose novels are couched usually in the collision of great ideas, but symbolically, like in *To Have and Have Not*, or in *For Whom the Bell Tolls*. All of which is ultimately about the bourgeois individualist off to make a revolution. A revolutionary off to a safari. To fight the good cause in Spain, but first the bullfight. Like Flaubert, Hemingway was a nasty man, personally, and it shows in his writing. Flaubert was totally alienated, but he wrote for the alienated. As he sought his freedom through his alienation, he sought ours as well, without perhaps planning to. He was completely twisted, crazy even, but he sought his, hence my, freedom. That ultimately is the purpose of writing.

Mauriac? And before him, Céline?

Céline really belongs to the nineteenth century. In any case, he did apply weird, granted, but particular principles at the beginning, in his great books, like *Journey to the End of the Night,* then flipped out during the Nazi occupation. No one reads what he wrote then. Like Dos Passos and Steinbeck; totally meaningless writers once they gave up their commitment to their fellow suffering human beings. You mention Mauriac, a very convinced Catholic believer, yes, who claims to write to help his fellow beings find god. But you like what he writes, yes? So do I. Why? Because we search for god? For meaning? No, of course not. We like Mauriac because he struggles with his demons to give himself, and hence all of us, peace. He cares about human beings. Never mind his god. Just like Ivan or Stavrogin. Here on earth, in the midst of everyone's absurd existence. Like Keo in Malraux's *Human Condition* [*La condition humaine,* now usually translated as *Man's Fate*], one of the great novels of the twentieth century.

I certainly agree with you on that. I am appalled at the fact that none of my students have read it, worse, even heard of it, before I make it required reading. Their lit teachers tend to make them read American psychological novels, not ones that reveal Hegel's great theory of literature as the collision of great ideas, not even Dos Passos's *USA* trilogy.

What a shame. *Manhattan Transfer* [by Dos Passos] is surely one of the great American novels of all time, on a par with *American Tragedy* [by Theodore Dreiser], or *Absalom, Absalom!* [by William Faulkner], or that book on the Civil War . . .

The Red Badge of Courage [by Stephen Crane].

Right. Which has that universal collision seen through the psychology of that poor soldier. But some of what you call the typical American psychological novels try to do likewise, and some are pretty good, mainly, yes, I agree, because behind the psychology, there is that collision of great ideas, like in [Joseph Heller's] *Catch-22* and some of [Philip] Roth and Malamud. But that is never stressed by your critics, at least the ones we read here. It's as if to admit that we live in an absurd world with no grandiose meaning would be a sacrilege.

Quite so. America is a fundamentalist state, no matter how much they pretend to have separated church and state. Even our coins read "In God We Trust," and kids in public school have to swear allegiance to America, "and the flag for which it stands," "under God."

Oh yes, I remember that flag business. I've never visited a country with more displays of its flag, not even Russia. You have it everywhere, on people's front lawns, on private buildings, like telling you, Hey, don't forget you're an American and all others are enemies.

Actually, that is what it says, at least to most ordinary Americans. That helps most Americans tolerate our imperialism, like the [William] Walker story.

What was that?

He was a dentist, lawyer, nineteenth-century filibusterer, that is, an adventurer who raised a private army, with the money of the First Boston Group which became United Fruit Company, and conquered Nicaragua, turned it into a slaveholding state, and tried to get it annexed to the United States. He then tried to conquer British Honduras, but the Brits defeated him, catching him alive, and handed him over to the United States to be tried for violating our neutrality laws. He was tried in New Orleans, and his main defense was that it is better to be a slave and part of America than to be a non-slave but independent. The jury applauded him as they shouted "Not guilty." But to get back to the issue, your writer ultimately writes to help create the classless society, because only then can he live with his angst, his absurd existence.

Correct. A classless society means that we would live in collectivities, in which our sense of the absurd would be tolerable because of our identity with our fellow beings.

But then there would be no need of writers?

The classless society must be able to look at itself.

Meaning that the writer would then be only a spokesperson for the common, like he would write about the cane cutters for the factory workers and vice versa, so that each would understand the other?

No one has yet formulated convincingly a theory of the classless society that encompasses the role of the writer, the artist. But it would surely specify that the writer would write for all, since ideally, there would be no elites. Neither Marx nor Lenin explained how, or better, who. [Antonio] Gramsci tried, of course, and came close to concocting a theory of the proletarian intellectual, but he set it in a transition phase. As for Rosa Luxembourg, unquestionably the most democratic of all communist revolutionaries, she nevertheless writes for her comrades, to stimulate action.

Result: the CP ignores her.

The CP is stupid, period.

Yet they didn't attack *What Is Literature?* did they?

No, but that was because either they didn't read it or they didn't understand it, or their bosses said, Oh don't attack Sartre right now, we need him, or something like that.

And [Gyorgy] Lukacs?[2]

A royal poseur.

But he was the first to explain, contrary to general erudite opinion, that [Honoré de] Balzac was much more of a revolutionary than Zola.

True. Zola was really merely a reformist. Give the miners more food and a bigger salary and they'll be OK. I'll give Lukacs credit for that much. But his attack on my work had almost nothing to do with what I wrote (I wonder if I read it). Basically, he wants to maintain, in his convoluted prose, which few can fathom, that communist writers write for the masses, not the communist elites.

In fact, we all write for elites, do we not?

Yes, but once removed, so to speak—that is, through the intermediary of the petit bourgeois who read us.

There are no intermediaries when you write for *La Cause du Peuple.*

No. There I am able to write, and be read by the militants all over France and to some degree in Germany and Italy as well, yet I have written, and will continue to write, hundreds of pages on Flaubert. What I do for *La Cause* is exercise my profession as a writer. But *Flaubert* is a creative work, and its prestige guarantees that when I write about the outrages at the Toul prison, the world listens.[3]

But you're not going to tell me that you spent fifteen years writing *Flaubert* in order to be able to attract a readership for *La Cause?*

Of course not. But in a way I knew that such would be the consequence. After all, I had spent twenty years writing literature that gave me the opportunity to write my "J'accuse."[4] Besides, all my plays were committed plays. I did not write the plays in order to sign [petitions and manifestos], but I can sign because I wrote the plays.

And which act is more valuable?

To society? Signing. To me, the plays. But in both cases, am I not saying that the writer is the one who believes that the world has been freely chosen by whoever lives in it, to be given the meaning it deserves for all its inhabi-

tants and by all those inhabitants who respect it, irrespective of its disasters, wars, and outrages?

If so, we're back to Stavrogin's search for the god that does not exist. Or Malraux's definition of life as trying to swim across the river knowing no one can make it and that we'll all drown, yet swimming just the same.

Yes, as a free choice.

Only an elite can believe such a harsh reality. Ordinary folks who suffer daily from the exploitation, greed, avarice of the rich, have to believe that they will somehow be avenged, like the Christian credo that it is easier for a camel to go through the eye of a needle than for a rich man to get to heaven. Actually, I prefer the Buddhist notion that a poor man will be reincarnated as a butterfly while a rich man will come back as a cockroach.

You just made that up, didn't you?

Yes, but I like it. Anyway, every religion has to offer some such vengeance, or it won't spread.

The Jewish doesn't.

Which is why they don't proselytize. And why it's not just a religion but an ethnic entity, so to speak. Which is why most Jews carry out their tradition, but in fact are atheists. Or at least the elites. And these elites are just as bogged down trying to make sense of our absurdity as any other elite, and they, too, conceal their metaphysical alienation, just as all other elites.

Fact is, there are different levels of elites. The top, what my grandfather called category one, know exactly what the score is. They are either the greedy bastards of the world or the revolutionaries, that is, they either say, Well, since existence is absurd, let's enjoy it and the hell with others, or they say, OK, there's no way out of our absurdity but let's try to make everyone as comfortable and satisfied as possible. But then, said my grandfather, and he was quite right, there is the secondary elite, which either mimics or follows obediently—well, he didn't put it that way, I did. And finally there is the third level of elites, to which he thought he belonged, educated bourgeois who try to divulge, explain, translate, make palatable. That elite is caught in between self-awareness and self-deception. Exploited and abused, dominated and harassed, it has a need to believe in some kind of retribution. But need and conviction are not synonymous. And it really is not convinced.

Like CP functionaries.

Precisely. They need to believe that by following Stalin, or anyone else's

orders, they are helping humanity reach a higher level of happiness. And that their dedication makes them in fact one with humanity.

Like all those fantastic communist rank-and-filers who went to Spain to fight Franco using false names, false papers, leaving behind false stories. No one would know that they died in Spain fighting for humanity, but to them it was an act of advancing that humanity of which they felt part.

Exactly. They felt that in their act they were representing all. Like the man who seized the bus in an act representing all those in the queue.

But in so doing did he not establish himself as a leader? A member of an elite-in-fusion, so to speak.

No, I would say that his act was genuinely democratic, an expression of people's will, like any decision by an AG.

I have a problem with AGs, at least where I teach. Most of my students, and I dare say most of the whole student body, work. Many full time. They come to Vincennes, and I presume Nanterre, Jussieu, et cetera, to gain a bit of knowledge to improve their dreary life. They don't have time to attend AGs, much less to participate in the workshops and investigation committees set up by the AGs. Then also, there are scores of students—I know three personally—who are absolutely brilliant but extremely shy, and won't open their mouth in an AG, confronted by hundreds of other students. So I have doubts about how democratic "direct democracy" really is.

What's your solution, then?

Very complicated. As far as students are concerned, I would make the AGs much smaller, maybe just by class, but even then, my class in the United States had sixty-five students, so we'd have to break that down. Maybe all students should be given free room and board, and stipends. But how do we deal with the rich ones, or those who not only work for their keep now, but also to help their very poor, often unemployed families, which is true of many of my Algerian students. Obviously the problem of direct or participatory democracy now, in our level of capitalism, is part of the overall problems of our capitalist society. I think the example of people seizing the bus and hence creating a group-in-fusion has problems both ways, since after they all get home and return to work the next day, they're all serialized again. They would have to start again, and again and again. Too demanding, too taxing. I'm perfectly willing to grant Marx and you that there is no such thing as human nature, and grant you that there is a human condition which we have to take into account to better our society. But I think that part of that condition, as real as our eyes, nose, two arms, et cetera, as real as the animal's condition of speed or fear or flight, et cetera, is the fact that both humans and animals can take only a limited amount of pain or stress or exertion. We may not know what that limit is, but I think it does end up defining our potential.

Very true, but no one claims revolutions are easy. If we define progress as the increase of people participating in the decisions that affect their lives, there can be no doubt that, despite the massacres, genocides, mass murders that have consistently plagued human history, there has been progress. There may be dictatorships all over the world today, but no historian, or almost none, would claim today that dictatorship is better than bourgeois democracy, just as almost none claimed before that a divine ruler was better than a parliamentary royalty. Each stage may get crushed temporarily and the world may regress temporarily, but once instituted in humanity's ethos, the notion of progress becomes endemic in the world's people. Look at the Cultural Revolution, for example. It apparently ended up in horrid excesses. (I say "apparently" because I do not trust our mainstream, that is, establishment historians and media.) But the fundamental characteristic of the Cultural Revolution is that people make policy and administrators administer that policy. This notion is now part of our world, part of our understanding of what people call human nature. Not all the king's men, all those propagandists in Washington and London can erase that. Mao said two steps forward, one step back. Perhaps now the money-governments of the world have succeeded in taking two steps back. But once a man tastes honey, he cannot deny its sweetness. So, yes, it is a defeat each time a group-in-fusion deteriorates into a serialized conglomerate of individuals. But no one will ever forget how fantastic they felt while living out that fusion.

You should explain all that in detail in your ethics.

If I write it. You know, I've lost a lot of my energy. I'm sixty-seven, and aware that if we have a revolution, my work will become meaningless. And if we don't, ah . . . My passion to write is gone. As you know, all my life I kept up my incredible pace by taking speed, which my doctor now forbids me to take, so I have slowed drastically (although I can still get some). Still, I just finished a thousand new pages of *Flaubert*. But it bores me now.

I don't think it's age. It's the times. For me, it's disappointment. You know, we came very close to a revolution in the United States, the night Martin Luther King was killed. The blacks were so angry that they took over one hundred cities—yes, a hundred. A hundred cities were burning that night. And the whites? Watching it on television. If we had joined the blacks, who knows. So me too, I just don't have the spirit anymore. My students think I do. They talk about my passion. I overheard a great compliment the other day, one student telling another, "Oh Gerassi, he's either a communist or an anarchist or crazy or all three, but you never fall asleep in his class." But maybe that's just my training. I started writing, I realize now, for three reasons: to make money, to gain fame, and to change the world. But now that I feel I'm not going to help change the world one bit, fame and money aren't good enough motives to keep me going.

I understand, but you should try to remember our old Mao Tse-tung. "A single spark may start a prairie fire." Look at '68. We almost had a revolution here, and it all started because the government built a stupid swimming pool at Nanterre.

Did '68, its failure, change your work habits? When did you decide to write *Flaubert*?

By a fluke. A friend had his correspondence, so one day when I was in her apartment I picked up the book and started reading. That was in '45. Then, sixteen years ago, old man Garaudy, who was still struggling with his soul, came to see me, basically, I think, for help. He suggested we work on the biography of someone each on his side and then compare. I said OK, and suggested Flaubert. That was in 1954. But I didn't do anything, as I was then rereading Marx. I had been disappointed by volume three of my trilogy. I had also decided not to continue my ethics. Anyway, I started reading everything I could on Flaubert. And it began to amuse me. When I got to his last novel, I suddenly realized I had to deal with his death, which meant with my own death. And that's when '68 happened.

So '68 put everything in question?

No, not in '68. I didn't really understand '68 until '70, until now.

And what do you understand about '68 now?

That to write is simply to exercise a profession. Somebody makes shoes, somebody becomes a soldier, somebody writes. Today I write three hours every morning, except Fridays when I talk to you, and write three hours after lunch. The rest of the time I do what they want me to do.

And what did you understand of death, first of Flaubert, then of you?

For Flaubert it changed nothing, because he was terrified of death all his life. But understand, it wasn't a fear of a state of death, if one can speak in

such contradictions, it was a fear of nothingness, which is why he tried to believe in some form of hereafter, and which is why all the commentators and biographers said he was religious. He wasn't. He wasn't stupid, quite the contrary. He was putting up a show for himself. His gods always deceived him . . .

Like Emma's lovers.

Indeed, and he always failed, like her, to escape the clutches of those who would destroy him, and her. The choice to commit adultery is Emma's only means of exercising power over her own destiny, and of course it leads to her death. His choice to condemn the bourgeoisie, of which he is part, leads him to seek a salvation he cannot believe in, and he too ends in despair. Fear of death often leads to seeking it. Flaubert's god offered him no solace.

And yours?

My god? My death? In my case it was not to escape death, but to encompass it that I wrote about it, through him of course.

You feared it, or better put, you were never to let it affect your vision of life, your choices, your priorities?

I never thought about it as *my* death. It is there, in me. It colored my relationship to politics, insofar as I would not do at forty what I did at twenty, or now that I am sixty-seven what I did do at forty.

You mean the resistance?

No, what I mean is the interior significance of my acts. Example: If we had a revolution in 1945, after the Liberation, I would certainly have taken part, and probably had gotten killed or in some way suffered from the ensuing terror. I would do the same now at sixty-seven. But my conception of my behavior would be different. At forty I would expect to see the result, good or bad, of my acts. At sixty-seven, not. In other words, knowing that one dies means that at a certain age one cannot see the consequences of one's actions, whether in fact one does see them at twenty or forty, since one can die at any time, especially in a revolution. But at sixty-seven, one knows that one will not, even if very lucky.

Does that not affect your behavior?

Of course, insofar as the possibility of dying at twenty or forty is an injustice incorporated into my actions. But it does not change the actions, only adds, if you wish, to my being not only a revolutionary but also a rebel. Today, at sixty-seven, I can only be a revolutionary, for if I should die in the revolution, there would be no injustice.

But the injustice of seeing so many innocents die, not the ones caused by human greed, but the others, like earthquakes always killing the poor.

Like Freud wanting to believe in god just for a moment to tell him off.

Like my friend François Charlot, who was in the hospital with me last Tuesday—he got beat up by the cops worse than I did—saying, I sure wish there was a god so I could punch him in the nose for being so pro-rich.

Is he OK? That was quite a demonstration. Of course the Algerians got the worst of it, didn't they?

They sure did. One actually lost an eye. Charlot's OK. Not a word in the press.

La Cause will have it in full, with ten pictures, a special issue. _Politique Hebdo_ will also have some great pictures. What did the doctors do to you?

Nothing much. They took X-rays of both my legs and my head, which was bleeding a lot, but no fractures or concussion. They patched me up and I went home to sleep it off. But tell me, not knowing the outcome of all your actions, and knowing that you won't know, does that not at least make you anxious?

Sometimes. In fact, last night, I woke up to go piss, and when I went back to bed I couldn't sleep, thinking about death and old age. I'm an anxious type anyway. So anxiety always reverts to death, doesn't it? But I did fall asleep after half an hour, not very deep sleep, and in the morning I felt a bit woozy until I had my coffee. So it wasn't like the other times.

You had three attacks.

Yeah, one in October [1970], a small one in May, and another in July [1971]. I call them attacks of old age. I guess they were mini-strokes, since I couldn't walk up stairs or talk very clearly. It didn't last long.[5]

I remember, since you canceled our interview.

Just one, right? Then I was OK. It didn't affect me psychologically, I don't think. Well, I did start thinking about being incapacitated, stuff like that. But not about what surveys claim old folks think about, namely being abandoned. I still have my friends. I work every day with young people. I am still useful. But I feel, at the end, that it will soon be all over.

And that doesn't provoke more anxiety?

No. What does is suffering. Like after the war, when I was flying everywhere, yes, I was very anxious for a while, I was afraid that the planes would fall, catch fire, that I would get burned up, that kind of stuff. My first flight, boy! There were no real seats. It was a bomber with sort of benches along the

sides and a hole in the middle for parachute jumps, and we were in the thick of a storm, flying very low, to Bermuda because the pilot didn't think he could make your East Coast. You were pretty scared of planes too, I remember.

At the beginning, yes. Once I was so nervous flying over the Andes that my wife got fed up and said she wouldn't sit with me anymore. So I said, OK, no more anxiety, and took a newspaper and started reading it, calmly from left to right. Suddenly she burst out laughing: I was holding the newspaper upside down.

Ha-ha ha! That kind of anxiety disappears with old age. That's the good part. The bad is being treated as old. Three days ago, Foucault, Mauriac, and I joined the GP in a demonstration in front of the Justice Department to protest treatment of prisoners in jails—well, you know, since you were there—and after our press conference we all sat down, remember? Right there on the steps. When our protest ended, a big burly guy sitting behind me—I guess the GP had asked him to be a sort of bodyguard—saw that I had a bit of trouble standing up and picked me up like a sack of flour. It reminded me of Proust in *Remembrance of Things Past,* when a young woman offers him a seat in a crowded trolley, and he ends up feeling so dejected because he obviously looked old. That's how I felt. Oh yes, worse. When the cops began to push and club a bit, one jostled me, then said, "Excuse me please."

He had recognized you.

No, that's the point, he saw I was old. I didn't feel insulted, but . . . Sure, OK, I'm old, but I don't feel old, I mean, I forget stuff, I have a hard time getting up from the floor, but I can still work, I can still analyze Flaubert's sentences.

That's the key, to keep the mind going. Like all those disgusting old geezer politicians, de Gaulle and Adenauer, who lived nice long lives, then retired and boof. Or Churchill.

How old is Fernando now?

Seventy-two.

Still painting? Still taking those long walks in his beloved Vermont hills, despite his cancer? How bad is it?

It's bad. It's cancer of the esophagus, which is deadly. But yes, he still walks those two miles to his studio, you remember, the old little red schoolhouse, which the town of Putney has loaned him [for thirty-five dollars a year]. With his faithful dog. He wrote me for the new year. A strange letter, I guess in response to mine, which complained, sort of, of being in exile from the revolution, which of course isn't taking place anymore, not since the whites abandoned the blacks after they killed four white students at Kent State last year. I guess he interpreted that to mean that I was putting my life in question and he told me that it was perfectly acceptable to do that, that he had done it at each phase of his life, after the Spanish Civil War, after being discharged from OSS, after moving to Vermont and becoming a teacher, and so on.

Sounds like he has become bitter, no?

I don't think so. He told me in that letter to like what I do, that was the key to life. Like he liked painting, whether he sold or not, that he loved colors, that they were his buddies. He just hoped that his cancer wouldn't hurt too much for him to paint.

I think that's the key. Those who are afraid of the suffering involved in death are not really afraid of death. Those who are afraid of death have regrets about their lives. And that applies to me. I had a good typical bourgeois life for a typical bourgeois. Schooling, profession, friends, travel, plus in my case a bit of glory and fame. That part was not liked by the bourgeoisie, but even if I tried to refuse the bourgeois honors for my anti-bourgeois work, I guess the satisfaction of having been relevant within our absurd existence gave me satisfaction.[6]

Like [Bertrand] Russell.

A queer bird, that one. An aristocrat who became better and better as he aged, like good whiskey. He made the War Crimes Tribunal happen by sheer conviction, at ninety-five yet.

When I went to see him in Wales, after I got back from North Vietnam, he talked almost like Fidel, on and on into the night, about his pet tribunal. I asked him at one point what kept him going like that. Remember, he was also writing his memoirs then, a good six hours a day. He poured himself another shot of Scotch, I think it was, held up his glass, and quipped: "A bottle a day."

Quite a warrior.

Yet after the war, he had advocated a preventive war against Soviet Russia.

That was a weird period, indeed. We didn't know that radiation does not dissipate, and we tended to believe most of the propaganda fed to our newspapers by the CIA. That's why we created the RDR, a colossal mistake.

You were even good friends with Arthur Koestler then.

Not really. I didn't like him all that much. He always talked about himself in the third person, "Uncle Koestler . . ." "Papa Koestler . . ." But I liked his wife. She was pretty, jovial, warm, maybe perverse along the edges, corrupt a bit. I went out with her some. She had been Camus' mistress, and sometimes the three of us went out. And *Darkness at Noon* was a fascinating book. Merleau did a great job analyzing it in his *Humanism and Terror.*

Koestler was part of the RDR, wasn't he? *Darkness at Noon* was published in 1947, the same period when you wrote *Materialism and Revolution,* which by the way I still make required reading in some of my classes. I think it is the best politico-philosophical analysis of communists' so-called objective path of history.

It wasn't meant to be political. Don't forget that I was not political then, I was an intellectual, trying to show what is really happening in our world and why. Even the creation of the RDR was not a political act for me—of course it was for everyone else—but for me it was an intellectual's need for independent cognitive understanding, and hence, since to name is to act, action. But not a political party. I didn't become political until last year, when I understood the political significance of '68 and when I joined with the GP as a militant.

But whether you thought of yourself as political, your activity from 1945 on has always been political and, perhaps more important, since as you say, hell is each other, interpreted by your peers, and probably by ordinary Frenchmen, as political, right?

Unquestionably. From the end of the war until '51 or '52, we tried to stay nonpartisan, and of course that got us attacked by both right and left . . .

Who's "we," then?

Camus, Merleau, and what you or the press, or even Castor, calls the family, Bost, Pouillon, Gorz, and Castor, at a distance so to speak. I mean they were always there, at the rallies and meetings when we staged them, but, once we started the RDR, never really members. Even Camus, though he was a member, he stayed a bit distant, as did Merleau, who did not want to alienate the communists, who attacked us quite ferociously. He always insisted that the RDR could never become significant unless it became a party, and if it did it would get absolutely nowhere, because the French voted for the big parties only, the communists, the socialists, the Gaullists, and the non-Gaullist rightists, period. And he was right, of course. But none of us, I mean those of us on the left in the RDR, wanted it to be a party. It was in that sense that I saw myself, as head of it, nevertheless as an intellectual and not as a politician. By 1951, we had about ten thousand adherents, and it was growing. The rank-and-filers were on the same wavelength as Merleau and I. The active leadership, Rousset, [Georges] Altman, and others, were more anticommunist than anything else—by the way, you should interview Rousset—

I did.

Good. And they wanted more money than our ten thousand could donate even if they wanted to, so Altman, who had been a communist but was now director of the rabidly anti-communist daily *Franc-Tireur,* went to America to get money from the CIO [Congress of Industrial Organizations]. We knew that the CIO's foreign bureau, under [Jay] Lovestone, was getting its money from the CIA, so that's when I asked the members to vote to dissolve the RDR and they voted almost unanimously to do so. Camus was out of the picture by then, and Merleau was too preoccupied with his writing. He would come to 42 [rue Bonaparte, Sartre's apartment] with the family for the editorial meetings of *Les Temps Modernes,* but that was it. And he would write articles for it occasionally, of course. But then the world had changed. It had become clear that America wanted to Americanize France, and all of Western Europe for that matter. CIA meddling in our politics and media, and even more so in Italy, and England's total subservience to America, had all become too evident. And France was waging an imperialist war in Indochina, which had to be condemned. That's when the sailor Henri Martin refused to sail on a ship taking war material to Vietnam, and faced mutiny [charges], perhaps execution. The CP asked me for help. I agreed. So began my fellow-traveler phase, 1952–56. But in 1956 came another Russian invasion: Hungary, and my denunciation caused another break, which lasted until the Algerian War. The communists were very soft on that issue, but I did go to Russia then and, as you know, got entangled in a very passionate and serious relationship, which made me go back many times.

Lena [Zonina], your translator?

We traveled throughout Russia a lot together, sometimes with Castor, the three of us. She was, and is, a fantastic woman. Her father had been a revolutionary from the beginning, but Stalin executed him, and also her brother. Her mother, a devoted communist, was kicked out of the party, and she was herself, though never charged with "anti-party" activity, but often interrogated by the NKVD. During the trial of [Yuli] Daniel[7] she was harassed a great deal for having signed a statement supporting him, and at various times refused an exit permit to visit me, but she persevered and did come to Paris, and returned without a problem. We live in a disgusting capitalist system, but those who suffer are the poor. In Russia, the government is afraid of every intellectual, not the poor, because they are guaranteed their livelihoods, but people like us because we might be too critical about something they do or say, and then what? They never figured that out.

I think the explanation is that those opposed to the capitalist system still, by and large, accept the electoral process. In the United States, the press, the media in general, is so controlled by the industrial-financial-military complex that the only real voice of dissent is limited to a few journals or magazines read by intellectuals, who are barely respected anyway. Here, intellectuals are respected, and their statements, like yours, are carried in the established media. Your government tries to stop *La Cause du Peuple* and jail GP militants precisely because they have given up on the electoral system. Like Matzpen [the Israeli Socialist Organization] in Israel. America's way of silencing dissent is by depriving dissidents of jobs, so very few ordinary folk can risk it, and no one pays attention if, say, a Norman Mailer says capitalism is no good. Intellectuals often sign statements in the *New York Times;* they sometimes even pay for full-page ads. It does absolutely no good unless half a million folks then march on the Pentagon. And you will never get a thousand marchers in favor of nationalizing the biggest gangster companies in the world, namely the insurance and health industry. Here, if the government wants to privatize a public hospital there would be ten million marching. Americans have been convinced by the corporate media that public companies are less efficient than private ones.

All very true, but for us, you, me, the "family," if we were Russian, doing our thing, we would be in gulags, wouldn't we?

Yes, precisely because our dissent would have mattered.

And that's why the communists kept after me. I guess, until I understood, after '68, that everything is political, my whole trajectory was determined by the communists, by what they said, what they did, how they treated me, and how I opposed them.

February 1972

GERASSI: You said the other day that you became a fellow traveler in '52, with the Henri Martin affair. But what happened when the Korean War started? Were you silent?

SARTRE: That was our first big crisis at *Les Temps Modernes,* I mean between Merleau and me. The others were natural: Aron was a right-wing social democrat, so he had left. Malraux wanted to be part of de Gaulle's team, so he left. But the first really significant issue was when the guns started in Korea. First of all, we believed most of America's propaganda, that the North [Koreans] invaded without provocation, that Syngman Rhee was a good democrat in the South, that Kim Il-Sung was a fanatical bastard, et cetera, et cetera. It took a few months before we began to get the whole picture, that there had been skirmishes between North and South ever since the Russians pulled out of the North and the Americans did not in the South. Then we found out that Kim was a resistance hero while Rhee was a semi-collaborator, who had sworn to unify Korea under his tutelage. But when the guns began, we didn't know all that. We didn't even know that [General Douglas] MacArthur was the old fascist general who had ordered his troops to fire on the vets of World War I who had congregated in Washington to demand their bonuses because they were starving. We simply said: "Here we go, World War III."

But be silent about what?

Until we got all the facts, Merleau, like the rest of us, believed the propaganda, and hence he thought this was Stalin's way of circumventing the Yalta agreements, by conquering the whole area by proxy, yet did not want to criticize Soviet communist policy because it would be interpreted as an attack on our own communists here in France, who after all spoke for the exploited proletariat.

Like today, if one criticizes Israeli policy, one is immediately accused of being an anti-Semite here at home.

Precisely. So he wanted us to be silent on Korea. I think it was his upbringing as a bourgeois democrat yet very Catholic. His mother had been a very strict Catholic and had just died, so he had her buried with all the religious fanfare. He was a very strong advocate of personal freedom, but as an abstraction, if you will, not the freedom in context of a capitalist world, the freedom of owning a pair of shoes. In other words his democratic principles were very bourgeois, but resting in an inferiority complex about his class. He absolutely hated it. But there was also the question of his career, which he did not want to jeopardize. He longed to be appointed to the Collège de France, and he was eventually. That lust was unconscious, of course, but I think that was in part the reason he did not sign his editorials, for example.

But neither did you.

I only wrote one, alone, precisely about Korea after we learned the facts, and I signed that one. Then after Merleau and I split, and I wrote *Communists and Peace*, which was serialized in the review, I wrote another and yes, did not sign it, because it was the view of the whole staff. But he was political editor of the review. He wrote almost all of our editorials, and never signed them.

That's normal. After all, editorials are meant to state the point of view of the review in general, and if a staffer disagrees, he or she either writes a dissenting statement or, if the review won't publish it, resigns.

In any case, Merleau was very pro-communist yet always careful not to engage the university in his politics. Like Camus, the personal colored the political.

Camus? I thought his politics were determined by his being a piednoir?

That too. But much more important was his wife, Francine. She was quite bright, a mathematician, and extremely pretty. But she was equally extremely reactionary, pro–"Algérie française," pro-OAS [Secret Army Organization, created by right-wing nationalist officers to fight de Gaulle's plan to grant Algerian independence]. She actually testified at [General Edmond] Jouhaud's trial.[1]

How could Camus put up with that?

By the time of the trial, Camus had died in the car crash. But he had treated her abominably. We often went out together, Castor and I and them. He was having an affair with [the actress Maria] Casares [Quiroga] then, and everyone knew it.[2] She was playing then, and intermission was at ten-fifteen, so every night, no matter whom he was with, ignoring Francine's visible pain, he would excuse himself to go call Casares. And then, if Casares was up to it, he'd take Francine home and go clubbing and whatever with Casares. He was very nonchalant about it, yet was wracked with guilt just the same. But then none of us were very normal after the war. Consider *Les Temps Modernes*. Merleau, the political editor, was very close to the communists. I, as cofounder and co-editor, was constantly attacked by the communists, yet I was certainly on the left. Not so with Aron, [Albert] Ollivier, and [Jean] Paulhan, both of whom I knew from the resistance. Ollivier had been active in Camus' *Combat*. Paulhan, whom I knew well before the war, had been with me in the communist resistance movement. There were disagreements all the time, and not just over Korea, though that's when Ollivier and Paulhan left the review. But we had serious fights over such issues as punishing the collaborators. Camus wanted Brasillach executed, for example. Mauriac did not. Nor did Castor. I was in America, so out of it, and I thought of myself, as I told you, as not political. The whole country was then equally turbulent. Don't forget that after de Gaulle quit, we were ruled by a tripartite government, the right-wing basically Catholic MRP [Popular Republican Movement], the mealy-mouth socialists, and the communists who had refused to take over from de Gaulle. And in the middle of all this, when I returned from America, there was me, famous, looked upon as a spokesperson for the noncommunist left, and totally befuddled. It was then that the mass media began to actively attack the CP, and I was constantly asked to explain, give interviews, debate the left and right, go on talk shows, even host a talk show. There's a great difference between being famous and being a celebrity. I knew I was famous—as an intellectual. But what does a celebrity do? Camus used to kid me that I could not blow my nose in Paris without it being talked about in Rio de Janeiro. In 1947, a weekly rag called *Samedi Soir* sprang up whose only business was to tell tall tales about celebrities, you know, like who sleeps with whom, and so on.

And then Pierre Lazareff, that disgusting press mogul,[3] launched *France Dimanche,* which was almost as bad. Somehow they found out that I had the mumps, so they reported that Wanda had come to visit me to prove that the side effect of the illness—it's supposed to make a man impotent—was not true, and as gratitude I gave her the role of Jessica, Hugo's wife, in *Dirty Hands.*[4] I ran into that scumbag later at some club; he came up to me and said: "I know you despise me, but I greatly admire you." But the other side was almost as bad. Dominique Desanti, for example, did a hatchet job on me in *Action.*[5] But you have to put everything in context: once the center of the world, France had been cut in two by the Germans and basically ignored by all. So after the war, the world began to exist for France and France began to exist for the world. Couple that to the development of the mass media, and you have a sort of free-for-all, everyone trying to find a niche, or fame, or goals, or a purpose. And in that chaos, the main attraction was "Existentialism," and me as its founder. Wherever I went, also Castor, who was dubbed La Grande Sartreuse,[6] we were photographed, asked for comments on anything, preyed upon to help get gigs, solve conflicts, save the sick—it was maddening.

No doubt, but let's be honest, you kind of asked for it, too. You were constantly seen in Left Bank *boîtes* [clubs, not necessarily respectable] drinking until the morning.

True, but so were my attackers; they usually got there before we did, so they didn't come to write nasty things about us; they were there getting drunk on their own.

Did your fame cause jealousies at *Les Temps Modernes?*

I don't think so, certainly not with Merleau, who shied from our public life. I wrote about that in "Merleau-Ponty Vivant." As for the others, no, I think they enjoyed going out with us, that is, those who became what Castor calls the family, and they weren't egging for fame as writers.

They were mostly your old students, weren't they, like Bost and Pouillon?

Some, yes, but not all. Lanzmann had not been my student, nor were you, when you joined us in '54, and Castor included you in the family. I remember you loved to hang out in La Cave du Vieux Colombier with us.

That's because of Sidney Bechet, who played there with Claude Luther's band. I loved that kind of jazz.

So did we, and you loved to dance with Michelle Léglise [Vian]. You two made a great team.

But that was later. The great upheaval period, during which your fame, and celebrity, spread across the world, ended with the Korean cannons, as Merleau used to say. Aron, Ollivier, Paulhan, left then. Camus remained a close friend but was no longer interested in the political debates. Who ran the review then? Jeanson?

Jeanson became the boss then, but that meant nothing because we all wrote what we wanted, with no interference. For legal purposes I was "responsible director," meaning that if an article in the review was deemed treasonous by the government, they had to arrest me. But a lot of very good work was done by Lanzmann and [Marcel] Péju and of course Jeanson, though his views were a bit soft until the Camus affair.

You didn't plan that, did you?

Absolutely not. When the advanced copy of *The Rebel* arrived, I asked Jeanson if he wanted to review it. He had written a very favorable article on Camus before, so I felt he'd do a nice job on the book. None of us had read it yet. In fact, I didn't read it until after Jeanson's article was set in type. When I did, I immediately thought, Uh oh, he's going to hit him back, meaning at Jeanson, of course. That's because I always knew that Camus was very egocentric; he once told me that he should have received the Nobel Prize just for *The Stranger*. Anyway, it never occurred to me that Camus would attack me, personally, in a letter to "Monsieur le directeur des *Temps Modernes*," totally ignoring Jeanson. And when I responded to the letter, I did so not out of loyalty to Jeanson, but because I completely agreed with his criticism of the book and with his right to say so. And the incident helped at least in one way: Jeanson thereafter ran the review carefully, adroitly, and acutely. He was always on the correct political wavelength, which allowed Merleau to care more for his philosophical works.

Do you think that Camus' letter to you was motivated by that egocentricism you mentioned?

More complicated. Camus was always in a dilemma: Algerians have a right to independence, but the settlers made that country thrive; Russia has a right to fear America, but the buffer zones it creates in Eastern Europe end up being satellites; Henri Martin has a right to refuse to participate in an imperialist war, but the elected government has a right to impose its policies. His personal life ran the same way. Then there was the question of death. He had various bouts with tuberculosis. He was terrified of it. He lusted for immortality. Like all who fear death, he courted it. Everyone claims that it was Michel

Gallimard who was driving the car that killed both. I wonder if in fact it wasn't Camus. In any case he would have egged Michel to go faster and faster. But Camus knew that immortality is a joke; no matter how brilliant a book may be, how long will it remain in our intellectual consciousness? A thousand years? Two? Ten? Ridiculous. The quest for immortality, and Camus knew it perfectly, makes sense only while one is alive.

What happened to *Les Temps* once Jeanson left to work full time for the Algerian FLN?

By then Gorz, Pouillon, Bost, Lanzmann, and of course Castor kept the magazine flowing smoothly.

Merleau was gone by then?

Yes. He had distanced himself quietly during the 1950s.

Precisely when you got closer and closer to the CP? *Communists and Peace,* which came out in '52, pleased them a great deal, I gather, yet as I reread it the other day, I found in it the germ of your eventual rupture.

The ending? Indeed. The forewarning of what is to come is there.

But much later, in '64, with the *Ghost of Stalin,* correct? It certainly seems to me that you were very political during that whole period, first with a great play, to me your best, namely *The Devil and the Good Lord,* in which you seem to argue for the notion of the end justifying the means, that's in '51, then *Communists and Peace,* and your book on the Henri Martin affair in '53, and of course that very funny play *Nekrassov* in '55.

But my approach was always ethical. Whenever I condemned the communists, or anyone else for matter, it was always from a moral point of view. And don't forget that my major effort during that period was *Saint Genet,* in which I tried to show how society both ruins a man and creates a genius by its stupidity and prejudices.

I had lunch with [Jean] Genet last week, and he complained, jokingly perhaps, that your book had so completely dissected and analyzed him through his novels and plays that he couldn't write anymore. It's true he hasn't written anything for a long time, has he?

Ha-ha! Don't blame me for that. I think that he simply does not feel like fighting for a cause that he has won. The intellectual world, if not all the French, now accept that homosexual passion can be as vivid and meaningful as any other kind. And that any victim of prejudice can become a criminal, as a way of fighting back against an unjust society. But you'll see, he'll write again. In any case, my analysis of Genet and his work was purely moral, as is

my analysis of Flaubert. Just because I condemn their society and the bourgeois class that oppressed Genet or that Flaubert hated but lusted after, has political significance, does not mean that I analyzed it politically. In my mind then, before I understood that money is politics, just because a capitalist was greedy, selfish, avaricious, et cetera, was a moral judgment, not a political one.

You operated like our universities do. They separate economics from politics. There's no department called political economy in the United States. I think it's the only country in the world where that's the case, as if economics has nothing to do with politics, and in the United States a student can get a degree in political science without taking a single course in economics, and vice versa. In your case it was morality over here and politics over there.

Quite so, though of course my works are all very political. I just didn't think that way consciously. But I think that was because my training, and original interest, was philosophy.

And that didn't change with Budapest?

Not very much with Budapest, but certainly with Prague. But you know, I was always there, even if I didn't realize it. As early as during the resistance, in our group, which was called Socialism and Liberty—I was the one who named it that, by the way—I always resisted the communist idea that freedom, liberty, comes only after the classless society has been established. That's my objection to Goetz in *The Devil and the Good Lord.*

Yet he is the most sympathetic character of all, even more, I think, than Hoederer.

Well, Lenin was a sympathetic character, wasn't he? [Nikolai] Bukharin even more so. And [Karl] Radek. Even Gramsci languishing in Mussolini's jail.

True, but then there's always my darling, the greatest democratic communist until Che, namely Rosa Luxembourg.

Is that why she failed? Like Hoederer? But that was always my commitment: socialism and liberty. And that was always why, no matter how much of a fellow traveler I was at different times, my objection to the communists remained firm—socialism and, very important, *and* liberty, even in the process, on the way to the classless society.

And you thought of that as a moral issue, not a political one?

Until '68, yes. Once I understood the roots of '68, precisely the lack of meaningful liberty in our societies, then I finally understood that everything is political.

What was the core of that understanding?

That to capitalists, liberty means to say what you want, but never to do. Capitalist society holds all the important purse strings. You are free to yell, to demand, to condemn a particular policy, to agitate so it will change, and indeed, it sometimes does change, like the 1961 referendum in which a majority of the French expressed their desire that Algeria be granted its independence, and it was. But freedom from poverty, freedom from prejudice, freedom from the police, from oppression, is out of the question. Such lack of freedoms destroys human beings. It eats away at their guts, their desires, their goals. That's why middle-class kids in '68 wanted to overturn the government. And that's why, when they marched down in front of the Ministry of Interior, where all the repressive files were stored and the cops guarding the joint yelled, "There's no one inside, come and seize it!" and made the fist salute, [Daniel] Cohn-Bendit or Geismar, I forgot, yelled back, "We don't want power." That's when the communists decided to try for a compromise with de Gaulle. They understood that the kids would not bring down the government, no matter how many millions of them marched against it. And when that sank in, Castor and I finally realized that we are all political animals.

You then eventually joined the maos. Did Castor also?

You know, she had always shared my views, my political views, even if we discussed them as moral. But '68 changed her, too. She became aware that there was a lot that women had to do, actions I mean, that writing about women's liberation was not enough, that change, real democracy, has to be fought for in . . .

In the streets.

Exactly. So she did. They started demonstrating, occupying, et cetera, and did often join the GP when they thought that the struggle was common. But from then on, Castor went to her meetings without me; I was not allowed. And it changed her relationships with my "women," as they say.

Why?

Because they live off me. You know, these women live off me. I consider it normal since, after all, I was so demanding when we started our relationships, that they ended up doing nothing else but living it. So today, Wanda, Michelle, Arlette, my [adopted] daughter, all live off my writing, and while it is normal, Castor doesn't feel comfortable with it anymore.

Olga, too?

No. She did her own thing, and teamed up with Bost.

I hear that there are five young writers who receive monthly stipends directly from Gallimard at your order?

Who told you? Robert [Gallimard]?[7] **Don't tell anyone. I don't want them to feel obliged to me.**

Are any of the five women?

I'm not going to tell you, because you're too good a journalist, but I'll tell you this, I sure wish we had our own Rossana here.

Rossana Rossanda?

Yes; she is the most magnificent communist, not in the party mind you, that I know, and a great feminist, who loves to cook, and does so for [K. S.] Karol, as well as any visitor.[8] **I love to see her. She is my ideal of a committed feminist and revolutionary writer. And I love her cooking.**

March 1972

GERASSI: France went through a very agitated period from 1945 to 1962, yet that was your most productive period as well.

SARTRE: The end of the resistance, war in Indochina, the collapse of the tripartite ministry, the RDR, the war on Algeria, and if we go to 1966, the destruction of the left in France. We, in *Les Temps Modernes*, and I personally, responded to each crisis, each phase. We made some mistakes, like the RDR was a bad one, but we were more or less on the button during each phase, internationally, which was the most, but not only, crucial issue then, based on our fundamental anti-imperialist commitment. We were right to join the communists in the campaign against the Americanization of NATO—we still are of course—and the "Ridgway Go Home" demonstrations, we were right to side with the communist labor battles, because the party did represent the vast majority of workers in France, we were right to join the CP in its agitation against the colonial war in Indochina, but we were right to condemn Russia for its invasion of Berlin, Prague, and of course Budapest in '56, right to condemn the whole left for its stand on Algeria, both the CP, which was wishy-washy on it until it became clear that Algerian communists were fighting with the FLN and that Massu was torturing their militants. But even then, support for Algeria was weak, and it destroyed the credibility of the left.

The tripartite government did not collapse because of Algeria. What really went wrong?

Squabbles. The socialists represented, and still do, France's petty functionaries, basically the petite bourgeoisie. They sought a few reforms here and there, but god save them from any semblance of a revolution. Just a bit more liberalism, a bit more bourgeois freedoms. The communists didn't want a revolution in France either. They never did, either on orders from Stalin, or because they were worried that the United States and England would invade if they took power. At least that's what their militants claim. But there's also the fact that all the top leaders are also petit bourgeois, enjoying their status as deputies or senators or union chiefs, and they don't want to sacrifice that. So socialists and communists agree: just give us more reforms. And, obviously, when two major parties agree, they squabble. They find issues to shout insults. Like the CP is opposed to the Common Market, even though Brezhnev is for, while the socialists are in favor, though not in the form presented, so in the referendum, they will abstain. The CP orders its adherents to vote no, thus validating the referendum. And so on.

Why then did the left not create a genuinely leftist party during this period?

First, because the resistance got all the young anti-Nazis to join the CP. Once Russia was at war, the French CP waged a great fight against the occupiers. It was well done, well led, hard and just. So most of the young with a political conscience, who fought with the communists during the occupation, then joined the CP afterward. To these kids, the CP was papa. Like most children they remained loyal, even if disappointed that their papas were not more militant. Which is why they loved so much that old-time warrior André Marty. As you know from your father, I'm sure, Marty was mad but . . .

Fernando said his nickname was "the butcher of Albacete."

Indeed. But the party's rank-and-file knew only that he had led the 1919 Black Sea mutiny [when the French navy had been ordered to fight the Bolsheviks], fought in Spain, led a formidable wartime resistance force, and, with that other great resistance hero Charles Tillon, advocated a more revolutionary stance as a member of the CP's Politburo. Many of those rank-and-filers favored Marty's stance, thus threatening the old established leadership, so in 1952 Marty and Tillon were tried for treason and in 1953 thrown out of the party. The CP never fully recovered from that.[1]

So why didn't those who left the party during that period, objecting to its reformist position, form a new communist party, or a revolutionary one? Something like *Il Manifesto* in Italy.

France never had a left as intelligent as Italy's. But also the French war on Vietnam brought the CP new adherents, or rather held the old ones, the ones who wanted to quit, because the CP was solidly in favor of Vietnamese independence, and since there was nothing else, I mean the goddam socialists were colonialists—imagine!—as they were later in Algeria! So gradually we, at *Les Temps Modernes*, got closer to the CP, and I wrote *The Communists and Peace*, then came *The Henri Martin Affair*, then I attended the Vienna peace congress in December 1952, and finally *The Devil and the Good Lord*.

And you started cooperating with the party?

No! We simply agreed on the major issues and coordinated our responses. But we never denied that there were two major antagonistic powers, which were likely to confront each other militarily, and blow us all up to smithereens. The difference was that it was the United States that was edging toward war, not the USSR. There was the Ridgway business, the McCarthy witch hunts, American intervention in the Korean civil war headed by the well-known fascist general MacArthur, the missiles deployment in Turkey, and on and on. No one had any doubts in France, or on the European continent in general, that America wanted to destroy Russia. Many, of course, agreed, but no one doubted America's intention. What most Europeans didn't realize was that the land war would be fought in Europe, mostly Western Europe, and that if so, France would no longer exist.

And you continued to go to peace congresses sponsored by the communists?

Yes, it was harder and harder to push my line, which was that the world would benefit from unarmed cultural confrontations. Of course, that wasn't their view at all. They believed that culture and politics cannot be separated. And they were right, of course, as the kids of '68 showed me. But I was then pressing that position, and the Russians did not treat me as a weirdo. Actually, at the next congress in Moscow, they scheduled a workshop to debate the issue, with two teams. Ehrenburg was on my side. The debate continued for a while, at the congress in Poland and Finland. I was suspect, of course. And Elsa Triolet warned them that I would fink out eventually. And of course I did, when the Russians stormed into Budapest.

You also attended a peace congress in China?

Not a good trip. First, because Chou En-lai, who was in charge of the

event, thought we were Russian spies, because Moscow had indeed recommended us. He even avoided us on the platform and did not shake our hands. Mao did, but that's probably because no one told him who we were.

Us? You went with Castor?

She was very eager to go.

You didn't write anything about your trip, but she wrote *The Long March*.

But except for a few first-person descriptions of sites, she could have written that book here in Paris, at the library. Like me, she didn't understand what was going on. You know, we don't speak Russian, and we always had official translators. But Russians are European, in the sense of expressions, cultural responses, what have you. You can sense when a Russian is lying, especially intellectuals, who don't like to lie. But we could not read the Chinese. There was no way to tell if they were telling us some fantastic tale or the truth. So Castor's book ends up dependent on documents and other books, which are all at the library.

Didn't you travel in China? How long were you there?

Six weeks. We went everywhere, Peking, Shanghai, Canton. Nanking. OK, we saw a lot, but in fact nothing. When we asked if we could wander in a typical village, they took us to one that was so clean, I thought we were on a stage. Every little house was painted white. There was no mud in the streets. And everything was so alike we got lost. So we asked where was the Hotel de la Paix. They applauded. Again and again. Obviously they had heard the word "peace" so often they thought we were preaching it, or whatever. Eventually, the guy who had been following us, the secret service agent dressed as a villager, came forward and showed us how to get back.

Didn't you have discussions with intellectuals?

Sure, dinners, lunches, the works. If we raised the question of Korea, silence. If we asked about party policies or anything interesting, they responded by asking us if we had tasted such and such a dish. What I remember most is the congratulations I got from intellectuals everywhere for writing the life of Nekrassov. Yep. Seriously. Someone in Russia must have told them that I had laid bare his treason, forgetting to tell them that it was fiction, a play. So wherever we went, I was hailed as the man who exposed the famous Nekrassov's fraudulent masquerade.

Didn't you visit factories, have discussions with your translators . . . ?

We would be taken to factories where we were served tea and told, by

the director, that China is working very hard, and they were at this factory, in order to catch up with the West. With our translators, we could talk about the opera we saw, and compare it to ours, or about which city he prefers, or about past history, and even there, without talking about current events or the revolution. Nothing else. If we tried, say about the Japanese invasion, it would embarrass him or her. So we stopped. We ended up saying we saw nothing in China. That was your experience as well, wasn't it?

But I was in China for a very few days, just trying to return to France from my two months in North Vietnam, and that was 1967, with the Cultural Revolution in full blast. And there, when every group I saw was carrying Mao posters and red flags, I was totally confused. I was quite anxious. When I got to Nanning there were no planes leaving or coming. And the red guards kept looking at me suspiciously; I speculated that they thought I was Russian, so I spoke nothing but French.

How did you finally get out?

It's a long story. In short, I managed to get on a military convoy that was going to Shanghai, and there I found the French embassy. I claimed I was Roget Dumonville, had been stripped of all belongings, including my French passport, and all my money. They gave me a laissez-passer and a ticket on an Air France flight.

Why didn't you write about that part of your China visit?

I didn't want Dumonville to get into trouble. I will someday. It was actually a fantastic trip, including three days in the back of a truck with soldiers who spoke English but with whom, by then a firm Frenchman, I had to speak English with a terrible French accent.

Ha-ha! But in Vietnam, as I read in your book, you had no trouble communicating or understanding the people?

The Vietnamese are completely different from the Chinese. First of all, they speak French, or most do. And then they were raised under French customs. They like to sit and talk in cafés, they argue, they shout. And they like to laugh, that's the best part.[2]

Like the Cubans. You speak Spanish, so you never had a problem. But I don't, and it didn't matter. I wrote seventeen articles about Cuba and its revolution, some quite critical, and even the Cubans printed them all.

Not in the United States, unfortunately. But Karol's book, *Revolutionaries in Power,* was, and in Cuba too. And it is quite critical as well.

That's something that our Stalinoid communists could never fathom,

that one can be critical yet supportive. I remember once a dinner with Aragon and Cocteau, wherein Aragon was attacking Jean Genet, maybe because I had written my study of Genet by then, and it was very favorable, and I had broken with them, as this was after Budapest. And Aragon said that he was sick and tired of that fucking faggot getting so much attention, let him go rot with those blacks and Palestinians. Cocteau almost cried, and of course repeated it to Genet. Stupid. They lost the support of a great writer and a wonderful humanist right then and there.

That's rather typical of communists; they never understood that under the rebellion lies a revolutionary.

Precisely. Even before I became really political, I understood that in a capitalist society all prisoners are political. So when I was invited to talk at a communist rally for Henri Martin, I was shocked to see a huge banner proclaiming the CP "The party of honest folks." What's worse was, his wife, when she spoke, she complained that they had jailed her husband with common prisoners.

And that's also what bothered communists about Cuba, because many of the *guerrilleros* had been common prisoners, like [Juan] Almeida, who became a general and head of the Fidelista army, or in the United States, Malcolm X.

Even some of our maos make that mistake. For example, when they staged a hunger strike to protest the disgusting treatment of prisoners in our jails, specifically at Toul, their complaint was the treatment of political prisoners. Even Geismar could not avoid the distinction between common and political prisoners.

And that's the argument, turned around, that I have against your support of Padilla. He's arrested because he feels privileged. A poet is above the law. A poet can smoke pot, because he's a poet. If you want to proclaim that anti-pot laws are lousy and should be repealed, like I do, fine. But a revolutionary government seems to think, yes, mistakenly, that pot smokers become counterrevolutionary. So everyone who smokes pot is pursued. Down with such a stupid law! But to sign a special petition for the sake of one poet who smokes pot is like saying, please treat political prisoners more amiably than ordinary common prisoners.

Well said.

April 1972

GERASSI: At lunch last Sunday, you referred to Malraux as a pig. Was it because, as Castor wrote in her memoirs, he tried everything to get Gallimard, your and his publisher, to dump *Les Temps Modernes*?

SARTRE: In general, yes, he's a pig. Everything about him is phony. I mean, *The Human Condition* is a fantastic novel, one of the really great ones of this century, certainly, but he, himself, is a phony. An adventurer who went to Cambodia to steal its artworks and sell them. He's always been a money man. OK, I know, he saved your father from execution by the Comintern.[1] I'm not saying that he didn't do some great things. But his so-called great leadership in the resistance, Colonel Malraux! When I went to see him, right after the Germans entered Paris and split France in two, to suggest we start a resistance group, his answer was: "What can we do? We don't have tanks or planes. Let's wait for the Americans to get involved." And he waited and waited, all the way until they landed in Italy. But what Castor was mad about was his maneuvers about *Les Temps Modernes*.

What happened?

I don't know if you remember: Trotsky's widow had petitioned the French left to stage a "tribunal of honor" about her husband and his assassination. When Malraux was head, or a leader, of Writers and Artists Against War and Fascism, or whatever that organization was called—ask your father, he was a member—he corresponded or something, I don't remember, with Trotsky. He had some kind of particular relationship with Trotsky. So the tribunal asked him to testify. When he refused, and he did so because by then he was ass-licking de Gaulle in his lust for power, his widow sent us a copy of the letter, and we were going to print it. So he went to Gallimard, that was Gaston, the old man, and threatened not only to leave that publisher if Gallimard continued to subsidize us, but also to expose Gallimard's collaborationist attitude or perhaps its actual pro-German acts. So Gaston gave in and pressured us, and when we refused and went ahead with our plan to publish the letter, he stopped his subsidy. So we went over to Julliard, and after the old man Julliard died, Claude Gallimard, who took over Gaston's house when papa semi-retired, took us back.

What was in the letter?

I don't remember, nothing earthshaking, but I think it was embarrassing to Malraux because it showed him to have been a Trotskyite or sympathizer, which would not do well, he thought, with his drive for power. He was wrong, of course. It didn't do him any harm.

And how did Gallimard collaborate with the Nazis?

Like all publishers who continued to publish openly during the occupation. Of course, Gallimard was the biggest, so it got more attention. But it was never ostracized for making Pierre Drieu la Rochelle, a known fascist, editor of NRF [*Nouvelle Revue Française,* the most famous prewar, wartime, and postwar literary review] to comply with German censorship demands. Some of its editors were secretly in the resistance. So nothing came of it.

And your feud with Malraux?

Nothing came of that either. But everything he wrote from then on was crap.

Including his work of art and his anti-memoirs?

Crap.

But you know, during those anti-fascist committee days, and all the way up to and through the civil war, Malraux was very close to the communists, yet when he turned right, Gaullist, he never revealed any of the secrets he knew. He told me, when I asked him in '54, that what he had learned back then was because he had been trusted by the party, so he wouldn't reveal anything later. I remember him saying "not like that scum Koestler."[2]

OK, so I'm a little hard on Malraux. But he could have done wonders for

France, besides having its old buildings cleaned. **He wanted to live in luxury, so he aimed for that, and he was smart enough to know how to fool the critics into praising his books, especially his anti-memoirs, which are really shit. You're frowning. You don't agree?**

I agree on his postwar novel, and on his anti-memoirs because I know where he made things up, or even worse, just plain lied. But I liked his work on art, and I was one of those critics who praised it when I was art critic at *Newsweek*. But OK, so Malraux wrote bad stuff, wanted money and luxury, et cetera, but for someone with his experience, his previous commitment to the good guys, how could he move that far right, when France was behaving so abominably, in Africa, in Vietnam, in . . .

At home. Right here in the north.

What was that?

The miners' strike. That was very important. In 1948, under the tripartite government . . .

Didn't the communists quit in '47?

Oh, yes. The communists had left the government in May '47, but not because of the horrific massacre in Madagascar, but over the attempt to privatize Renault.

What happened in Madagascar?

The natives rose up demanding independence and killed maybe up to a hundred French colonizers. So the French army responded by slaughtering at least ten thousand, although some estimates went up to ninety thousand. Socialist Paul Ramadier was prime minister and Maurice Thorez, the head of the Communist Party, was his deputy. Just like the massacre at Sétif, Algeria, in May '45, when the French army admitted killing six to eight thousand Algerians, while Foreign Minister Georges Bidault said the toll was at least twenty thousand. No one gave a shit. Well, some intellectuals did. Camus denounced it. The French cared only about their wallets, but the socialists didn't, refusing to vote for a general raise even when it was their own people doing the demanding. They sent the CRS [Compagnie Républicaine de Sécurité, France's tactical police force][3] to crush a major strike by the miners in the north, miners who were not agitating for a revolution, or even a change in government, but just better pay. Food. And the CRS opened fire and killed some of them. These were the same great miners who had staged a strike against the Germans during the war. The Germans had rounded up a few and

executed them by firing squad, right then and there. Now these great heroes of France wanted a better livelihood, and the socialists sent the CRS to kill them.

The north? That's where the socialist boss Guy Mollet is from, no?

Yes, Arras, that's his fiefdom.

And he and his party were responsible for Indochina too, right?

And how. And no one cared about that either, at least until the CP finally got involved, but thanks to Henri Martin. To be fair, the media were partly responsible. They covered it so badly that most of the French thought we were fighting the Japanese over there. They weren't even shocked when, later, France and the Vietminh were in the midst of negotiations to end the war, some air force bastard named Thierry d'Argenlieu bombed the port of Haiphong; we denounced it as an act of piracy in *Les Temps,* and almost all the dissenters went to jail for sedition.

France had the full support of the United States then. Obviously, our leaders were coveting all those territories already. The Dulles brothers certainly wanted Indochina and Madagascar; it fit right in with their grandiose plans of dominating the world, at that time mostly with bases and armies, not quite yet with capital, but dominating just the same.

I always wondered about them. I mean, Eisenhower turned out to be OK. He stopped us and England from seizing the Suez Canal. Why did he not get rid of those two fascists?

First, because they were very important to the Republican Party. Next, because they represented the cream of the ruling class. John Foster Dulles, who was Eisenhower's foreign minister [secretary of state] from 1953 to '59, had been a trustee of the Rockefeller Foundation, and an outright supporter of the Nazis in the '30s. He pushed "containment" as U.S. foreign policy, advocated a NATO and SEATO as a way of dominating Europe and Southeast Asia, and helped create them once in power. It was he who ordered his brother Allen, head of the CIA, to prepare the coup to overthrow the democratic leader of Iran, and to prepare the coup to overthrow the democratically elected president of Guatemala. He defined neutralism as "immoral." Big business loved him, and Eisenhower didn't realize how his policies would lead to an "industrial-military complex dictatorship bent on worldwide warfare" until his final days in office. Like his brother John Foster, Allen Dulles was a prewar partner in the powerful law firm Sullivan and Crowell, and concocted the vicious agreement whereby just about all the good arable land of Guatemala would belong to United Fruit Company, actually one-sixth of the whole country. But unlike his brother, Allen was not pro-Nazi before the war, but had many contacts with Germans on both sides, which ended up being very useful for him later when he successfully managed to bring many of Hitler's scientists to the United States under phony IDs and documents. As head of the CIA he was always planning new weapons, or getting his capitalist pals to develop them, the most successful of them being the U-2, which the Russians finally shot down at over fifty thousand feet in the air. But Sartre, when you say that Eisenhower was so good to stop the French-English-Israeli invasion of Suez, you don't realize that was both Dulleses' policy. They didn't want you or England to be major colonial powers anymore. It was time, they were convinced, for the United States to dominate the world. And incidentally, it was Allen who arranged for Nasser to die of a "heart attack" two years ago. For me, the most disgusting coup that both Dulles brothers fomented was the one in Guatemala. You traveled there with Dolores, if I remember, and before the coup.

Indeed, I went there three times, but the big trip, in '49 with Dolores, was really memorable, not so much Guatemala, although we saw all the fantastic Mayan ruins, but our trip to Haiti was outstanding. This was of course before [François] "Papa Doc" Duvalier's dictatorship. The president then was a guy called [Dumarsais] Estimé, a black man, the first since the U.S. invaders were taken out by Roosevelt. But real power was in the hands of the taxi drivers' federation, yep, taxi drivers, and they took us everywhere. To voodoo ceremonies, to hidden farms behind stark mountains, to meet Haitian communists dreaming of a return of someone like their great hero, Toussaint Louverture, who fought the French so magnificently at the beginning of the nineteenth century, and to meet the Americans, engineers hoping to make a fortune, as racist as any French colonialist in Algeria or Madagascar. My memories of Haiti remain very strong. We went everywhere in Central America, down to Panama, which was, and I gather still is, a totally subjugated American province, and we went to many places in the Caribbean, but it's our few weeks in Haiti that I remember most—well, with Cuba, which was, and is, as I have gone back, absolutely enchanting, but back then it was also a completely corrupt American colony.

You actually felt and saw the corruption?

And how. With bribes you could get anything and everything. A ten-year-old girl, or boy for that matter, if you wanted. Anything. We went one

night to the Shanghai, the famous, or infamous, nightclub where the show included couples fucking on stage. That really upset Dolores, who pretended to
be shocked, but I think because she was worried about being taken for a black
woman, hence a local woman, since she assumed, probably correctly, that a
white man like me would never come from America or France with a black
woman. She was wrong. Her skin was too light or else no one gave a damn.
She was never insulted or asked an embarrassing question.

You broke up with her shortly after that trip, no?

No, much later. She came to France and began to bug me. First she
wanted to divorce her husband. OK, I gave her some money so she could do
that. Then she settled in a villa in Cannes. Ha, I remember the owner, his
name was Pissarro, because he was a descendant of the painter. Then she
came to settle in Paris. That was too much. So we split.

You mean you told her to go away? That's not a "split," which is
mutual.

OK, I told her it was over, and she went back to America. It was a very
busy period for me.

Including a lot of attacks and lawsuits, I gather. In fact, what happened
to your suit against Nagel? [As the publisher of *Dirty Hands,* Nagel autho-
rized a translation of the play for Broadway titled *Red Gloves.*]

It lasted for years. In fact, I just won one phase, but there's more not resolved yet, although it is clear that I'm going to win. As you know, when I
found out that whole passages had been added and some taken out to make
the play more anti-communist, I tried to stop the production.

I saw it on Broadway. It didn't come across that anti-communist to me,
but then I had read it before seeing it. What were the worst changes?

I don't remember now. The one everyone talks about is when Jessica
says "il a du chien," they translated that, "he's vulgar," instead of, what? "he's
sexy"?

One could actually say "he has dog," though few would understand.
Better to translate it as "he has sex appeal."

As if a communist can't be sexy! But there were more important
changes, some wanted by [Charles] Boyer [who starred as Hoederer], who
knew he had to appear as a very hard leader, but wanted to be very charming
as well. Details. Anyway, the play was a flop on Broadway, thank god, and
when Boyer came back, we talked things out, and everything is OK now. But
it's a period piece; it has no value now.

I disagree. I think the play says a lot about party politics, party loyalty, ends versus means, et cetera. I like the play. Not as much as *The Devil and the Good Lord,* which I think is tremendous.

It has never been produced in America. It may be put on in England, though the translation is not very good, but not for political reasons this time.

Speaking of attacks, though, I noticed that Mauriac was really blasting you back then. Was that a personal feud? It sounded like one.

We have to be clear about which Mauriac we're talking about. The old man, François Mauriac, who got the Nobel for literature in 1952 and died two years ago, was a fanatical but tormented Catholic, a fairly good novelist, a very moral man who condemned France's role in Indochina and its torture in Algeria. He wrote for *L'Express* [a center-right weekly]. Then there's his son, Claude, not so Catholic, not as good a writer, not as polite, who wrote for *La Figaro* [a right-wing daily]. Claude edited the journal *Freedom of Spirit,* and he did attack me feverishly and often personally, but also sided with us in confrontations with the government, which he deemed racist, authoritarian, and devoid of moral scruples. He never assumed that his personal attacks on me were in fact personal, and greeted me as a friend.

Yet I read some in his journal that were vicious.

On the other hand, he was with us [for a sit-in occupation] in the Goutte d'Or and then at the press conference made us look like a bunch of do-gooders from the Salvation Army. Still, because he was there, *Le Figaro* ran an article about the event. What Claude really lusts for is a reformist leader who wants a beautiful republic that would give housing to all and exploit no worker, where there would be no racism and no violence, yet no unions and no socialism.

At your demonstration at the Palace of Justice the other day, where he had a seat and you didn't, he saw the tremendous effort you made to sit on the floor, and he quickly came to help you into his seat. Nice.

How did you know that? You weren't there, nor were any militants.

Michelle was. But tell me, you never write in the café anymore?

Impossible. The Flore, Les Deux Magots are always full of curious tourists. Until recently, I wrote quite a bit at Les Trois Mousquetaires [on avenue Maine near rue Gaité, one of the most culturally diverse streets of Paris]. But they've modernized the place, and it has lost its charm.

There's still Le Liberté at the corner of Gaité and Edgar Quinet.

Too busy.

Actually, I always wondered how you could write in a café. Novels, plays, OK, but philosophy, *Being and Nothingness, Flaubert*?

I always felt I had to stay in contact with the world, with my world. Ever since Marx, philosophy must lead to action. Otherwise it is irrelevant. So a philosopher does what he has to do, then sits down at his desk, wherever it is, and "retakes the thread of his anger," as Valéry once said. The distractions don't matter as long as I could retake the thread of my anger, anger against this system, against all those who believe that they have a right to be greedy, who feel they are superior to others, like the French in Algeria, in Madagascar, the Americans in Haiti, in Puerto Rico, the whites in black New York, the Dulleses in Guatemala or Egypt. Philosophers must be angry, and in this world, stay angry.

Do you think this is true about all artists, or only committed writers?

As I wrote in *What Is Literature?* I think it is true about all *good* writers. We discussed that already, how Malraux, Dos Passos, Steinbeck, et cetera got real bad when they gave up on changing the world. You know more about artists; what do you think?

Good artists want to change the world in a different way, but I think it's true for them as well. It's like when I asked [Willem] de Kooning how he could have kept it up, especially his wonderful women, since the early '40s, he answered: "Revenge, my boy, revenge." But let me turn it around: must a writer be committed to be good? And of course by committed we mean to the poor, the exploited, the subjugated.

I think so. Now at least that we know why the poor, the exploited, and the subjugated are so.

Is [Pierre] Courtade [a communist author and journalist] a good writer?

Being committed is a prerequisite but not a sufficient element for a writer to be good.

Are you suddenly talking about talent? Let me remind you that you have said that "talent is drawing the chair to the table."

Very true. But in that act of drawing the chair is also the commitment, the experience, and especially what we were talking about a minute ago, the anger.

May 1972

GERASSI: I reread "Merleau Vivant" since last week, as well as his major works, and was struck by how careful you were not to imply that you were not great friends.

SARTRE: Yes, I was a bit hypocritical. Have you read his *Phenomenology of Perception?* So you realize how close it is to much of what I wrote in *Being and Nothingness?* He had read some of that work, and had asked me not to publish it until his book came out, chapters I had written during the war, before his, and he was hurt that I did not wait. For him it was a question of his career . . .

And since it wasn't for you, why didn't you wait?

You think I should have, huh? Well, maybe. But to tell you the truth, I wasn't moved by his career concern. Like on *Les Temps Modernes,* he did not want his name on the cover, as co-director, because he thought it might affect his career.

But he did accept. I've read many articles signed by him in the review at the time.

Articles were OK. It was a strange period. Our magazine was seen with jaundiced eyes, as a whole. Suspect. But to be published in it was considered a career plus. It was weird. Intellectuals from all left-wing variants submitted stuff to us all the time, but the same intellectuals criticized the overall "purpose," as they said, of the magazine, without ever stating what that purpose was. Anyway, Merleau's pieces were very Husserlien; remember, he was a phenomenologist to the core, and politically a Mendessite. He even wore the Mendès-France tie.[1] In other words, Merleau was a bourgeois who favored an honest and "pure" bourgeois state. He was also somewhat religious.

Now you sound like you disliked him a lot.

Let's face it, we were never close friends. At school, I thought he was intelligent and perhaps even interesting, though I was already by then reluctant to talk about ideas, which seemed to be the only thing that interested him, at least when he was with me. Castor, of course, was much closer to him, since he was dating her best friend, Zaza. But then, as you know, Castor blamed him for Zaza's death when he broke up with her, not knowing that her parents had threatened to expose the fact that he was illegitimate if he didn't. But there was other stuff that bothered us. He was sleeping with some ugly girl who kept for him all the papers he wrote, unsigned of course, in her pad, so when the Nazis raided her place and she courageously refused to say who had written them, the Nazis believed it was she and took her away to a concentration camp. There was a lot of stuff like that which bothered us, like Camus.

Camus? What do you mean?

Using women. Camus was like that too.

Like what?

Well, he would try to seduce every woman we knew, and then dump them, unless they rejected him, in which case he hounded them, like Juliette Greco . . .

The great singer?

Yeah, and they always dumped him, because once he sort of succeeded, all he talked about with them was himself.

But you and Merleau pretended at least to be good friends, no?

Yes, but he wasn't really part of our group, you know, what Castor now calls the family. I'm not sure how to explain it. I remember one day, he came up to us at a café and said, I'm not doing anything for dinner, can we team up? Castor said we were to have dinner with Giacometti, but he could join us if he wanted to. He did, and later, after he left, Giacometti said, "You know, he's not our people." And that said it all, although I can't really explain what it meant, something of the sort that we think about different things.

Yet you've written that he influenced you, politically at least, more than anyone.

Yes, that's true.

Specifically on the Korean War.

Indeed, he helped me see the issue clearly, that America was willing to risk war to have control, which Russia was not. And then he became neutral, so to speak.

Yet in *Humanism and Terror* . . .

See, that's one of his many contradictions, as was his role in the RDR. He was in, yet out. He liked our "third way," yet supported the communists . . .

So did you then.

In France, because that was the party of workers. But Merleau's approach to the CP, in fact to everything, was always philosophical.

And you claim in various places that you were extremely influenced by him.

I was indeed, the whole nonparty left was. But today? Well, who cites his works now?

Oh come on, lots of intellectuals still do. His analysis of Bukharin's downfall I think is brilliant, as is his critique of Trotsky's tactics.[2]

I agree, but that's all old hat now.

Yet it's in that text that you quote his famous sentence, with which he sort of whitewashed Stalin's crimes, and hence so did you, the sentence: "The values of communists are our values, in spite of them." Do you still stick to that?

Yes and no. I mean, globally speaking, yes, like [Louis de] Saint-Just's famous slogan: "A patriot is he who supports the republic completely; whoever fights it in detail is a traitor." Of course, today, we would have to say, "whoever supports the revolution," not the republic.

If you stick to that, you can't criticize Padilla or Mao . . .

Well, certainly Merleau would not have.

Of course not, because he, like all good Marxists, would put the revolution in its contingent situation, which is how he gets to say that there can be no revolution without terror. You don't buy that argument. I remember that in my interview with you for the *New York Times,* you said that what you wanted was a revolution without terror, but you concluded that was a contradiction. Yet in "Merleau Vivant" you insist that to always criticize, which after all was also Merleau's position—another of his major contradictions, yes?—is not enough. Yet that is precisely what you do in the RDR, no?

All very true, but you have to remember that at the time of the RDR I am a flaming bourgeois, petit bourgeois. In fact, I don't really stop being one until after '68 as I told you.

But in '47 you wrote that a writer who does not commit himself is a bad writer. Commitment is not just criticizing, it is taking a position.

Absolutely, but taking a position, sticking one's neck out, is not necessarily being a revolutionary, yet anyway, since eventually it does lead to that; to criticize is either meaningless, as the government says, sure, go ahead, that's freedom, and it does nothing about your criticism, or else it silences you, because your criticism threatens it, like during the witch hunts. McCarthyism was not just the ambition of a politician. It represented a whole group of people who were afraid of losing money, or not making as much, as you yourself wrote in *Les Temps Modernes*. There was a rivalry between those who wanted to trade with Soviet Russia and those who did not, who made money from war, or the industry of war . . .

The military-industrial complex.

Right. That's why you had witch hunts in America, and why we had them here, like our ridiculous pigeons affair.[3] That should have made me chose right then and there, but I waited. I was a bourgeois and did not dirty my hands too much. I had to have a more flagrant incident. And it came, with the General Ridgway affair, when the United States was much too obvious in trying to make France a colony. Even de Gaulle thought that was outrageous, which is why he kicked NATO and all U.S. bases out of France.

And made his famous statement, "No nation is free if it allows a foreign base on its land."

After that we had to choose.

And so your famous phrase, "Not to choose is a choice." But you chose to be anti-U.S., not pro-communist. What then pushed you to go all the way? The Rosenbergs?

Wasn't that later?

They were executed in '53. Castor writes that you were in Venice at the time. They had been found guilty in '52, lost all appeals, and were executed in June '53. You then wrote *Communists and Peace,* which actually is kind of mild, considering your rage when you read in Venice that they had been electrocuted.

But you see, I never thought that Eisenhower and the American government was that stupid, that horrendous, to actually go through with their execution. I wrote *Communists and Peace* before they were executed, in '52, when I was still thinking that America would come to its senses. And then we had our Henri Martin affair. It hence became impossible to believe in bourgeois democracy. But I was sill reacting as a bourgeois myself. I would say the execution of the Rosenbergs was an outrage. The Henri Martin affair was a violation of the right to dissent. You see? I was making moral judgments.

Did you not know that the right always uses terror when it feels threatened? That the execution of the Rosenbergs, who were guilty, really, of nothing more than being communists and hawking the party paper, *The Daily Worker,* on the Lower East Side, was an act of terror to frighten all serious dissenters?

Not really. I mean, theoretically, I knew that. But in practice, the right is so adept at using courts, juries, the law, to conceal its terror, that we bourgeois are always fooled, at least somewhat. But you're absolutely correct: the right will always revert to terror when it feels threatened, and always has.

OK, as a bourgeois, you were gullible, as was Merleau, as full of contradictions then, in the '50s, as was Merleau. What about now that you claim to be solidly a revolutionary, committed to the GP, which does not believe in bourgeois elections. Is a revolution without terror possible, and do you support such a revolution?

Wow, you really want to put me on the spot today. OK, first issue first. Yes, I believe that a revolution is impossible without terror, precisely because the right will resort to terror to stop it.

But there has been no terror in Cuba. Repression, yes, but no terror.

That brings up another aspect of revolution, which is this: to succeed, a revolution must go all the way. No stopping in midstream. The right will always use terror to foil it, so the revolution must use terror to stop it. Now, you mention Cuba. True, there has been no terror in Cuba. Why? First, because, as you have said, Castro allowed popular tribunals to judge the Batista torturers as a way of getting the hatred out in the open, as a cathartic cleansing of the lust for revenge. But more important, because of circumstances: first, the rich Cubans had a lot of family and friends in Miami; second, the United States let

the rich come in at will—precisely because they were rich, hence of the same upper class as those for which your government exists; third, because Fidel let them go. Anyone could leave with two suitcases of belongings, no gold and no money, correct?

Correct. Add to that, U.S. stupidity. At first the United States was convinced that Castro was a bourgeois reformer. I was an editor at *Time* then, and the top editors immediately understood that Castro was genuine when he allowed those trials to take place. Even our correspondent in Cuba, who turned out to work for the CIA, kept saying, The trials are fair, the trials are fair. But my bosses understood: sure the trials are fair, but if Castro is willing to execute the torturers, it means he's serious, and if he's serious, he'll learn quickly enough that behind everything that Batista did was an American capitalist. When he did learn that, he told our secretary of state, Christian Herder, that he would not guarantee the inviolability of U.S. businesses in Cuba. That did it. But by then, Castro's bourgeois front men, remember, the temporary government he put in while consolidating his power with the military and by creating militias everywhere, were out. So he didn't need terror.

OK, that's the exception that proves my case. A revolution must, absolutely must go all the way to have a chance of succeeding in a world dominated by powerful capitalist countries ready for war. Lenin and Trotsky knew that very well, and they went after the counterrevolutionaries with vehemence. The Red Army built by Trotsky had to be superior to the fourteen capitalist "volunteers" and the two White armies. How? By making the rank-and-file choose their officers, with total recallability, and political commissars who explained the meaning of each operation. So the same grunt soldiers that the Germans beat over and over suddenly became ferocious revolutionaries.

And then Lenin and Trotsky lost the revolution because they turned on their left?

Exactly. Like Robespierre, who had the backing of the sans-culottes, then wanted stability in the streets, and turned on them. Stability is a cry of the right. It should never be sought by revolutionaries. Once Robespierre lost the streets, he was doomed.

As was Mao, or the Maoists in China. Another revolution without terror, although the West keeps trying to argue that the Cultural Revolution was terror.

Agreed, there was no state terror. Excesses? A lot. But that's not state terror, like Stalin's or Franco's, which are obvious, but also, the state terrors of witch hunts, and phony trials, and legal executions like Sacco and Vanzetti, or the Rosenbergs. The state terrors of the established capitalist countries never have to be as pervasive as the terror of revolutions for the simple reason that the capitalists have all the weapons of suppression, the armies, the police, the media, the courts, et cetera. In China, Mao should have let the Cultural Revolution run its course, let the kids purge the party hacks, let them purge the army hierarchy. Basically it was a fantastic grassroots rebellion by people who said, We set policy, the bureaucrats administer our policy. But Mao got scared that even he might end up being sent to hoe potatoes on some collective farm, and the so-called Gang of Four did not feel strong enough to go all the way. So, they perished, and with them, the revolution.

So how do you deal now with Saint-Just's statement? Who were ultimately the traitors, Mao or the Gang of Four?

We don't know anything yet, except that, to me anyway, the leader of the Cultural Revolution was Lin Piao, and he certainly never tried to escape to Russia. Once he was killed, probably by the army, the revolution was doomed; the Gang of Four became powerless. We'll see. What is certain is that either Mao or the communist apparatus, his or the army's or the party's, have basically stopped a move to the left, which means that the original revolution, you know, Mao's, Lin Piao's, Chou En-lai's, is over; they failed, and China will move radically to the right. I'm absolutely positive of that. A revolution that assumes that to survive it must crush left and right, like Robespierre did, like Stalin did, must fail.

So what is your role in all this? I mean, to go back to Saint-Just, what is the revolutionary intellectual's position when he sees the inevitable?

To remain faithful to his, to the revolution's, principles.

And since you, now that you are political, a revolutionary intellectual, who hopes for a revolution without terror, do you condemn the terror, when it comes? If terror comes to Cuba, do you condemn it? You are certainly guilty of the second part of Saint-Just's statement, since you criticized the forced self-criticism of Padilla.

Where the Cuban revolution went wrong was not its fault. The mistakes were made by incompetents. But that's because most of those with education, training, technical skills, et cetera, were from the top bourgeoisie . . .

And mostly white in a country 85 percent black or mestizo.

. . . and they fled to America.

They fled Russia, too.

But Russia then had a civil war, and during that war, a lot of rank-and-file communists gained a tremendous amount of skills. Plus there was a long history of communist literature written by Russian intellectuals, of all sorts of revolutionaries, anarchists, Decembrists, all sorts of thinkers, and doers too.

That didn't stop Lenin from complaining that his closest team was full of incompetents. Remember Lenin's great sentence when the invaders were beaten—"We've defeated the counterrevolutionaries, but we will never get rid of the imbeciles."

Indeed, that's good, but yes, leaders always think they know best, which is one reason that they try to stay in power.

OK, so the revolutionary intellectual criticizes, say, a detail, like Padilla, only on the basis of revolutionary principles and in the name of those revolutionary principles—in other words, did the revolution act here in conformity to a global ensemble of principles that are the basis of the revolution. Correct? Whew! That's some task.

OK, what I criticized about the Padilla case is that the tribunal that judged him to have a "counterrevolutionary attitude" was not based on such principles.

Ha, so it wasn't the verdict, "counterrevolutionary attitude," but the tribunal itself, which was not what, in your mind?

Ouch! I guess I have to say, a tribunal set up by a ruling committee of some sort, not one emanating from the revolutionary struggle.

You're getting into trouble there, because had it been a people's court, like the one I witnessed, made up of his neighborhood folks, his maid if he has one, the guards on his block, his street cleaners, the repairfolk in his building, all folks who either fought Batista's army or joined the militia after Castro won, he could easily have gotten ten years of cutting cane "for the people."

So what's your answer?

Criticize from within, not from without.

And if from within only gets you in trouble, and doesn't do any good?

I don't have an answer. Get out, like Voline and write a great book explaining it all [*The Unknown Revolution*]. Or wait it out and confess, like Arthur London, and explain later [in *The Confession*],[4] or as Merleau explained about Bukharin, criticize from within, then accept the court's judgment without reservation. So what are you going to do about your situation at *La Cause du Peuple?* [An editorial in the paper had called for the assassination of a particular informer. Sartre reacted with fury, accusing the GP of not being able to tell the difference between a situation and an individual.]

I told them to change their position or I would quit the GP.

If you quit, you lose your efficacy.

And if I stay, I lose the power of my political voice. The GP is the only party or group or gathering, since they are not a party, that tries to be both revolutionary and ethical, Marxist and moral. That's what attracted me to them in the first place. Now, when you think about it, the idea of vengeance is a moral idea. But now what? Is popular justice to be translated into lynching? If that's the case, it's all over.

But, to get back to the basis of our discussion, as long as the capitalist world wants to continue to subjugate the masses, make the rich richer, while the consequence, the poor becoming poorer, is inevitable, revolution is not possible without terror, until the whole world is revolutionary. Right?

Right!

And who sets the terms? Precisely the subjugated masses.

Yes, but the masses do not do the choosing. That is the result of a bunch of petit bourgeois intellectuals who create a proletarian definition of justice.

And if they don't, who will? Popular justice was very popular during Robespierre's time; the *charrette* [the cart used to transport victims to the guillotine] was loved by the masses.

Very true, as long as Robespierre incorporated the violence of the masses into his terror, he and that terror were popular, as were Cuba's trials and executions of the 375 Batista henchmen. But Robespierre substituted popular terror with juridical terror, and he lost everything, including of course his life.

Did you express this to your Cuban hosts, when you were there?

Oh yes, I told them that they still had their terror in front of them. Meanwhile, it was great, really great to be in Cuba in the '60s, not so?

And how! I'll never forget in 1967 finding everyone armed except the cops, and those beautiful traffic cops, all gorgeous young women in miniskirts. You should have seen the traffic jams.[5]

That was the period when Castro got rid of the old communist apparatchiks, too.

Ah yes, the so-called mini-faction of Anibal Escalante, who was packed off to Czechoslovakia. A great period in Cuba.

So what went wrong? Or, let's put it in context, why is it not today, just a couple of years later, as wonderful as it was?

Money. The U.S. embargo hurt, no doubt about it, and the educated bourgeois elite continues to leave. Also, after the missile crisis, Khrushchev lost interest, and when Brezhnev took over, that loss of interest grew wider. It's tough in Cuba today, and a lot of people try to get to the United States. But the only terror is that generated by the United States, planes dropping poison in the lakes, bacteria in the cane fields, sabotaging shipments, a lot of stuff like that, yet still, Castro's intelligence service is nowhere near as brutal as the ones taught by AID [Agency for International Development] and Civic Action, the two U.S. CIA agencies that train friendly police forces all over Latin America on how to torture. In fact, I think Castro's intelligence apparatus is first class. Did you meet Barbaroja when you were there?

No, who's that?

[Manuel] "Redbeard" Piñeiro, Cuba's chief of intelligence, a brilliant, simpatico, extremely efficient cop, and a very nice guy.

Boy, you surprise me: a nice cop?

A revolutionary cop. Anyway, no terror so far.

It will come, as the population suffers more and more from lack of food or clothes or whatever. Like in China. Well, maybe there was a terror during the "let a thousand flowers bloom" period or whenever. And there was a sort of mini-terror during the heyday of the Cultural Revolution, but if so, it apparently wasn't bad. I wonder if one reason, probably the main reason, for the terror is that the revolutionaries do not completely dismantle the old regime apparatus.

That's what Lenin said, yet he himself did not dismantle it. He used it, and look at the consequence.

The question is, did he have a choice? Two White armies, fourteen capitalist "volunteer" armies, a recalcitrant peasantry, famine, plots, god knows what he didn't have to combat.

Yet, by your own definition, he did not remain true to the revolution's principles. Not only by crushing the Kronstadt sailors, but by playing power politics, by not aiding the Béla Kun revolutionaries in Hungary, by closing the border with Iran to its rebellious Tudeh communist party guerrillas in exchange for British recognition of his government, and on and on.

All very true. Still, the only party in France in 1952 that systematically opposed American imperialism and represented the proletariat was the com-

munist, so there's no other position but to be a fellow traveler, critical, but allied.

Until Prague, and then?

Two things happened. First, I wanted to go to Russia because of my enormous . . . ah . . .

Because of Lena.

Yes, but also, and this is crucial, Algeria. The CP was not pro-FLN. As usual, the party wavered between its stupid nationalist and opportunistic stance with which it hoped to gain votes, and its reluctance to side with Muslim fanatics.

The FLN was not a fanatical Muslim sect then; it was nationalist, yes, but as we always said, nationalism in a developed imperialist country is fascism, nationalism in an underdeveloped, imperialized, or colonialized country is revolutionary. You said that yourself in your preface to Franz Fanon's *Wretched of the Earth*.

Indeed, but what party could be moved to be pro-FLN in France in 1962, besides the CP? I mean a large party that could have some influence on the government? There were a lot of independent leftists back then who were in favor of the FLN, and a lot of rank-and-file commies, and quite a few CP intellectuals too. So I hoped, and I really worked at it, to push all these leftists to back the FLN. My thought was that if enough leftists proclaimed themselves in favor of Algerian independence, and were loud about it, you know, demonstrating in the streets and staging pro-FLN rallies, then the CP would feel obliged to join in. The FLN gave us a chance to unify the left, to save the left in France. OK, it didn't work. But it created a germ for what was to come. It was then, in our support of the FLN, that the new left was born in France. It then deepened as we became more militant in our support of the Vietnamese against American imperialism. When you convinced me to join Bertrand Russell's International War Crimes Tribunal, you argued that it would help Vietnamese morale. I agreed. It was a moral position on our part, right? But it also hardened our backbone. And from those moral positions, a young, noncommunist, militant, street-oriented left was born, a left that scoffed at establishment compromises, a left that had no respect for leaders. And that all crystallized in '68. What I did not understand when you talked to me about the tribunal was its significance in the minds of the young. They saw in our sessions that we were appealing directly to the people, to the masses. A sort of fancy, because of the big names involved, people's tribunal. It didn't get

much press, and the American media scoffed at it, if they even bothered to report it. But it said to the young, the hell with their courts, with their laws,
which always defend the rich and crucify the weak and the helpless. What we
said, fundamentally, is that their "rule of law," which they herald from their
capitalist rooftops, is a farce, a way of subjugating the poor, the needy, the
weak, the just. We always knew that, but the tribunal, precisely because it en-
compassed intellectuals and pacifists of world renown, got that message to
the young. They knew all that instinctively, of course. But the tribunal said:
Russell believes that, too, so do Sartre and Beauvoir, Dave Dellinger and Lelio
Basso, Jimmy Baldwin and Stokely Carmichael, Lázaro Cárdenas and Isaac
Deutscher, and all those Nobel winners, people the young respected. That
was extremely important.

Basically, that was the beginning of the GP, too, wasn't it?

The tribunal was held in two sessions in '67, in Stockholm and Copen-
hagen, and the fact that the United States and England would not allow it to
be held on their territory helped a great many young people all over the world
to realize that America and England were now allied in a fascist imperial policy. It was extremely stupid to have banned the tribunal from their point of
view, and it sure helped the flourishing of the new left, which then the communists had to support, in the May '68 events, when communist workers
joined the students and the young in their battle against the de Gaulle government.

And their subsequent betrayal.

But that was because the kids did not want to overthrow the regime—
that is, they didn't want power, and the CP then had no choice but to maneu-
ver for some gain for their members. That's when the GP was really born, a
movement to seize power, but not by the ballot, which elects only rotten
politicians, but by revolution.

Indeed. Everywhere. Including in Israel-Palestine, which created a
major contradiction for you, didn't it?

We're not so far apart. I've always been in favor of one Israel-Palestine
state, in which all are equal. Trouble is that the religious right is too powerful.
They want a Jewish state, whatever that is, with all the historical crap enmeshed into their constitution, which of course alienates not only all Mus-
lims, and all Christians, but also all nonreligious Jews as well. So, OK, in that
light, I'll be for two independent states, equal and free.

But the GP supports the revolutionary actions of the Palestinians.

So do I, and so does the Israeli left, when Israel subjugates the Palestinians, takes away their land, stops them from being able to live free.

But they support the armed struggle, they consider the suicide bombers "freedom fighters."

I have always supported counterterror against established terror. And I have always defined established terror as occupation, land seizure, arbitrary arrest, and so on, as does the Israeli left, Matzpen for example. I have always had very close ties with Matzpen.[6]

That I know, since you were the one who put me into contact with them. By the way, did I tell you that they were really great with me during my trip in '69? They showed me everything I wanted to see, introduced me to the fedayeen, even got me to talk to the rabbis who oppose Zionism. And now most of their leadership is in jail.

We sent a formal protest to the government and to our Israeli friends on that. The charge is that they are in contact with the fedayeens, which is against the law.

So much for democracy! You know that Lanzmann broke with me when he heard that my trip was sponsored by Matzpen. How do you get along with him now?

I had a very serious problem with him for a while, because he asked me to sign a letter at the time of the Six-Day War begging both sides to stop. That was OK, but then Lanzmann organized a conference based on that letter, which was signed by all the usual suspects, to support Israel. That's when he cried that if [Lyndon] Johnson supported Israel he would shout, "Bravo, Johnson!" This is in the midst of the Vietnam War, when Johnson was sending more and more troops, and bombing and burning poor peasants with napalm. That put a damper on our relationship, but he wasn't involved in anything we were doing, so I let it go.[7]

You weren't embarrassed by his journalistic activities, like his writing for *Elle*?

Not really. He was a bourgeois who wanted the good bourgeois life. He paid his dues as a young resistance fighter . . .

Whoa! As a good Maoist you know what Mao said, that one is never finished paying one's dues . . .

Very true. Still, OK, he didn't do any harm at *Elle*. One can be a revolutionary and write for *Elle*, no?

And *France Dimanche*?

That was in '48, I believe. I guess I wasn't very politically conscious then. I do remember that when I was with Fanon one day then, and Lanzmann showed up, and Frantz jumped and said, "You write for *France Dimanche*? Are you crazy?" Yeah, that was embarrassing. But now, well, he's a good bourgeois, researching a film, and praising Israel, but his praise, in his head, is the consequence of the Holocaust. He really doesn't see what is happening to the poor Palestinians, chased from their land, their houses seized without compensation, their children driven out of schools, harassed from morning to night, beaten by heavily armed strangers. Lanzmann thinks of Israelis as Holocaust victims. And to him, anyone who criticizes Israeli policy is an anti-Semite. Period. And any Jew like the members of Matzpen, and Pierre Bloch, and you, are all self-hating Jews. He's old enough to have been part of the Holocaust, and would have been had he been caught during the occupation, so that's where he's stuck.

Is Israel debated within the GP?

No, on that issue, they're united, they're solidly pro-Matzpen, as is the whole new left, and the Trots, and the *anars* [anarchists].[8]

But there is inner trouble at the GP, no?

Yes, but not on policies. Those who have quit did so because they don't like the way their chiefs treat them, haranguing them, calling them incompetents when something goes wrong. And the chiefs, especially Pierre [Bloch], treat them that way out of frustration, I believe. A tremendous amount of the left, just about everyone that shows up at Renault to demand fair wages for workers, or picket the elite schools, or demand military bases off farmland, et cetera, agree with the GP, but no matter how right the cause, no matter how much their paper *La Cause du Peuple* is read across France, they don't join. That is very frustrating to Pierre and his fellow self-appointed leaders. The GP numbers four thousand active militants today and cannot seem to grow. Most new leftists are too reluctant to join any party.

Except, it seems, La Ligue [Communiste Révolutionnaire].[9]

I don't understand why. They don't do anything. They're incredibly dogmatic and Stalinist in their organizational structure. I can't figure out where they find those who join. [The party's leader Alain] Krivine has asked to have a meeting with me, and I will go, because I will do my best to unite the whole new left, and despite its ways, most of its adherents are young, the product of '68.

Quite a schedule you have these days: Flaubert, volume two of the *Cri-*

tique, articles for *La Cause,* and you still spend time at the cafés and with all your women!

Paris, France, would be something completely different without cafés. To sit calmly, ogling passers-by, making comments . . .

Nasty?

No, not necessarily. Like, Oh, that's some hairdo she's got. Or how about that coat?

So, you're at the café with women, I gather.

Absolutely. Café life with men is no fun. I know we agree on that: pleasant conversation is about emotions, senses, perceptions, discoveries, not ideas, or politics.

And who do you spend those "pleasant" hours with? Arlette. Michelle, Wanda, Castor.

No, actually, those ladies I see usually in their homes. For one thing, you can't enjoy hash in a café, can you?

That reminds me, how much do I owe you for that last bunch?

Forget it. I got it from Arlette or Wanda. It was good, wasn't it?

Great. Really great. Where did it come from?

I don't know, but it costs one hundred thousand francs for a hundred grams.

That's five hundred dollars! Twice what I pay in the United States.

But as good?

I can't tell. At home, we smoke grass. The hash here is more powerful. I was gone after one joint.

So was I, or two maybe. Perhaps you mixed too much with the tobacco. But it's very nice, isn't it? Arlette and I or Wanda and I really go off on it, especially if we're making love.

You don't take speed anymore?

Corydrane? No. The doctors said it's dangerous now. Too bad, because I loved it. It doesn't create a high. It just speeds things up. Do you know that I wrote the whole of the *Critique* on corydrane? It made my hand move so fast, I couldn't write any faster.

Did you ever try it with cocaine, or making love with cocaine, which really heightens orgasms fantastically?

No. Never tried coco, opium, or heroin. Or LSD for that matter, although I gather that it has some of the same effects as peyote, you know, mescaline, which I used to take. I think that's how I first started hallucinating

my crabs and lobsters. But it wasn't nasty. They would walk along with me, on my side, but not crowding me, very politely, I mean, not threatening. Until one day I got fed up. I just said, OK beat it, and they did. I liked mescaline a lot. As you know I am not a nature lover. I much prefer to sit four hours in a café than wander the Pyrenees, like your father.

But not me. I'm a city man too.

I know. Still, with mescaline, those Pyrenees hills take on so many different colors, it's really art.

OK, so you get stoned periodically. When do you go to *La Cause*?

By and large, this is my schedule: Flaubert every morning until lunch. As you know, we have lunch late, from 2 p.m. to 3:30 or so. Then I write pamphlets, articles, whatever, for the GP, or I go there and get embroiled in their squabbles. Evenings, unless there are rallies or meetings and the like, I spend with either Castor, Wanda, Arlette, or Michelle.

And where does Pierre fit into all this?

Right now, because the squabbles are serious, I am more often involved than I should be, or want to be. The GP risks getting dissolved. A whole bunch have quit, mainly because they consider Pierre too authoritarian, too hard.

But that's not what is breaking up *La Cause*? It's the article on Bruay, right? [On April 5, 1972, a young girl named Brigitte Dewevre had been murdered in Bruay-en-Artois, and a "peoples' article" in *La Cause du Peuple* (May 17) had accused a local notary public of the deed, in effect calling for his lynching. Sartre responded in the paper (May 26) with a vehement criticism, reminding the editorial board that "innocent until proven guilty" is not a bourgeois principle "but a peoples' victory," "not to be abandoned by a peoples' Justice."] Pierre had nothing to do with that.

But his people wrote the article. The others, the "democratic revolutionaries," were the ones who quit over that.

I had dinner with Claudine [Trouvier, a GP militant] two days ago; she called it fascism, pure and simple fascism. Yet it fits with the GP's notion of "popular justice," doesn't it?

There's an article by Pierre in the next issue—it's out today—which tries to say that, but with many concessions. The problem is that Pierre, and the hard core of his followers, want to push toward armed struggle. And of course, we aren't there yet, nowhere near. But these kids are anxious, very anxious. And Pierre is convinced that the intellectuals in the GP, those who have a good education, like Geismar, are to blame for moving too slowly, for finding too many "ifs" and "buts." The strange thing is that they are all intellectuals, including him.

He's an Egyptian Jew, isn't he?

Yes, but raised in France. He studied with [Louis] Althusser and is extremely well read. You know, he founded the Union of Communist Students, and then the GP.

Where is Geismar in all this? He's the paper's editor, no?

I saw him last night at the meeting for [Paule] Thévenin.

So did I. He spoke very well but said nothing.

So you noticed that all the leftist groups were represented, the Jewish student association, the PSU, the Ligue, *La Cause du Peuple*, but not very many people to hear Paule Thévenin . . .

She was great though, condemning [Interior Minister] Marcellin directly for the murder of her son [killed by police during a demonstration]. But I was stunned that Geismar could not rise to the occasion.

He's not that solid at the paper, either. He behaves like a political commissar. He and [André] Glucksmann, who does all the work, are the force behind the editorial board, but they exhibit a sort of triumphalism that bothers me. Although their fight for the occupation of the empty apartments in Paris was great, and quite a victory for many families. There are 165,000 empty ones in Paris today. And how many homeless?

Now what? The GP is disappearing. *La Cause du Peuple* is closing. And now every social advancement has to be fought in the streets, just like in the United States.

Ordinary people, dissenters, oddballs, anyone who has a legitimate, or illegitimate gripe for that matter, no longer has a voice in France. Democracy, I mean bourgeois democracy, is dead.

The Fifth Republic wiped out proportional representation?

Oh, we haven't had that for ages. But at least we had a lot of different parties, different movements, all with their newspapers. Now we're like you. Our Republican Party is the Gaullist, with its various sects, and our Democratic Party is the Socialist, with its communist, Trotskyist, green hangers-on. Even from a capitalist viewpoint, we no longer have a soul. We have become a crass, consumer-oriented, racist, ageist, uncaring society, an appendage of America.

You need another de Gaulle.

Not again! Stop with that goddam bastard. What do you see in him, anyway?

I know you hate him, but look, he was the only statesman who knew that France, perhaps all of Western Europe, was more threatened by the United States than by Russia, the only one who warned that "No nation that has a foreign base on its soil is free," and ordered French missiles to be pointed both east and west. He kicked the U.S.-NATO out of France. He agreed to talk to the FLN and for Algeria's independence. He fought the fascist generals who did not. He proclaimed an agrarian reform that kept farmers and their families on their land and solvent. He repeatedly vetoed Britain's entry into the European Union. And when he resigned, he was perfectly willing to turn over the presidency constitutionally to his vice president, a communist. What more do you want from a French leader?

With his ridiculous "grandeur" he was an insult to France. He appointed Pompidou as his prime minister, and that scumbag eventually did allow the Brits to become members and ruin it so America could dominate us better. And worst of all he arranged for Pompidou in May '68 to promote Marcellin to interior minister so that fascists could destroy our civil liberties, *à l'américaine*.

Did you at least like his statement, when you were hawking an illegal paper right in front of police headquarters and they didn't arrest you, "La France does not arrest its Voltaires!"

See! That idiot didn't even know that Voltaire was indeed arrested in France. He and his heir ruined France. But it doesn't matter who is most to blame: they all are, so that today we have massive censorship, or self-censorship, no art worth our heritage, no literature, no self-esteem. We've become the lapdogs of your capitalists.

You still have the daily *Libération.*

For a while. Have you noticed how the paper has moved to the right?

It was started with your money; don't you still have influence?

None whatsoever.

Wait: France's most viewed program is one on books, ninety minutes of discussions about books and ideas, the most popular show on French TV. In the United States such a program on national TV wouldn't last a day. And there are still some producers who want to put on your plays, which they wouldn't do unless they thought lots of folks still wanted to see them. That would be out of the question in the United States. There, independent thought attracts no one, no popular critic, no one.

You're referring to *Nekrassov*? OK, but it won't make a bit of difference with our public. The play is a condemnation of our press, but do you think it will make it change for the better? Ha. By the way, I wanted to ask your advice on that play. When it was written and produced, everyone got its two main themes, namely that the press is corrupt as hell and is part of the Cold War machinations, and that communists do fight for workers. You've seen it, you've read it. What will it say today?

The same, I think, but it might be colored one way according to the actors. I heard that you were thinking of Louis de Funes [a slapstick comedian] for Palotin [a caricature, meant to be taken as play's idiot but who turns out to be the socially hip winner].[10]

Wouldn't that come across as too pro-communist? The times have changed; I don't want the play to be communist propaganda.

I would cut the end a bit. It's too long, and there the triumph of the communist daughter can come across as a bit preachy, especially since she's not a party notable, only an ordinary militant.

Good point. Especially now, after Prague, Budapest . . .

And your own *The Ghost of Stalin*. It's okay to be allied to the communists in their fight for better wages for the workers, but it's also important to make sure that your viewers know that the Communist Party does not necessarily represent the interests of its members. And that does come across in the play, although it gets a little fuzzy by the length of the ball at the end.

Do you know that there's also a producer who wants to put *The Witches of Salem* on stage? I don't know if that'll happen.

I liked your movie much more than Arthur Miller's *The Crucible* because it was much more political, in my sense of being class conscious. Miller was fighting the witch hunts, of course. But you put it into its class-war situation. But you know, you were historically wrong, as was Miller, of course.

In what way?

Historically, the class war was between the poor folk who had no access to the river and were stuck paying huge fees to the Putnams, and the rich ship owners who also controlled the ports. Reverend Parris represented those poor, who accused the rich, even the governor of Massachusetts, of witchcraft, which was defined in those days as being out of the ethos of the

"City Upon a Hill." The original leaders, the famous preachers, John Winthrop and John Cotton, believed in communalism, everyone flourishing together, and Parris was their disciple. In fact it was the preachers, John Cotton's son-in-law Increase Mather and his son Cotton Mather, who got Parris to call off the attack, because it was getting out of hand. The confrontation was the rich against the poor, and the accusers were the good guys, but remember, to be accused of being a witch in those days was to be charged with being an individualist who didn't give a damn about others.

Shows that neither Miller nor I did our research, doesn't it?

No one got that. Historians still don't write about the class war in Salem. We got it by accident when we were researching our book *The American Way of Crime*. We came across, in a basement of the Salem courthouse, a list of people in Salem and what they owned, and it showed that 85 percent of the people in Parris's church were dirt poor. By the way, the irony is that, when New York Times Books, which was the original contracting publisher, sold our contract to Putnam Publishers, we ended up being published by a descendent of the original Putnams. They printed five thousand copies and refused to print more when they sold out. I asked Mrs. Putnam, the owner, one day, why not, and she honestly replied: "I didn't like it. It's a commie book."

It's not, of course, but it shows that capitalism and organized crime worked together right from the beginning, and I can well understand that the American establishment wouldn't like that spread about. But in France, *Le crime à l'américaine* was a best seller, wasn't it?

And how! I'm still living off it. What about *L'Engrenage* [a play by Sartre, called *In the Mesh* in English]? I hear that, too, may be revived on stage.

Actually, it has been playing a lot recently, twice in Germany and Switzerland, in Italy, and here last year. You know why? It comes across as a parable on Cuba, the revolutionary country trying to be independent and being blackmailed by its powerful neighbor. And to think I wrote it in '48.

But it was meant to be a film, wasn't it? You wrote it as a scenario.

Yep. I even signed a contract with some producers, but they eventually told me that their backers, the big buys, had changed their mind. Then the Italian communists wanted to do it. I even had a nice talk about it with [Palmiro] Togliatti [leader of the Italian Communist Party].

Oh yes, that famous long dinner with him and Gina Lollobrigida, the most beautiful actress in the world. I was madly in love with her at sixteen.

But you got it wrong. That famous dinner was in '54 at the Piazza Santa Maria in Trasteverde, and she was eating with a group at another table. But it sure was a memorable dinner, although not so much because of her, rather because of the genuine interest that Togliatti had about what was happening in France. I was amazed that he really listened, and wanted to learn . . .

Yet before we go gaga over the Italian communists, let's remember that they too, and specifically Togliatti, as much as we may like him personally, and Fernando did indeed in Spain, they, and especially he, were faithful confirmed Stalinists.

True, but unlike his French counterpart, he never personally insulted his critics. He always responded politely, and he listened to those critics. Our dinner lasted three hours, and during most of that time, he asked questions, not only about what I thought of such-and-such, that could have been just out of politeness, though I believe he really wanted to know, but especially about French politics, French communist tactics, French government policies, and so on. I looked at him as a de-Stalinized Stalinist.

And what about Gina?

We were in a very popular sector of the city, full of restaurants, all open air, almost one next to the other, and hundreds of people, rich and poor, strolling by. Our restaurant was reputed to be one of the best, and it was.

Indeed. [Film director Gillo] Pontecorvo took me there in '67. He's the one who told me that this was the restaurant where you had your famous dinner with Gina and his party chief.

Boy, how stories are concocted! Gina and her group were sitting about three tables away from us, and of course the strollers recognized her and started yelling their appreciation, their love even. But then someone recognized Togliatti, and the whole crowd moved over, shouting "Viva Togliatti," clapping, saluting. It was something to see: people hailing a communist politician so much more than Italy's greatest sex symbol. In fact, it got so noisy, we couldn't talk anymore, so he suggested we go to a nearby café. He waved to the crowd, shook a few hands, and we walked on. The café was a hangout for many working-class communists, and they cheered him as well, but after a while they left us alone to talk. That is, until a famous local singer walked in and asked Togliatti if he wanted to hear some old songs. Sure, he

said. And the troubadour began to sing some lovely old songs, songs from the 1830s, all papist songs. I even remember one or two lines, like, "Careful, the devil has landed, Garibaldi is at the gates of Rome!" Togliatti knew the songs, and began to sing with him, then everyone in the café did also, all these communists singing these old royalist and papist songs, laughing and genuinely enjoying themselves, and me too, as I picked up a few refrains, and sang along.

Castor tells me you have a great voice, basso.

I used to, but I did OK that night. Anyway, can you imagine Thorez, or any of our communist leaders, walking through the crowds with no body-guards, singing reactionary songs, listening for three hours to criticisms about communist tactics from a foreigner? That's Italian communists for you, willing to be teased, respecting their enemies.

No longer, I fear.

Result? The good ones broke away and launched *Il Manifesto* . . .

That's also the period when you went to see Heidegger. Did he impress you at all?

Nope. There was one session that did not impress me, but I found interesting. It was with a whole bunch of German philosophers, very important ones, asking him very profound questions, I presume. I understood nothing. But my time with him alone, naw, it was a waste of time. Anything he said I attributed to Husserl.[11] I was much more influenced by Husserl than Heidegger. Actually, I had already written *Being and Nothingness,* which people like to say was inspired by Heidegger's *Being and Time,* when in fact I only read it during the war. Incredibly, I found it in the library of the stalag where I was a prisoner. He did help me make a few of my concepts more precise, though. He was pretty shrewd. Which is why he played footsy with the Nazis and survived.

And this is the period when you go rather extensively throughout Russia. How could you not realize what a disgusting regime it had?

You know, I was blinded by my understanding of world politics. Because I knew that Russia would never start World War III and the United States would, I didn't see the internal realities of Russia. You know, when I got there the first time, in '54 or '55, my host, the head of the writers' federation, I forgot his name, told me, "Monsieur Sartre, you are free to go anywhere you like, except the concentration camps because they don't exist." Don't forget,

Stalin was dead and our old friend Ehrenburg had published *The Thaw,* about the de-Stalinization process.

A terrible novel.

Yes, but important. He was the first. [Konstantin] Simonov, for example, was still being careful.[12]

Didn't the folks you saw then, and later after Khrushchev's de-Stalinization speech in '56, talk openly to you about the real conditions?

Yes, but guardedly. Castor will put many of the comments in her next book of memoirs, when she talks of our trip to Russia, but since Ehrenburg is now dead, she will attribute all the comments to him, so as not to endanger those who made them. But you know, even with the writers we got to know well, telling us how it was, and mind you, most were Marxists and genuine revolutionaries, they didn't really want to say too much that was bad. They would find good points, like that [Osip] Mandelstam was now being published . . .[13]

What about the memoirs of his wife? They are fantastic.

Yes, everyone made a point of mentioning that.

And that convinced you?

Of course not. To my credit, I never came back from Russia and shouted, like Nizan, "I have seen the future and it works."

Nor did you denounce it, like [André] Gide.[14]

In fact, I never wrote anything about Russia, good or bad. But yes, I wanted so much to believe that the revolution takes two steps forward, one step backward, as Mao had said, that I hoped the Soviet system would pull out of its terrifyingly repressive stage.

And yet, privately, even if you didn't say so publicly, you were fooled a great deal. How come?

I went to Russia with all my bourgeois preconceptions, which of course included my hatred of bourgeois morality, or I should say, lack of morality. Because the bourgeois media lie so systematically about everything, or, to be more accurate, tilt all news to the defense of bourgeois life, I obviously was predisposed to believe that anti-bourgeois counterpropaganda was more truthful, or less fictitious. I was too used to the usual articles, which always went like this: "In Timbuktu yesterday protesters complained that French paratroopers beat up the main pro-independence groups, but what we saw was the paratroopers, in stifling unbearable heat, fixing the road and drilling

for a new well to bring water, and a bit of relief, to the poor inhabitants." That's typical: mention the real issue in passing, quickly, then praise our side with glowing details.

That was certainly true about the media during the U.S. invasion of Vietnam. Nor did anyone, either the *New York Times* or the *Washington Post,* report President Eisenhower's warning about the "military-industrial complex." Our media even faithfully reported without comment the number of Vietcong soldiers killed, without ever adding up the official figures, which amounted to hundreds of thousands.

So, I took all the criticisms of Soviet Russia in the Western media either as outright lies or vast exaggerations, and wanted to believe as much as possible of the rejoinders by communists or by Russian propagandists. OK, so when I got there, I quickly realized that they lied too. But I knew that in the West, workers were exploited and their protests vastly repressed.

Actually, compared to the United States, your workers are in heaven. Do you know we have no law that guarantees workers paid vacations, or pregnant women that they will have their jobs back after giving birth, or that they must be paid while delivering and afterward? We have no law that guarantees the worker his investment in a private firm's retirement plan, even if his contribution is mandatory. We don't even have a law forcing companies to pay fired employees compensation and no law giving them health coverage, and let's not forget we have no national health system. Unions fight for these, but don't forget, in the United States, the government can abolish a union outright, and jail and fine its leaders for leading a strike, which the government can declare illegal.

Your capitalism is terrifying, no question about that. We have solid unions and a national health system and laws that guarantee a certain amount of security, all true. But from our point of view, work conditions are pretty bad. Don't forget that except for a few bourgeois leaders, like Jean Moulin, most of those who fought the Nazis, and so many died doing it, were our workers, especially the railroaders, and most were solid communists. Our factories are probably not as dehumanizing as yours, but they're awful. So I expected that the factories in Russia would be so much better. I asked to see some. Of course I saw them as a tourist, but they were clearly no better, even though everything I was shown was probably the best they had. I knew about the Stakhanovite system [of production quotas for workers], but of course I couldn't ask questions, or rather, when I did, I depended on the

official interpreter that they gave me. And if a worker, or anyone, said something, if it was not to the translator's ideological liking, what would stop him or her from telling me, "Oh, he saw you on TV yesterday, and shouted, Hoorah for Sartre." Add to that our prejudices, inherited from years of our media concoctions. Like, one day in Prague, Castor and I went without a translator to the main library, and the librarian immediately started yelling at us how terrible life was under the communist regime. We immediately assumed he was an official provocateur of some sort. Or, in China once, where Castor wanted to read up whatever she could in French or English on feminism and women's issues, especially on the rumor that the government had a program to kill off the newborn females. The librarian recognized her and said one thing in Chinese for the interpreter to translate and another, how unhappy she was and how dominated women were, in her little French when the translator went to the bathroom. Again, we assumed the incident was set up, to see our reaction.

What about once you teamed up with Lena? You went everywhere with her, and once you two were lovers—I presume she didn't lie to you about what you saw.

No, of course not, but all those great trips were after the de-Stalinization, and before the return to Stalinization with Brezhnev.

And in Cuba?

Everything is different in Cuba. For one thing, everybody disagrees publicly with everyone else. I remember the first time I went, at the beginning of the revolution, in '60 or '61, I was on TV with Castro, and we disagreed about something. I can't remember what it was, but for two days afterward, everyone gave me their opinion, in Spanish, of course, but my translator translated all the views, Castro was wrong on that, Castro was right on this, you got the best of him on that, et cetera. And for you, it must be even better, since you speak the language.

And yet I get suspicious, too, sometimes. I remember in '67, a beautiful young woman approached me in the street. She had seen me at the press conference when the Cubans had caught five CIA agents planting bacteria in the sugar fields just before the harvest and where President [Osvaldo] Dorticós had chastised the American press for not believing the agents. Some Miami reporters had asked such questions as what was on the kitty-corner from where you lived in Miami, or what is the name of the bodega on the next corner, stuff like that, and when Dorticós got mad, I intervened to explain that U.S. reporters are trained to ask embarrassing questions like that when they are reporting a story favorable to the opposition. So this young woman asked me if I could help her get to Miami. She had asked five times for an exit visa, but had gotten no answer. She handed me a list of her relations. I assumed that she was a spy, because of my intervention on TV, and ignored her request. Lo and behold, eight months later, she looked me up in New York to thank me for helping her, assuming that the reason she got an exit visa was because I interceded for her with the government. She was completely genuine, and boy was I ashamed. And by the way, she quickly got to hate the Cuban-Miami exile community.

You see, that's how our media brainwashes us. So we have no choice but to remember that all governments lie, that all media lie, in order not to lose the advertising where the press is purely capitalist or to be in good with the government and keep getting the licenses where they don't live off ads or where the governments hold Damocles swords over the reporters and editors. Where I'm at now, with all my condemnation of Stalinist regimes and parties everywhere, is to never forget that no one becomes a communist of any stripe unless he or she really wants to fight for a better life for the poor, for the workers, and for the colonized. Revolutionaries are made by the greed of capitalists.

June 1972

GERASSI: I've just read the new issue of *Les Temps Modernes,* which is dedicated to the maos in France, just when the GP and *La Cause du Peuple* seem to be crumbling.

SARTRE: Don't confuse the various groups. You went to the meeting of *La Cause?*

No, but I heard those who quit the paper let loose on Pierre.

They really admire him, his knowledge, his analytical skills, his tenacity. But they consider him a dictator and they stuck to their decision to quit.

The whole editorial board? All seven?

Yes.

And then, in *Les Temps,* Glucksmann praised Pierre.

He's really the only one who does. And I don't understand why. Is it because he wants to take over the paper himself completely, because Pierre isn't going to? Or is it because he's on a centralist kick? But did you read Foucault's article? He is completely in favor of popular justice.

But not popular or people's trials.

That's because he rejects trials as a creation of the ruling class.

So how does popular justice work?

Ask him next time you see him. But the merit of his article is that it

shows how the ruling class was able, generation after generation, to turn justice into an arm of rule. That analysis is first-rate.

What I like about Foucault's analysis is that it ends so logically on the viciousness of the state, how it will resort to massive violence, all nice and legal, of course, to have its way. But boy, is he pessimistic.

He's right, I'm afraid. Things are bad everywhere. And no one seems to give a damn anymore, like all those massacres in Bangladesh, in Tunisia, in Iran. Over a hundred thousand people killed in Burundi, and no protest. Why aren't there protests in your country against the systematic tortures in Colombia, in Uruguay, in Brazil? Everyone knows that they're organized, even carried out by the CIA, but no one seems to care.

The approaching end of the war in Vietnam, the assassination of Malcolm X and Martin Luther King, the failure of the Weather Organization to spark massive armed incidents, and especially the total moral and political corruption of the media, which cannot get the balls to blame the CIA or the FBI, the two greatest organized crime syndicates in the world, for teaching police forces everywhere how to torture, are having their effect.

And the worst is to come. Like in Chile. They'll move before there can be a civil war, you'll see, they'll make a coup, and murder thousands. The Chilean CP will do nothing, you'll see. They'll sit on their asses and call for patience, votes or referenda.

I wonder if they really understand that the class war is between rich countries and poor countries. Russia clearly will end up with the rich. The big question is China, and I'm afraid it too will side with the rich.

As Foucault wrote, I fear the worst. Four, five years ago, China gave us hope that it would join the Third World against the First and Second. Its Cultural Revolution, with all its excesses, was a revolutionary movement without the state, a genuine people's war against bureaucratic terror, at home and abroad. But now, with Lin Piao gone, we see a foreign policy that has no relationship to what was developing internally. The Chinese are repeating what we had in France, centralist rule by the Jacobins instead of popular rule by the sans-culottes. Chinese revolutionaries now seem to be studying the various economic indexes, like the gross national product, the rate of exchanges, the balance of trade. Once that becomes the test, it's all over.

That's true for France too, isn't it?

Yep. Our small businessmen have adopted the American standards for everything, without understanding that it applies only to the dominant enter-

prises. They have a sense that something is wrong, which is why they have created all those associations of owners. But they're doomed. Actually, they started these associations in '56, even before de Gaulle's return, with no understanding that it would eventually lead to economic chaos. America can sustain, for a long time yet, a capitalist drive to make more and more profits at the expense of less and less productivity. But France cannot. Already, our major industrial firms are folding, like steel.

Didn't de Gaulle's economists try to offset that by a form of "dirigism" (not public ownership but some form of public control or co-control of major industries)? That's how he got the Airbus industry launched, and the new bullet trains.

None of that can solve our basic problem, which is that our CEOs want to be richer and richer, like yours. And of course, the only way to get richer is to produce shoddier and shoddier products, or better yet, produce nothing, become a service industry economy. So we have more and more banks, speculators, real estate firms, combinations and buyouts, and of course delivery folks, salesmen, advertisers, and coffee-getters.

What we call gofers, from "to go" and "for," in other words, a flunky whose job is to get things for the boss.

I guess you can survive a long time in America on that kind of economy, but we can't. As it is, we have three types of workers now: the one who gets up in the morning, travels an hour to his job, gets paid well enough to feed his family of four and allow his wife to be a consumer, travels another hour to get home, and is too exhausted to do anything or read anything, just watches stupidities on TV.

That's the one the song is about: "dodo, Métro, boulot, Métro, dodo" right?

Exactly. He's a member of the CGT or CFDT [the largest labor union confederations] because the unions get him paid vacations and a decent salary, but he'll never make a revolution, though as we saw in '68, he might join one after it has started and he thinks it can succeed. The second type of worker is the young, who lives in the city centers, hates his job but likes his life; he goes to the movies twice a week, eats in restaurants, doesn't read, not even the newspapers, and blames foreigners for whatever goes wrong. Then there's the third category, mostly the foreigners that No. 2 hates, who do the work that No. 1 or 2 won't do, like cleaning the streets, picking up garbage, and running the errands, the gofers as you call them. They live in the projects outside town, where their brothers and sometimes their fathers are unemployed. Many of them are illegals, mostly from Algeria and Morocco, but the government won't harass them because no one else will do their jobs, and therefore they won't complain, until the day when they are beaten too brutally for not calling the local racist cop "sir" or, unemployed and hungry, for stealing an apple, and then their whole neighborhood explodes. But when it does, the rest of the workers, the No. 1 and 2, will denounce them as ingrates. The result is that we will not change. We are doomed to perpetuate the same disgusting society until your economy, in America, collapses, and affects us all.

Like 1929?

Except in '29 or a few years later, you had a president who knew how to save capitalism, by signing contracts with producers. And even then, he needed a war to get the whole country going. This time, it may not work. Much of the world is too wise about America's intentions and its need for perpetual enemies. And the capitalist economy no longer produces real stuff. Germany and Japan still do, and unfortunately China is feeding your, and our, consumer needs, but the United States? Does it produce anything that we need? Besides war material of course. It will collapse, and then, perhaps, a form of humanism will reemerge. But not in my lifetime. Nor in yours.

And yet, there continues to be some movement, some understanding among the young that there can never be genuine dehumanization via a capitalist state. That's a bit of legacy the Cultural Revolution has left the world. I think now the youth of the world has understood that capitalist bureaucracy, capitalist parliamentarism, will never solve the ills of this planet.

I'm not so sure. Look at Germany, where a violent revolutionary group, the Baader-Meinhof, behaved perfectly correctly. They never killed an innocent. They went after the vicious pigs of their society, and the American colonels who fawned over them. Yet popular sentiment was against them.

Still, it seems that there are young people everywhere willing to put their body on the line, so to speak, to fight for genuine meaningful changes.

I'm not so sure. The Baader-Meinhof group were bourgeois kids.

The Tupamaros [an Uruguayan guerrilla movement] weren't. Most of them were exploited sugar workers.

Led by a socialist deputy. And how did they get caught? By being turned in by the poor.

Because the government got enough money from the United States to offer $100,000 for the capture alive of a Tupe. That kind of money can feed five poor families in Uruguay extremely well for ten years.[1]

Perhaps. But most ordinary folk don't relate to bourgeois self-sacrificers. The Tupamaro leadership was made up of doctors, architects, lawyers, and I think, with no proof whatsoever, that workers just sympathize or perhaps don't trust people who act, or so they believe, out of bourgeois frustration. Still I'll grant you this: the Red Guards may have been created by the students of Peking University, but the vast majority, and many of their spokespersons, especially those fantastic young women, were workers, or sons and daughters of workers, and their legacy, as you say, has remained, somewhere. As for everywhere else, well . . .

Africa! The beginning is great. It will be completely crushed, yes, but the people will remember their Fanon, Mulele, Gizenga, Lumumba, Nyerere, both Cabrals, Moumia, Nkrumah, Hawatweh, Ben Barka. Especially Amílcar Cabral, who was a bourgeois, yes, a trained agricultural engineer, but who returned to his tribe, led it in the fight for [Guinea-Bissau's] independence against the Portuguese, and wrote some fantastic essays about intellectuals, therefore bourgeois by definition, committing class suicide. Morocco's [Mehdi] Ben Barka was certainly one of the best and most forceful of all African revolutionaries, who started the nonaligned movement, and I'm sure every African will remember him.

And who killed or bought all these folks? Ben Barka was murdered by de Gaulle. The CIA got Mulele and Lumumba. And what did your "ordinary folk" do about that? Heh?

OK, OK. (Well, not all, not Cabral yet.) But they didn't forget them. I don't know a single American black militant or revolutionary, not a single rank-and-file [Black] Panther or Muslim, who does not revere Fanon, or Malcolm X.

Maybe, but what are they doing? Now. Here in France, what's happening to all those flaming radical intellectuals from '68, huh? All of Althusser's students?

Althusser does not advocate violence. To him communism is a stage, a passage from one type of society to another, so unless we know what kind of society communism will lead to, and what the costs are, it doesn't seem worth it.[2]

The problem is that the communist revolutionaries, that is, those who are still revolutionaries, and there aren't many of those left, have a bourgeois

mentality: they act out of bourgeois guilt, which means that their conviction is purely moral. As mine was until '68 shook me up. And I still am much too bourgeois, despite the fact that I've given up on writing my ethics for precisely that reason. But I'll tell you, Pierre does not think, or no longer thinks like a bourgeois, which is why he's a genuine revolutionary.

We'll see. He's certainly not a democratic revolutionary. And didn't you tell me that what attracted you to the maos was precisely that they were moral revolutionaries?

Yes, but not bourgeois morality. Bourgeois guilt leads to revengism. That is Castro's greatness, that he knew the dangers of revenge and let those trials get it worked out. Moral revolutionarism is fine.

Isn't that what leads to such articles as the one that so shocked you in *La Cause*?

That was revengism, pure and simple. Nothing moral about wanting to break somebody's balls.

Is that the reason you don't like *The Condemned of Altona* anymore?

Yes. The whole play is based on culpability.

That's not how I read it. Or even saw it, in the De Sica film. [Sartre's play was made into a movie directed by Vittorio De Sica in 1962, starring Fredric March and Sophia Loren.] To me it said that when you eliminate the feeling of personal guilt, you end up with the guilt of a whole class.

That is it precisely. But a real revolutionary does not want to wipe out the bourgeois class because of its guilt, but because historically it is compelled to exploit the proletariat.

OK, so class guilt is to be sequestered. That means it cannot be moved, or saved for that matter, by art. And since it is the bourgeoisie that reads, literature is useless. Yet you continue to write. Why? You've said that you do not have the motive of gaining immortality since, you claim, you don't consider your impending death in anything you do. So?

It's true, I am not a Flaubert who wrote, he claimed, because it pleased him. Why does Fernando paint?

When he realized that art served no purpose whatsoever in the larger scheme of things, that he would never be famous because no art dealer wants to exhibit an unknown at the end of his life—it doesn't pay—he did go through a small hell, for three months, alone in his studio, staring at a particular painting, a really great one, I must say, of colors dancing, until he suddenly said, "Painting pleases me. It gives me personal pleasure. Period."

I can't say the same about writing. I don't know if it serves anything. But I hope it does. And you, why do you write?

I started for three reasons: fame, money, and to change the world. When I realized I would never change the world, that nothing we do, we writers, painters, dancers, actors, would ever change the world, I stopped writing. I wrote ten books before signing a contract to write your biography, and as I warned you, I really had no intention of writing it. Everyone told me the same thing: The revolution isn't going to happen for fifty years at least, don't waste your deal. Go back to France, write the biography, explain to the world why a bourgeois who has never suffered for being a bourgeois, who never rebelled against anything or anyone, has become a revolutionary. That's incredibly important for the revolution, which you will never see or experience.

And I think that's true. It's important for revolutionaries and for the bourgeois who might become revolutionaries to know how a writer of the twentieth century was led into the revolutionary camp, in spite of himself, since politics bored the shit out of him. And did it. But every time I got involved in something literary I ended up in politics. I think it is extremely important to show that if a writer thinks and writes honestly, he ends up a revolutionary.

But so few have, in the past.

In the nineteenth century, Victor Hugo at least demanded amnesty for the Communards. But not even Zola followed suit. And those who condemned them, like the Goncourts [the brothers Edmond and Jules de Goncourt] and Flaubert, should have been shot.

You've said that a writer should always be against. I quite agree, always against the government, as Malraux said. So did Hemingway, by the way. But what is a writer's position under a revolutionary government?

He cannot be against, but must not be for. He must not join the government. He must never exercise power. He has to keep his independence, never become a bureaucrat.

So you disapprove of [Roberto Fernández] Retamar being head of La Casa de las Américas?

No, that's not an official agency, even if it gets government money.

What about Alejo Carpentier?[3]

I think that was a special case, because if he hadn't joined the government as its representative outside Cuba, I think he would have defected. I

knew him fairly well, or at least I saw him often, since he lived in this neighborhood—he always seemed to be sad, morose even.

Well, he was suffering and dying from cancer. So if a revolutionary
government suddenly took over France, you would not join it, and you'd oppose Aragon, Eluard, and others working for it?

**Your question implies that the CP is revolutionary. OK, let's say it was,
hypothetically. Yes. Their job then would be to make sure that the government
sticks to its and their revolutionary principles, to make sure it does not become opportunistic. But our CP could never be revolutionary, nor could its intellectuals ever be leaders of a revolution. They're too closed, too pedantic,
too didactic, too phony. You can't talk to them, nor do they want you to. Only
listen.**

Unlike Italian communists, right? That's a mistake; no matter how
charming they are, they still belong to a party with a particular structure that
does not allow rank-and-file input in the policies, in the core of a CP. And
if they can, like Togliatti, or [Yugoslavian president] Tito, or our good common friend [Vladimir] Dedijer, it does not and cannot change the party struc-
ture.4 It was precisely against this secretive, closed centralism that the kids
launched the Chinese Cultural Revolution, and when they went after the
party hierarchy, they got crushed.

**So you want to be a _spontex_ [French leftist slang for spontaneous mili-
tants]?**

That's what your maos are, aren't they?

**Yes, and indeed that's what I liked about them. In fact, that's what I ad-
vocated, so to speak, in the _Critique_.**

Your "group-in-fusion"?

**Exactly. But that's not the article at _La Cause_. We are all atomized in
bourgeois society. When a group suddenly fuses together and yells No! but
then follows through the No!—which is a moral reaction to extreme injustice—into group action, thought and action are joined, as is the group, now a
group-in-fusion. It explodes out of spontaneous rejection of an immorality,
but does not constitute a group-in-fusion until it translates that rejection into
an action that is for all.**

Like the group that seizes the bus on Third Avenue? But such a group
could also lynch. And it may not be popular justice. It may be that the victim
is thought to be guilty because he was different. So it could be a lynch mob,
racism, fascism.

It could. To make sure it isn't is the role of the revolutionary intellectual. The broadside writers. The dailies. The educational process. But when the group-in-fusion moves, the intellectual is just part of the group, neither led nor leader. The sans-culottes taking the streets of Paris, not Robespierre or even Marat, whom I know you admire so much. The *cocas* [black slaves] seizing Haiti from the French, not Toussaint Louverture telling them what to do, no matter how admirable.

They all failed.

Yes, and so will probably the next bunch. But success by groups-in-fusion someday remains the only hope for a fair way of life on this planet.

October 1972

SARTRE: **Tell me, how's Fernando?**

GERASSI: He's suffering a great deal, mainly because he won't take the morphine. He claims he can't paint with it. How about you, and Castor, how was your summer?

She's fine, as you'll see on Sunday. She traveled quite a bit in August; I just worked, mostly on *Flaubert*, then went down to Nîmes with Arlette.

I see the third volume just came out. I haven't had a chance to read it yet. It got rave reviews.

Yeah, much better than the first two volumes, with reason, I think—the third is much better.

So what's next, *Madame Bovary*?

Yep. The whole fourth volume, which will be the last, of course, is about *Madame Bovary*.

Is that book so important? I read it in school and I liked it, but only as another example of much-vaunted French nineteenth-century literature.

You should read it again, and focus on what it says about French customs and manners, morals, prejudices, and especially the stupidities of our prevailing bourgeois society. And don't forget, it was written by someone who was a petit bourgeois himself, and lived its ways completely, all the while insulting it.

I certainly remember his famous cynical comment that "To be stupid, and selfish, and have good health are the three requirements for happiness; though if stupidity is lacking, the others are useless." So you now work every day on *Bovary*?

Unless something else urgent comes up, like a demand yesterday for an article by the guys at *La Cause du Peuple*. But it has to be important. Like the Munich massacre. I wrote that in the morning, then went back to *Bovary* after lunch and never answered my phone until dinnertime.

I have to get the past issues of *La Cause*. What did you say about Munich?

I broadened it into an analysis of Palestinian terrorism. First of all, I recounted the history of how they got chased, and often killed, out of their land, dumped into terrible refugee camps, ignored or even repressed by the Arab governments, forced into a diaspora that got them being almost slave workers in Saudi Arabia, Kuwait, Jordan, and other supposedly pro-Palestinian countries, rebelling for a decent life and then condemned by every rich country because of their own guilt of having done nothing to stop the holocaust, of which the Palestinians were totally innocent and probably not even knowledgeable. Having said that, I drew the inevitable conclusion that the Palestinians have no choice, no weapons, no defenders, but to resort to terrorism. But I felt obliged to scrutinize that terrorism. I pointed out that the Lod Airport massacre, where a bunch of fanatical Japanese end up killing Puerto Rican tourists, was not only stupid but counterproductive. Puerto Ricans, of all people, who are dominated themselves, folks who have no alternative themselves to fight for their independence except by terrorism. But the Munich terror act, I said, was justified on two grounds: first, because all of Israel's athletes at the Olympics were soldiers, and second because it was an act meant to effect an exchange of prisoners. In any case, we now know that both the Israelis and the Palestinians got killed by the German police . . .

The world except Americans knows that. The media in the United States is so pro-Israel, the Israel lobby is so powerful, that everyone still thinks that the Palestinians killed the Israelis and the German police killed the Palestinians. We never, never get the truth about Israel-Palestine in the United States, unless we dig through the web, read the *Hindu Times* or the *London Independent*. But tell me, the GP has not condemned the Japanese assault on Lod, has it? I remember their claiming it was a great show of internationalism.

Stupid. We had some heated arguments, but Pierre convinced them to publish my article as is.

Glucksmann didn't object?

He's no longer there; he left while you were gone. He said he needed six months to think things over, which means, I think, he's out altogether.[1] The good guys have left too; you know, Le Dantec and [Michel] Le Bris are gone.

And Geismar?

I don't know, but he's nothing. He can't write, and he can't think well politically.[2] The only really solid one left is Pierre, and of course all the maos throughout France. And they write great articles about their local struggles. But the paper and the GP are on their way out, I'm afraid. It'll be the end of a great era with the demise of the kids in France, of those who started the Cultural Revolution in China, and of your SDS, of new-left movements everywhere, of the new generation that understood that party politics, indeed parliamentarism, elections and all that, are so rigged that reform is impossible. From now on, I fear, it'll be up to the genuine revolutionaries, like the *Il Manifesto* militants, to carry on the struggle, courageous but alone, and mostly ignored.

Have they given up on China?

Completely. They've even taken [the little picture of] Mao off [the top of] *La Cause.* They asked me a while back, should they get rid of him; I said I couldn't care less. In fact, I think Pierre struck Mao off the minute he heard of Lin Piao's death. Actually, I agree. When the Cultural Revolution started demanding that the party and the army be cleaned out, the old guard got scared. From Chou En-lai down. So they started arresting the most leftist groups, and then they had to get rid of Lin Piao himself, since he was very much active in bringing the Cultural Revolution inside the army.

But Mao was not threatened. Besides, he was getting a bit senile. The real power was Chou En-lai, and he was more afraid of the kids than anyone,

Precisely. And Chou was always a world-statesman type, the kind who would push Mao to view China as a world power. So last year Lin Piao is killed and basically Chou takes over, behind the facade of Mao, and arranges for Nixon to go there, and make everything nice. China's international strategy becomes just like Russia's, rivals aiming for the same goals.

And since there's a tradition in China not to execute political opponents but to send them to rehabilitation camps, that is, prisons, they couldn't condemn and execute Lin Piao. He was too popular, so they had to fake a crash, and just killed him. But claiming that he had plotted to kill Mao, then tried to escape to Russia, he who was the most anti-Soviet of all the Chinese leaders, is so absurd, I don't understand how the world has bought it.

Most folks just believe their government and their media. So they think Lin Piao died in an airplane crash trying to escape to Russia. That story suited the Chinese leadership, suited Kissinger, suited the *New York Times*. That's all. By the way, did you go see Jeanson in Bordeaux when you got back?

Yes. I couldn't see you first, since you and Castor had gone to Bruay. I had a fabulous lunch with Jeanson and his wife. They really overdid it, with a few dozen oysters and a big chunk of pâté de foie gras, then a luscious filet of turbot, followed by a chateau au poivre, the works. He told me he's working hard on your biography. He has a deadline in five months.

Did you tell him you were doing one, too?

He knew. There's no conflict; he is focusing on your struggle with your ethics, a sort of history of it, while I'm more interested, as you know, in your trajectory into revolution.

I have a small problem with it. Because everyone knows that we worked together very closely over the years, people will assume that I approve of his book, so I have to read it before he submits it. He wants me to, of course. I didn't, but I guess I have no choice.

Why don't you tell him? Now, before he sends you the manuscript, that you will write a preface for it if you agree and a postface if you don't.

Brilliant! No. I have a better idea. I'll do that for your book. And judging from our many arguments, it'll be a postface. Ha-ha ha.

So great, write a preface for his in which you talk only about your struggle with your ethics, explain why you will never write one, and that way, if there's stuff you disagree with, you can say so indirectly through your discussion of your problems of writing an ethics that depends on the situation and the dichotomy between object and subject, and the *en-soi* [in-oneself] and *pour-soi* [for-oneself].

Hey wiseguy, you want to write it for me? What else did you get out of your trip to Jeanson, besides a great feast?

I have to tell you that I liked him, a lot. His wife, too. And I would have even if they had served a pizza. I got the feeling that he thinks you feel guilty a bit about the 121, for not coming back from Brazil fast enough, hence avoiding the trial, his trial.

Bullshit. I had told him and the others to hold back until my return.

They decided to release the statement even earlier, and asked me to return quickly, barely forty-eight hours after I got there. I was scheduled for a whole itinerary of conferences. And when I did return I went directly to the cops and said OK, I'm one of the 121. You've arrested the others, arrest me.

No wait, I'm sorry, I confused the 121 with the network. Jeanson has a feeling that you feel guilty about not testifying at the trial of his network.

Ah, that's something else. Although the dates are almost identical.[3] Jeanson had asked me to testify at the trial, but I couldn't, so I wrote a letter, and it was read. It made a lot of noise. The next day, the OAS marched in Montparnasse shouting, "Shoot Sartre, shoot Sartre!" Anyway, after the war, and everyone was amnestied, Jeanson got a job as head of the cultural center of Chalon, near Bordeaux, and that separated us, not only because of the distance, but also because culture or not, it's working for the government. But, as you know, he came last weekend to read stuff and talk to Castor and me about his book. He stayed two hours.

He told me you were going to give him five interviews to help him along.

What! He made that up. I'm not going to give him a single one. I did help him last weekend. Well, I shouldn't be nasty: he fought well during the war, very well for Algeria, and ran *Les Temps Modernes* just fine. But on Algeria, let's not overstate our effect, compared to books like *The Question* [by Henri Alleg], and many others.[4]

But the French believed Alleg, and the others who also documented French atrocities, were telling the truth. In the United States, before the My Lai massacre was made public, we published scores of articles and even pictures we had managed to get about U.S. atrocities in Vietnam. Not only did the vast majority of Americans not believe us, but our mainstream media would never publish them. The self-censorship of our media is absolutely appalling, but worse, I feel, is the gullibility of the ordinary citizen.

How do you explain that?

Partly because they've never been occupied by a foreign power that then mistreated them. Partly because of that old puritan dogma that the successful are closer to god. But the main reason, I think, is because our ordinary citizen is scared. He's told from the day he's born that free enterprise, laissez-faire capitalism, is the best system. Struggle on your own, he's told, and you've got a good chance of becoming a millionaire like him, and her, and Joe and Jane, on and on. The ordinary Joe in the United States dreams long-range plans, repeats ad infinitum that America is the greatest country in the world because his dreams can come true, but lives day to day scared to his core.

I actually felt that in Tocqueville's book on America. Every commentator claims that it praises America, and considering what Europe was like at the time, there's no doubt he thought America was much, much better. But by stressing that money dominated the minds of all and that crass individualism and market capitalism had become the principle of the new culture, he also exposed the dangers to come, where the society's most flagrant behavior would be, as you say in America, dog eat dog. At the time, of course, his book was a formidable democratic cry for equality. But once our obscene aristocratic culture collapsed because of our constant rebellions, which could not happen without class unity, we moved closer to respect for the common man as part of a class. We have a long ways to go, and because of the power of America, which of course will do everything it can to stop us, we may never get there. But one thing is clear in Europe, all of Europe, east and west, that all human beings must live under a system that guarantees life, liberty, and the pursuit of happiness. That's your famous slogan, but life means health, and you don't guarantee it. Liberty means education, and you don't guarantee it; you have it but have it only for a price. And the pursuit of liberty means security, and that, as you just said, most Americans certainly don't have. In France, we simplify it all under the slogan Liberty, Equality, and Fraternity. The key is fraternity. Living together, not crass individualism leading to dog eat dog. OK, no country in Europe has established a regime that can turn that slogan into reality. But every politician knows that it is the ideal, and must at least pretend to strive for its realization.

Not so in the United States. But tell me, why didn't you accept the Nobel Prize and say all that, then give the money to the Swedish group Clarté, which is composed of Maoist revolutionaries?

I thought about that. But it would mean recognizing the whole show. I oppose any writer getting a prize from an elite, because as we agree, the value system of that elite, as much in Sweden as in America, is based on values we oppose, values which must be destroyed.

But a Nobel is never refused, only the money.

True, I'm listed as a recipient in all their mail, and most bios say "Nobel for Literature (refused)." I made some comment that the prize was too political, you know, after [Boris] Pasternak got it, so I had to abide . . .

What comes across as your reason for turning down the money is an individualistic act, one of personal honor, so to speak.

I agree. There's a mixed message there. When Lena came to Paris she gave me hell for that . . .

They let her come?

Part of a delegation, an exchange of writers, as their translator. During that early Khrushchev period, they were fairly lax. She stayed with me, not in their hotel, and that didn't seem to bother anyone.

Could she stay with you when you were in Russia, in a hotel?

No one seemed to care very much. She had to sneak past that big mama on each floor, but they knew, and no one said anything.

Do you still communicate with her?

Now and then. I send her books, mine and others, she sends me a nice letter thanking me and telling me what's going on. She got into a bit of trouble, nothing serious, for signing a letter in favor of [Yuli] Daniel and [Andrei] Sinyavsky.

She didn't want to stay in France?

She has a child and a mother to take care of. She does all right as a translator. The ideal for her was to get married, and she did ask me, because then she could stay six months in Paris and six months with her child and mother.

You refused? I thought you cared about her a great deal.

Oh, I sure did, but to be married, even only six months out of a year, complicated my life much too much.

Wouldn't it have been viewed by everyone here as a political act on your part?

Not by everyone. First of all, it would not have been good for her. In Russia, she has an excellent reputation as a translator, and earns well. Here, basically she would be a kept woman. Then there's Arlette, Michelle, and Wanda; they would be furious.

They knew you were having an affair with Lena, didn't they?

Yes, and I gather they may have been a bit jealous. But if I married her and lived with her here in Paris, boy! their jealousy could topple the Eiffel Tower.

When you talk about your women, you never mention Castor, as if you never had an intimate relationship with her.

First of all, we stopped having sex in 1947. Second, as you know, we had a different kind of relationship. There was no question that we were bound to each other for life, what we called our necessary relationship. We both had affairs all our lives, the kind we called contingent.

But they weren't of the same intensity, were they? Like Castor with Lanzmann; that too lasted almost their whole life.

No, not sexually; they stayed very close, and they still are. She's still very much involved with him, like right now financing a documentary he's making [*Shoah*], but they're not lovers anymore.

And you were never jealous of Lanzmann?

Never. As I told you, I was never jealous. Well, I did tell you that, but it was wrong. I was jealous of Olga. We were a very nice threesome, when Castor was teaching at Rouen, she, Olga, and me.

That's Castor's first novel, *She Came to Stay*.

Olga was Castor's student and around then Bost was one of my students. Well, I got jealous when Olga started an affair with Bost. I was jealous for six months. I discussed it with Castor, but her understanding and empathy didn't help. That was the time when I was being followed by more crabs than ever. It was all part of a serious crisis in my life, the first of two, right?

The second being '58 and the coup by de Gaulle.

Right. I was giving up my youth. I felt that very strongly. From now on, shit, nothing but responsibilities, obligations, seriousness. Terrible. And that lovely creature Olga going off with my student. I never said anything, of course. I mean to Olga or Bost. But then, I found a way out: Olga's sister, Wanda. They resembled each other, and Wanda was younger, all the better. The woman I loved had turned me down, so I got her spitting image, younger yet.

You're talking about possessiveness.

Yep, and Wanda was only twenty-two! Great for my ego.

You had no doubt that she would fall into your arms? I mean, she was, she is still, as I discovered last week when I had dinner with her, rather flighty, spontaneous, irascible, and unpredictable, just as you describe her in *Troubled Sleep*.

Do you know that almost all critics and biographers think that Ivich represents Olga? Shows how stupid they are.

Well, come on, everybody knows about your affair with Olga, because of Castor's novel. But no one has written about Wanda, so it's a sort of natural mistake. Anyway, knowing her, Wanda that is, I'm amazed that you could be so sure that she would fall for you, and stay fallen until now.

I just assumed that she was so pleased to be with me that if she was with another she would be unhappy. I still feel that. So I have never been jealous again. That's how I felt with Dolores, and Lena.

What about Michelle?

She ends up part of my second crisis in '58.

Wait, you were with her earlier, I remember very well, since I too fell in love with her in '54 when you asked me to take her dancing at La Cave du Vieux Colombier.

Oh yes, when you asked Sidney Bechet to play "When the Saints Go Marching In," and you and Michelle went crazy jitterbugging. She told me all about that. But you never made a move on her.

I was a nice bourgeois kid then, remember? Writing a dissertation on you, my mentor—how could I possibly move in on your girl, that is if she would have me anyway, which of course I doubted. But that was spring '54; I was twenty-two.

Too bad. It would have made a nice story, eh? Anyway, my crisis was in '58. I hated my life, I hated France, I hated Michelle. I would have hated anyone who was with me. First, because we had learned that our army was using torture in Algeria. Second, that neanderthal had seized power. Third, I had to stop writing the _Critique_ in order to denounce the torture . . .

That's why you wrote _The Condemned of Altona?_

Yes, and I hated it, because I was writing something against France, against the values that every Frenchmen should cherish.

You hated the play while you were writing it?

Yes, like Flaubert hated Madame Bovary. And to make matters worse, I had promised Evelyne that she could star in my next play, so I knew she would think this was it, but by then I had finished with her in my head—well, in my body too, since I was now impotent with her all the time. I hated the play for that, too.

Did you also want to end your relationship with Michelle then?

No no. I hated her because she was part of my life and I hated my life, living under that pig, having to accept torture as normal.

Castor told me she was really worried about you then. You were drinking much too much, she said, and taking speed.

She was worried, but I wasn't. I took corydrane for three or four months.

She claimed you were always talking about what happens if one of us survives the other, stuff like that.

Ha! It was she who kept bringing that up. I guess because she thought I was going to drop dead. I was pretty bad. Arlette told me that I wrote her a letter in which I placed one line on top of the other.

When did you start up with Arlette?

In '55 I think.

And when did you adopt her as your daughter?

Let's see, I came back from Russia in '62, then Lena came to Paris in '63, and the OAS was full steam then, so I guess I adopted her in '64.

Was that when they set off the first bomb?

No, it was on my way to Russia, in '62. I had spent the night at Castor's and had ordered a taxi from there to go to Orly [Airport], so we stopped at 42 [rue Bonaparte, where Sartre was living with his mother] on the way to see the damage. Not much. I had already rented a couple of rooms nearby. So we moved my mother, she was fine, and I went off. The irony was that the rooms were in a house where there lived an Algerian tailor who refused to pay the OAS—you know, they were gangsters, extortionists—so he asked the police for help, and they sent a whole bunch of cops, from seven in the morning to eight in the evening, but none during the night, when the OAS blew up all their bombs. So after another one there, Gisèle Halimi [Sartre's lawyer] found us an apartment in the fancy 16th [arrondissement], right on the Seine at Quai Branly. And the irony was that upstairs lived two OAS bombers. So as long as they didn't see us, we were ultra safe. But they said they were going to blow up Castor, so she called the Sorbonne and asked for volunteers. Scores showed up right away. They stayed at the windows and at the phone in shifts, and nothing happened.

But you had placed your mother in a hotel, right? Meaning you knew it was dangerous times.

Of course.

But it didn't affect you?

Not at all. By then my crisis was over. The war with Algeria was over, but

we were at war inside France. The cops wanted to try us for treason and the right wanted to blow us up. That kind of situation is the best medicine to get out of depression.

Did it get you to stop drinking, and taking drugs, and how about smoking?

I've never stopped drinking, but I did cut down, mind you, just to please Castor, because the alcohol was not what brought me down, or up for that matter; it was the situation in France, in the world. The drugs, yeah, I stopped. Smoking was later, and I didn't stop completely, as you know. I limit myself to one cigarette per hour.

That's caused some funny moments, like with Girardin, you remember, Jean-Claude Girardin, the student I sent you who was writing his dissertation on your theory of the state?

Oh yes, brilliant guy. I really enjoyed talking with him.

Well, when he left you we met for lunch and he told me that he must have really bored you, because you kept looking at your watch.

Ha ha ha! Did you tell him I was waiting to smoke? Arlette and Michelle sometimes forget why I keep looking at my watch and get mad at me.

But the root cause of that was health, right? Were you suddenly aware that alcohol, drugs, smoking, could kill you prematurely?

No, I did all that for Castor. She was preoccupied with dying—not death, dying. Her research for that book of hers on old age showed her that old folks don't think so much about death, but about the process of dying, and it wasn't true about me—I never thought or think about death or dying, but it was true with her, until Sylvie [Le Bon de Beauvoir], that is.

How did Sylvie change things?

By [Beauvoir's] adopting her as her daughter. We both like Sylvie a lot, and Castor had an intimate relationship with her as well. She's twenty-nine, so Castor knows that she'll be able to handle her affairs for a long time. She will leave her everything. It takes a lot off her mind. She can be more spontaneous now, more committed.

Did adopting Arlette allow you to be more committed? More hot, so to speak?

I think I've always been both, I mean hot and cold. In other words, I often wrote very angry, very violent articles, but coldly.

Like on the Basque trials, which I just reread in *Situations*. Boy, you were fuming.

Exactly. Who could possibly not hate Franco yet again for that trial and executions? Yet I was very cold inside when I wrote it, very composed, calculating. I wanted to be extremely effective.

Were you cold when you wrote that violent attack on the United States for executing the Rosenbergs?

No, I was hot then. I remember, I was in Venice when I heard the news. I immediately called *Libération* and asked if they wanted an article. When they said yes, right away if you can, I sat down and dashed it off as if I was condemned to die in five minutes. I then phoned it in. Both Castor and Lanzmann—we were together in Venice—thought it was bad, because it was so violent, but I didn't, and it turns out no one else did.

Oh no, it was great. It is still quoted by militants everywhere, in fact by everyone who remembers the great demonstrations, by their children who have been told that the execution of the Rosenbergs lost the United States respect all over the world. Do you know there are still all sorts of conservative writers trying to prove that, yes indeed, the Rosenbergs were guilty, academics who claim to be "objective," doing their best to try to save America's soul. The Rosenbergs' execution remains one of the darkest spots, proof, of the lack of justice in the United States, and your article is still quoted whenever the subject arises.

I'm very glad. Those murders turned my stomach, and convinced me never to trust Americans again.

Yet you didn't keep that "hot" attitude when you wrote other political explosions. Like your attack on the government's crucifixion of Henri Martin. Yet you continued to judge the work of others according to your criteria of hot and cold.

Cold inside, hot outside. Meaning that one must know well and calmly what one is going to say, then express it with the full vigor it demands.

You did that in your criticism of art, too. Like Titian and Tintoretto.

Titian is cold; I don't like him. Tintoretto, Picasso, Giacometti, your father, are all hot.

That's the point of your discussion with Fernando at the Mondrian show, in your novel, when he says Mondrian doesn't ask difficult questions?

Exactly.

Can you make a case that the "hot" painters are also all leftists?

I haven't studied the question, but let's see. Yeah, Titian ass-licked his masters, Tintoretto hated the system, Picasso was a communist, Giacometti

couldn't express his politics or he would get deported back to his native Switzerland, but he was certainly with us, a good friend. Your father, of course.

Velázquez?

Hum . . . he was Jewish in an anti-Semitic country.

Naw, doesn't fit. How about Nicolas de Staël?

I know, in 1939, before he joined the Foreign Legion, he made his living as a police informer and ratted on your father. But you have to consider his background, the son of a Russian general, a Baron von something. And he committed suicide. That excuses him, yes? No. OK, doesn't work. End of a new, thankfully unstated, theory.

November 1972

GERASSI: I hear the maos are planning a daily newspaper.

SARTRE: They're planning one for next year, February.

They have the money?

Yes. I don't know from where.

And they're calling for a boycott of the elections?

Yes. They hated Secours Rouge. Because it was composed of petty intellectuals, which is precisely what most of the maos in Paris are. Anyway, now they want to launch committees all over France called Truth and Justice, organized "at the base," meaning by and with the proletariat, which of course none of them are. The whole Maoist movement, it seems to me, is falling apart.

And where is Pierre in all that?

He's the only one left of the old guard. At _La Cause du Peuple,_ the only ones remaining are a bunch of young girls. Curious. And Pierre. I like Pierre, but . . .

Can't you talk to him, I mean seriously about the whole business and his anti-democratic role in it? It's because of his dictatorial manner that they've abandoned ship, no?

Undoubtedly. No, I can't find out what he really wants. He's very closed.

Yet the *gauchistes* [what the media called those who were to the left of the classic left] are still the main left-wing opposition to the system, the only ones who refuse to play the electoral game, get licenses to demonstrate, permission to publish, and so on.

Absolutely. You know, while you were gone, [Pierre] Overney [a GP demonstrator who was killed during a strike at the Renault plant after being shot by one of the company's officers] was buried at Père Lachaise [Cemetery]. No less than 250,000 followed his casket to its place in the cemetery. But when the GP called for a rally by the site, only two thousand showed up. They then created a new group called New Popular Resistance, which claimed it would kidnap the killer of Overney and try him clandestinely. Which of course never happened. That's the sad story of the gauchistes. Otherwise there have been some great rallies and demos staged by feminist groups. There was a very successful one defending a woman who performed an illegal abortion on a seventeen-year-old. [The girl's] mother was also charged because she publicly claimed that she had found the abortionist. She said she had asked her daughter, Do you want the child or no, and when the girl answered no, she arranged the abortion. Both the abortionist and the mother were found guilty, but thanks to the marches and protests, they got suspended sentences.

So who are your political friends now? You still see Pierre, I know, but you're not very comfortable discussing politics with him. Who else?

You.

Thanks, but I mean on a regular basis. You can't talk with Lanzmann. The young guys at *Les Temps Modernes* are great, but they don't quite fit, do they? I mean personally. There's Gorz, but he now spends most of his time in the country. There's Claire Etcherelli, who runs *Les Temps* day in and day out, but she's busy writing a new novel. I read her last one last month; it's really very good. I guess there's Bost, of course. Who else? How about your old resistance comrades; do you ever see them? Aragon?

I saw a lot of him, obviously, during the resistance. But also after, he and his wife, Elsa Triolet, often for dinner. We liked them, Castor and I. I also kind of flirted with Elsa; she was a bit of a coquette, and I liked that. We had invited them the day Stalin died, or was killed, and he showed up an hour late, all upset. He was gibbering. I couldn't understand him, and I thought he hated Stalinism, privately of course. Finally, it came out: he thought it would get much worse without Stalin, that whoever would take over would be much worse. And he claimed he was right when years later Brezhnev did take over.

He was a funny commie. Publicly very partyish. Privately very liberal. He told us a lot of party gossip, like that Marty was a real cop, not just in Spain, representing the Comintern, but here, in France, always reporting folks whom he thought were deviating from party doctrine. He told us that the party didn't like the way Francis Ponge wrote, his style, his prose, so they kicked him out. Stuff like that. But after Elsa died two year ago, Aragon came out of the closet, marched in gay pride rallies decked out in a gorgeous pink suit, and stopped seeing us. Too bad. He was fun, even more fun once she was no longer around to terrorize him. Otherwise, let's see. The Yugoslavs. Dedijer. He's great, and our dinner with him the other night was fantastic, wasn't it?

First time I've seen you so silent.

Well, you and he were doing all the talking. Ha! Otherwise, let's see. No, I never stayed friends with any of the *Lettres Françaises* group. Not those who stayed in the party. Those folks are absolutely impossible to talk to, and too rude, too pedantic, too know-it-all. Not like . . .

I know, the Italians.

And the Cubans, and even the Russians.

Simonov?

No, but Solzhenitsyn and Ehrenburg, of course. And the Cubans.

By the way, your book on Cuba has never appeared in French. Why?

It wasn't meant to. I had broken relations with *L'Express*, and there was no *Libération* yet, right? This is 1960, so I asked, via Lanzmann, to ask Lazareff if he wanted articles describing my trip. Sure, he said, and printed them all, eighteen I think, mostly very favorable to Cuba. I remember one in which he never touched Che Guevara's quote, which is now famous: "We are not Marxists, but it is not our fault if reality is Marxist." Nor did he contradict in another article my piece on *La Coubre,* the Belgian ship full of ammunition, which I said was blown up in Havana harbor by U.S. frogmen. And mind you, there were French sailors murdered in that blast.

You weren't there during the missile crisis, were you?

No, I was right here, in Paris.

Did the French go bananas—I mean, convinced we were an inch from World War III?

Not at all. First of all, most folks here thought that Cuba had every right to buy whatever self-defense weapons it wanted, especially since America was so bellicose. Second, we all knew that Khrushchev would never risk war, and that he would back down after Kennedy's speech.

What about you, personally?

I was very unhappy that the Russians did give in. I was opposed to what was beginning to look like peaceful coexistence. I had met Fanon by then, and I had been convinced by his argument that peaceful coexistence would be a disaster for the Third World, that it would mean no money for development. I could see that America, which even before peaceful coexistence always blackmailed Third World leaders to join the anti-communist phobia or get no money, and anti-communism meant not only kill your communists, which Nasser for example did, but vote as we tell you or else. There was no better example than the Aswan Dam, was there? No, I hoped that the missile crisis would lead to more confrontations, to create a rivalry between Russia and America, which would help the Third World develop. But because Khrushchev gave in, America felt free to invade the Dominican Republic and of course Vietnam. I remember Fanon telling me then, Russia has accepted its role in history as a second power. That means America is free to be militarily imperialist now, and we are going to suffer for it, badly. The money imperialism of Roosevelt is over, he said, or rather, it will now be accompanied by guns.

Speaking of Roosevelt's imperialism, have you heard of "lend-lease"?

That was America's program to aid those countries fighting the Axis, specifically helping Russia, right?

You heard about all the guns and cannons and stuff the United States gave them, right, and the food and tanks and so on we gave England, how generous the United States was.

Yes, we did hear about that, and it's true, isn't it?

It's true, all right—for 5 percent. Of all that money called lend-lease, the Allies got 5 percent, that's all. The rest was used to pay plantation owners in Latin America, the latifundistas, to stop growing food and instead plant coffee or bananas or sugar. It's the coffee agreement, the sugar, the cocoa, the soya agreements. Guarantees the rich their endless fortune, while making the member Latin American countries dependent on the United States for its food. Nice little trick, heh?

I had no idea. But it doesn't surprise me. I read that before the war, Brazil was totally self-sufficient in foodstuffs, but by '46 it was importing $500 million from the United States. Now I know why. Good businessman, that Roosevelt. But of course, we all know that he saved capitalism in America. It was on the edge, wasn't it, after the crash?

Yep. And the stupid capitalists in the United States hate him as if he

were a socialist, because one of the ways he avoided a revolution was by giving labor many of its rights, like the right to organize, to strike, the closed
shop—all those things saved capitalism. Still, he did help Mexico get its fair
shake from its oil.

**But even there, wasn't that because he foresaw the possibility of a
world war that would cut down on imported oil?**

Sure, but nevertheless, when Cárdenas nationalized Mexico's oil and
offered a pittance, whatever it was, I've forgotten, to Standard Oil, Exxon today, and Rockefeller demanded that the United States invade Mexico, Roosevelt said, Let's let the World Court decide, and he abided by the court decision, which ruled that Standard had been cheating Mexico by millions, just
as Cárdenas had documented. That's the only time the United States has
ever obeyed a judgment it did not like. On the other hand, Roosevelt made
the war with Japan inevitable.

How?

His ambition was to make the United States a "two-ocean power," as
he said. The only obstacle was Japan, which was developing so fast, buying
the raw materials from all over Asia. So Roosevelt kept putting embargos on
Japan, on the excuse that it was building a war machine, which it was. Steel
ingots, steel rods, and then oil were put under embargos. Japan has none of
that. So it decided to get it from Manchuria, then China, finally the oil from
Indonesia, which floats on oil. Not all Japanese leaders wanted all-out war.
[Isoroku] Yamamoto, the naval chief of the attack on Pearl Harbor, tried to
get a truce immediately after the attack, on which by the way he refused to
send the final wave of attack planes. His condition was simply open seas and
free market. Roosevelt refused, of course.

**America is always in favor of free trade when it benefits America, and
never when it does not.**

Correct. But to get back to what we were talking about, friends, Ehrenburg, you know that a lot of folks, liberals, even leftists, think he survived because he was a fink. You obviously didn't.

**No. He went as far as he could, always at the limit. You can't condemn
him for that. You know, Lena's family was Jewish, and her husband was sent
to a camp. She was then dismissed from the university where she taught. She
went to Ehrenburg and he employed her as his secretary. That was very risky
for both, but he stuck to his guns until Stalin was gone. He got hell from Khrushchev for it too, but that's all.**

You didn't know her then, did you?

No, I met her as my translator when I went to Russia in '62. That was a fairly decent period there.

But not in France?

Politically? It was awful. We were in limbo. On the one hand, de Gaulle agreed to a cease-fire in Algeria; on the other hand, his police were vicious in putting down demonstrations. On the one hand, a good majority of the people said yes to Algerian independence in the referendum of that year; on the other de Gaulle wanted a constitutional amendment to allow the president to be chosen by popular vote, which we interpreted as his move to stay in power all his life, the nonhereditary king of France. I spent a lot of time at the Sorbonne in those days, talking with students who were very disappointing then. Half were impressed by the structuralists. I tried to read their stuff, which was incredibly boring. Have you read [Claude] Lévi-Strauss? Besides being wrong, he is so boring, I can't understand how any student can claim to have read him. As if that wasn't bad enough, I spent the rest of my time at the Sorbonne with members of the Che-Lumumba cell of the CP, and they had nothing new or interesting to offer, except to repeat the stupidities issued by Thorez and [Laurent] Casanova [then a member of the CP Central Committee in charge of "Intellectual Endeavors"], before he was expelled. That period, until Vietnam woke us up, was dreadful. But then, when we saw what America was doing to those poor peasants in Vietnam, we finally became alive. The Vietnamese woke me up, and our students made me political, made me understand at last that everything is political.

May 1973

GERASSI: So we've both been traveling quite a lot since we last met.[1] How did you enjoy Japan?

SARTRE: I can't answer except with stupidities, like this was beautiful, that was crowded. I mean, I understood nothing. We were taken everywhere. We met union leaders, socialist party chiefs, deputies, but so what? Everything by translation. Just fancy tourists. Israel was different. Everybody, almost, speaks English, which Castor understands quite well and I manage, and many speak French. Also we had many old friends there, with whom we could ask embarrassing questions.

And?

Doomed. The hope of one Jewish-Arab state is dead. If for no other reason than that Israel will never return to the Palestinians their possessions, their land, their houses, their belongings. Finished.

Doesn't some of the left still strive for such a state?

No. Well, some, but no one listens to them. The Israelis want a Jewish state, even the left. Just like Lanzmann.

I have trouble with that, especially "like Lanzmann." He's an atheist, like me. He does not practice Jewish customs, as I don't. He doesn't speak Hebrew or Yiddish, and neither do I. There is nothing Jewish about him, and under no circumstances would he ever go live in Israel. He's totally French.

But he doesn't feel comfortable being French.

So why doesn't he go live in Israel?

He may not be comfortable there either—who knows. But he feels close to Israel somehow, even if he doesn't know a thing about how to be Jewish. But he thinks about it, which you don't. Besides, you're only half Jewish, and your Sephardic father didn't even know what Yom Kippur is.

Come on, he was Chaim Weizmann's personal bodyguard for two years.

That was part of Fernando's political activism, not an act of Jewish solidarity. By the way, Lanzmann's film is ready; he's gone to Cannes to show it.

At the festival?

No, on the side. Anyway, forget Lanzmann. The point is that I do not see a solution, since what exists now is the right facing the right, because no matter what Mapam [the Labor Party, then in power in Israel] says it stands for, it is a right-wing political party, and of course the Arab governments are all right-wing.

You've given up on the left in Israel?

It has no power. I found that most Israelis are reactionary and racists. As far as I could tell, there's only Matzpen, and those are the kids mostly. No, I see no possibility for the foreseeable future, so Israel will survive only if it has American help.

You're in favor of that?

Yes, just as I approve of the Palestinian resistance.

Including its resort to terror?

The poor and weak have no other weapon.

You end up on both sides, so to speak. Does that not contradict the position of the maos?

Sure. But we're allied on so many other points; they try to overlook my position on Israel-Palestine.

So you expect that the situation will continue as is, Israeli bombs and tanks against rocks and occasional suicide bombers forever? Forget one democratic state, but also no more hope for two equal states?

I doubt it. Maybe in fifty years after another war.

So your trip was a disappointment?

But not, surprisingly. I liked Nasser a lot. It's easy to talk to him, and

argue, and ask embarrassing questions. That's not the case with Israeli officials. They repeat exactly what the official line is, almost by rote. They have no flexibility. Whereas Nasser comes across as really caring. He is afraid that a new war is inevitable but dreads it. He really doesn't want one.

Did you like wandering around in Egypt?

Yes and no. It can be very hot and humid. And there's tremendous poverty, though you get the feeling that Nasser is really trying to help his people. Also, Arabs are easier to communicate with. They say some very formal official statements, then switch to wonderfully personal reactions to what you say. Of course, Egypt is not very Arab. And they all speak English, thanks to British imperialism. By the way, Eldridge Cleaver tried to reach me. Do you know why?

He got edged out of Algeria by both his Panthers and the government. He is trying to get a permit to stay here, and he thought you might help. I gave him the names and phones of various lawyer friends, but he's a typical American who thinks that it's contacts that work. I didn't give him your number, though.

I know. He called my secretary, who told him I was away, which I was. But I can't help him.

Giscard [Valéry Giscard d'Estaing] might. Eldridge is having an affair with Catherine Schneider, or whatever her name is, Giscard's mistress; so I told him to ask her to intercede with Giscard.

He's only a minister, but maybe he could. He'll run for president next year, then if he wins, perhaps.[2] I hear Cleaver claims that the only solution for America now is armed struggle.

Cleaver changes with the wind, but usually after the wind has calmed down. Armed struggle makes no sense now in the United States. But I think his reasoning is that you can help him get residency in France. You support the maos. The maos are in favor of armed struggle. He is too. That's his reasoning.

Well, he's right on that score—that is, the hard core group of maos still advocate armed struggle, but what they really want is illegal activities.

Do you support that?

In the sense of occupations of empty apartments, spontaneous strikes, marches without permits, and so on, sure, but armed struggle today, I don't know what that means exactly.

It doesn't really make sense, does it? Armed struggle in France, in

Italy, in Germany. Perhaps in Spain against Franco, but what chance would it have today?

What is important is keeping the notion of illegality alive. And that is hard, with the CP totally enmeshed in the system, and acting totally legally. Yet the proletariat is hot now. No one forgets how close they came to an actual overthrowing of the bourgeoisie in '68. But we have to wait for a new generation of rebels, a new new left, because our "gauchistes" are not a new left, just a revamping of the old left without the communists but still thinking like the communists.

You, personally, didn't think that the kids were even that in '68, did you?

I saw their rebellion as a cultural struggle. I felt I had to support them, but I never imagined it would gather so much support with workers. Do you know that the strikes of '68 were bigger and more important than the one of '36, which brought about the Popular Front? Paris was fantastic in May '68. There were no cars, no Métros, no buses, no gas, everyone walked to wherever they were going. No newspapers except some student broadsheets. Even *Le Monde* failed to appear for a few days. And on May 27 or 28, I forget now, the two great marches, the millions of students and the million of workers, bumped into each other at Denfert, I think, and united. Only then did May '68 become clearly political, not cultural.

But not for you, huh?

Not yet. I was still caught up in Cohn-Bendit telling the prefect that they didn't give a damn about his swimming pool, they wanted to make love. I saw him quite a bit after that; he interviewed me for some radio program. He was far from being brilliant. I didn't like him very much.

But in May '68, you continued to work on your *Flaubert*. Yet you did go to the Sorbonne.

Because they asked me.

You had supported them on some radio broadcast, and they knew that. They received you better than any other intellectual, although there was still a distance, wasn't there?

On both parts. I tried to bridge the gap, once I realized that they were neither communist nor Trotskyist. Oh, some were, but the majority were anarchist. Cohn-Bendit was anar to some extent. I've always had a strong anar side myself, as you know. I found out that they were against all sorts of cultural, or let's say educational, policies that I was opposed to. We related on

that. For example, the requirements on dissertations, which were always horrendous, a way for the establishment to force students to accept its views and defend them in their work. Or the habit of magisterial lectures. They want to be free to interrupt and disagree.

You were alone in your support. Why didn't "the family" join you? Castor did not even accompany you to the Sorbonne.

Castor is not very political. She supports my views, but passively. Bost is in favor of direct action, period. He just wants to put a bomb there, and go. Otherwise, he's too lazy to be active, march and yell, that's not his way. He wouldn't last a week under a socialist regime. Pouillon is completely with us, but quietly; he can't say or do anything publicly as long as he is editor of the minutes of the Chamber of Deputies. He summarizes what they say, edits it, and has it published every day; a very well-paying job. He'll be with us if the day finally arrives. Gorz will analyze, dissect, and write about what we do, but he won't go talk to students. Michelle would have gone with me, if I had asked her. But you have to realize that I make all my decisions alone, first, then I explain them. Castor can make me change my mind, sometimes. But only after I have made my decisions. I never discuss the issue first. I decide, then I discuss.

Not very collectivist! And Pierre?

He came to find me. With a group of his maos. He asked that I take the editorship of *La Cause*. That was a Sunday, I remember, because I ended up late for lunch with Castor and you. So I invited him for lunch another day, and we had a very nice talk. I still like him.

You stay friends with people you like, even if they are political enemies, but you break with folks who waver just a bit off your line, if you don't like them. Your attachments, in the final analysis, are always moral.

Your conclusion is correct, but not the premise. I don't stay friends with enemies. Lanzmann is not an enemy; we disagree on Israel, true, but if a revolution came to France, and there were only two sides, we'd be on the same side. Same with [Pierre] Leroy . . .

The priest who was a prisoner with you?

He's no longer a priest. He got married to a librarian. We don't see each other very much; he doesn't live in Paris. But we didn't have a break. Merleau broke with me, not me with him. Same with Camus. Koestler, yes, I don't want to see him, ever. But my judgments are not based on politics, but on whether I can trust the person, personally. And I agree, that's a moral question. With

Pierre, I have no doubt that I can trust him, no matter where he ends up politically. Same with Arlette. Don't forget that I define trust not just as someone who would or would not turn against me, verbally. To me, trust is if in an emergency I can count on that person. Castor thinks the same way on that.

I agree.

I know. That's everyone in the family.

What about your break with Aron?

Did you read his book?

Yes, but I'll bet you didn't.

Ha ha! But that's because I can't see very well now. You saw Maheu yesterday?

Yes. Very short, because he told me nothing. I mean, he said nothing but nice anecdotes. When I brought up Castor, he waved his hand in such a way that I understood he didn't want to talk about her, but he did, in the anecdotes, describing the happy days together, the fun roaming around Paris. He knew that I knew about Castor [and him being lovers], but we both made believe I knew nothing. But you know, he had tears in his eyes when he mentioned her. As far as you were concerned, he said that since he became head of UNESCO, you had sort of crossed him off, that you never get together anymore. But tell me about your eye, what did the doctor say?

The tension is 30. Much too high. I have to take drops and all sorts of things. In general, I've become a pharmaceutical suitcase. So tell me about Aron. You interviewed him also when you got back, yes? How did it go?

Very interesting. He intimated that you two broke because of four reasons: first, because of the lecture he gave at the Sorbonne criticizing Merleau.

I remember that he gave a stupid lecture, yes, and I could have criticized him for that, but we didn't break over it. I didn't go.

Ah yes! That's what he held against you, that not only you didn't go, but you also blasted him for it.

I may have said something, but it was based on reports from people I trust, like either Bost or Pouillon, both of whom did go.

Second, that you gave a lecture titled "Is Nietzsche a Philosopher?" in which you stole his idea on contingency.

Ha! I was in my last year at L'Ecole Normale, and it was a lecture to Normale students, though granted, many did come, as did a lot from the lycées, from hypo-khâgne, where it was advertised. So he was there. He had graduated already, but he came for some reason. But I had no idea what he thought. We had very little contact then, and we certainly weren't great friends like I was with Nizan, who by the way couldn't stand Aron. And contingency, ha! That was my favorite subject then. I even wrote a song about it. I still remember one couplet: "I bring boredom, I bring forgetfulness."

The third reason was that Castor didn't like him.

That is certainly true. But my friendship with him had nothing to do with Castor. I don't think I liked his wife or vice-versa either, but that didn't affect our relationship. And the fourth?

That you two were very close friends but it was an intellectual friendship, and it broke when you two went in different directions.

Well, that's sort of correct, except we were never that close. Well, maybe we were, but not like I was with Nizan, or Maheu for that matter. We never went whoring together, or got royally drunk. We were very close intellectually for a while, but as you know, my attachments are more emotional. If I like someone, I will continue liking him even if he's a fascist, as Nizan was before he went the other extreme and joined the CP. But I have to feel a real emotional bond, which I didn't quite have with Maheu—well, some, but not enough to want to keep seeing him after he went to UNESCO and all those official tuxedo shindigs. I had none with Aron. Intellectual, yes, but when it became clear that he was an idealist, philosophically speaking, while I was a rationalist, it became clear to both of us that the political consequences of those differences would finish off our relationship. And it did. He moved right, while I moved left. But his book on me is quite favorable, I'm told.

At first glance. But it's full of little innuendos meant to deflate the praise he officially lays on you. I said so in my interview and he got a bit upset. Like what? he demanded. Well, I answered, like when you say that Sartre wrote the *Critique* without having read Marx's *Grundische*, which has passages right up your alley. It wasn't yet translated into French, I replied. Well, it is now, he added; he should make the corrections. I had a hard time not laughing, because I was sure you still hadn't read it—have you?

No! Ha ha!

He asked me if I had read the *Flaubert*, and since I didn't want to get into a discussion with him on that, I said no. Neither did I, he said, so let's read it this summer and get together in September. He was very pleasant with me, and came across as genuinely respecting you, even if he thinks you're wrong.

Who else did you interview when you got back? Did you see the commies?

No, I'm seeing a bunch of them this week, including Garaudy on Wednesday.

You'll have fun with him. He's a real weirdo, you know. A communist who wants to bring it into Catholicism, or join the two. I gather you also saw Pierre.

How's the book coming along? [Sartre, Pierre Victor, and an architect and militant named Philippe Gavi had decided to record their thoughts on the need for a revolution in France. Sartre's position was moral, Victor's Marxist centralist, and Gavi's cultural.]³

We're almost finished.

How are the discussions? Any juicy arguments?

No. It goes like this: a problem is posed. Pierre states his position, though sometimes he waits till the end; then Gavi explains his, always very personally; then I state mine, usually also somewhat personally. We talk about everything, but our purpose, which is unstated except in the title of the book, is that in this world, and specifically in France, there is no way a person can genuinely find fulfillment. I can get you a photocopy of what we've done so far next week.

And when do you have time for Flaubert in all this? Everyone I know talks about your financial generosity, because you keep three women—why, by the way?—and give money to struggling writers, and to all sorts of left-wing causes, but that doesn't impress me as much as your generosity with your time, which I know is precious to you. Give me a rundown of your schedule.

As far as the women are concerned, you know, when one has a long relationship, one ends up with responsibilities. They're cumbersome, time-consuming, sometimes irritating, but I think I have to go on with them. I don't mean the money, I mean the time. OK. I get up at 9 a.m., I have breakfast with an old friend who lives nearby, that's just a habit, but fairly quick, because by 10:30 I'm at my desk, three hours. At 1:30 or 2 p.m. I have lunch, Mondays and Fridays with Michelle, Tuesdays, Wednesdays, and Saturdays with Arlette, Thursdays with Castor, Sundays with Castor and either Sylvie or, if you're around, with you. From 4:30 to 9 p.m. I work, except Fridays when I leave home at 7 p.m. to spend the evening with Wanda until midnight. I tell her I'm going home, but I spend the night at Castor's. Monday and Thursday

evenings I watch TV with Arlette. Tuesdays, Wednesdays, and Sundays with Castor, Saturdays with Castor and Sylvie.

You never spend an evening with Michelle?

No. But I call Wanda and Michelle every day at 1:30, unless I'm going to have lunch with one, and every evening at midnight.

Wow! I think I'd go crazy with such obligations.

And it was worse when Evelyne was alive—she was number four of my kept women.

So, what about vacations?

Twenty days with Arlette at Junas, near Nîmes, you know, you've been there. She doesn't know I spend any vacation time with Wanda—well, she suspects, I'm sure. Anyway, this year, Castor and Sylvie will pick me up from Arlette and take me with them to Venice, and after a few days, Wanda will come down and we'll spend fifteen days there, then I fly to Rome, where I'll stay six weeks alone, or sometimes Castor joins me, mostly writing.

You like that schedule?

No. It's mostly very boring. I enjoy writing. But as you know, I prefer to be with women than men. I see men only on business, or politics.

And the only person you never lie to is Castor.

Yes, well, now Sylvie, indirectly, since Castor tells her everything I tell her. And as you know, the important trips, like to Russia or Egypt or Brazil, at least the first ones, before I establish my own contacts there, I always go with Castor. And to the big rallies or demonstrations, Castor and often Michelle go with me. But the routine is like I said, and not exciting at all.

What about the rest of the family, you never see them? Bost? Pouillon?

Maybe once every two or three weeks, either at Castor's or at an editorial meeting of *Les Temps Modernes*, but those are held at Castor's too.

What about Olga?

No, never, not since she had that affair with Bost when she was with me and I got really mad. All that is past, but we never see each other anymore, well, except when I bump into her at Castor's. Vlado Dedijer just called me; he's in town for three days and told me he'd like to see you. He's at his usual hotel, he said.

OK, sure, he's very sympatico. Crazy but sympathetic. Are you going to see him?

I guess so. I like him a lot, but it gets complicated. He had an affair with Arlette, maybe still does, so he ends up wanting to see us both. It's perfectly normal for him, but for her, and for me because of her, it's sort of awkward. But yes, I'll see him. He's on his way to America to give some lectures or teach or something. Of all my friends, Vlado is the only one who has read the *Critique,* besides you and Castor, of course, and you because you have to, right? Ha ha.

OK, let's deal with it a bit. Your "group-in-fusion" is fairly easy to pinpoint in history. It's the Parisians who charged the Bastille, it's the Communards, it's the Kronstadt mutiny sailors, it's the people of Petrograd seizing the Winter Palace, it's the students of the Cultural Revolution, the Paris students of May '68. How does the group stay in fusion? Historically, everyone becomes serialized by either its inertia or by its institutionalization. Correct? Inertia means inefficiency, which leads to defeat, like the Parisian sans-culottes who allowed an elite to talk for them and eventually to repress them. Efficiency, on the other hand, means institutionalization, which means organization, hence centralism, and again repression. So where in this process is your totalization? To avoid defeat the group-in-fusion must remain in fusion. How? The folks on the bus went home. The next day they were back in line waiting, serialized. The Kronstadt sailors rebelled again, but Lenin crushed them. The Communards did not get the support they should have and were devastated by [Adolphe] Thiers's Versaillais regulars. And so on. According to Marx, the Communards were too kind, stopped fighting to vote, in other words believed in bourgeois democracy. Had they been led by a dictatorial proletariat central committee that would have ordered the seizure of the national bank and all its assets, attacked Versailles right away, et cetera, it might have succeeded. In other words, if the group-in-fusion had been replaced by a Leninist-type party, it might have been victorious. And then what? The Prussians would have returned in full, probably helped by Britain, and instead of fifty thousand deaths, France would have suffered ten times that amount.

First of all, you imply that the process is circular, that, OK, the folks on the bus were serialized the next day and they had to start over again, as if from ground zero. But that's not the case. The sans-culottes stayed active until 1795; the Communards made possible the Congress of Tours [national congress of socialists in 1920, out of which grew the French Communist Party]; the Cultural Revolution is not dead, nor is its basic tenet, that policies are made by the people, administrators administer them; nor is the spirit of '68 dead, on the contrary, as you see yourself in your classes at Vincennes. Is there a single social science professor today who can get away with delivering magisterial lectures?

OK, the curve of progress is jagged, but it moves basically upward. Or, as Mao said, two steps forward, one step back. We started with gods, then divine kings, then hereditary monarchs, then bourgeois elites, and now that is cracking. True. I know that every century or two, more people have a say in the decision-making process that affects their lives. But if the group-in-fusion is always bound to fail, no matter how much of a residue it leaves around the edges for historians to contemplate, why risk starting again? And by the way, do you think ordinary people had more relevance in the rules for their behavior under Stalin than under [Pavel] Miliukov or [Alexander] Kerensky?[4]

Actually, I think perhaps so, for ordinary nonpolitical people, but that's another discussion, and has no bearing here. Progress is defined subjectively by the individual in situation. Objectively, we look at the context, which reflects our subjectivity. Is Cuba better off now than under Batista? You and I will say: And how! The Cuban capitalist who fled to Miami will say: Absolutely not! But even by your criterion, we're in trouble. The worker, who can now complain about his work, his neighbors, his hours on guard duty to his CDR [Committee for the Defense of the Revolution], obviously thinks he is more relevant today. The capitalist who doesn't even have a say in what his factory or his land is to be used for thinks Cuba is a total dictatorship. You and I cannot discuss anything with the capitalist. The question for us is how to maintain a group-in-fusion to its totalization, which is the permanent revolution. So far, in history, each group-in-fusion has been eventually serialized. The folks on the bus can only talk about how great it was to relate to all those strangers, the satisfaction they got from helping one another, to remember that great smile from the crippled old woman in a wheelchair when so many hands were there to get her into her home. Now, as they wait for the bus, all they can do is look around, hope to run into one of their fellow bus comrades. But they won't forget that ride, ever. And one day, as they wait for a bus with their son, they'll say, Son, you know what happened to me once? And perhaps the son will tell his classmates. And perhaps one of them will say, Why don't we organize a people's bus route; if we all join in, we can afford to charter a bus, and we'll stop to pick up all the old ladies we see waiting. And another will add . . . And so on. That's happening in China right now. Peasants, ordinary illiterate impoverished peasants, are complaining openly, talking to their neighbors for the first time about strange things, like the meaning of life, demonstrating, arguing. Look at what is happening in France. Students can no longer be taken for granted. They, too, have changed, and they are forcing their teachers to change. The government may be conservative, but it can no longer push them around. May '68 failed, yes, but it has changed France, and will continue to do so.

Beautiful. But with each failure, with each repression, a generation abandons hope. If the United States picks the right general to make the coup against [Chilean president Salvador] Allende, the general will kill a whole generation of teachers, students, and intellectuals. How many years before a new generation brings to the Casa Moneda [the presidential palace of Chile] another Allende? And will that Allende move so cautiously, out of fear, that there in fact will be no real progress? [Former president of Argentina Juan] Perón is no revolutionary, but he isn't a patsy of the United States, so if he runs next year and wins, the United States will overthrow him. You liked Nasser precisely because he is trying to help his people. That means the United States wants him out. And Africa? The United States will systematically overthrow any leader who might have a flower of socialism in his dreams, like [Kwame] Nkrumah [the first president of Ghana, deposed in a coup by the army and police in 1966]. So what kind of totalization can we talk about? Or let's put it in Marxist terms: do you envision the end of history?

Difficult. But yes, the Chinese Cultural Revolution, the May '68 events here, the constant stirrings in Africa, these are all the result of groups-in-fusion. There will be more and more, even in America. Actually there have been a lot there already, by labor, by women, by blacks, and most recently by the antiwar movement. And you can add to your definition of progress, the speed with which they come. Very slowly at first, perhaps a peasant revolt in Russia one century, a wildcat strike another, but look how fast they come now.

But most are not revolutionary; they just want some local reforms.

That's how revolutions start. The ruling classes never like to give in on anything, so they refuse even minor reforms and repress the complainers. That leads to stronger dissent, and stronger repression. Eventually, a simple statement like We don't give a damn about your swimming pool, we want to make love, leads to five million students marching on the seat of power.

But when it gets to that point, the ruling class comes to its senses and quickly does enact the reforms, and everyone goes home. And when it doesn't and the groups-in-fusion coalesce to become a revolutionary force, as in Cuba or Algeria, the groups evaporate and a ruling clique runs the country as it pleases—sometimes well, sometimes badly. I see no humanistic, no moral successful revolution as long as the United States is run by capitalists, or their henchmen, who want to dominate the world. And a humanistic moral revolution means fundamentally that each of us is relevant. That in turn means decentralization. And that means weakness, vis-à-vis the massive state power of the United States, or the USSR. Look how easily a puny dictatorship like Franco's has been able to wipe out Euskadi, the Basque autonomous movement, or the one in Catalonia.

For the time being.

I know. Eventually Franco will die, and new movements will occur. We don't always lose. But we're talking about a totalization of the group-in-fusion, that is, one where every individual counts, is relevant, where experiences are equivalent. People make policy and their elected, always recallable representatives administer those policies. Or to quote your people: "Power to the imagination!"

That is precisely the definition of the end of history.

Your group-in-fusion then is Hegel's thesis, the repressive measures of the capitalist state are his antithesis, and your totalization is his spirit or heaven, or to Marx, communism. Hegel and Marx were optimists. Are you? Every group-in-fusion has failed. Will they someday be successful? Do we need [Gilles] Deleuze and [Félix] Guattari to help us find new forms of consciousness?[5]

Absolutely not. The dialectical process does move toward the end of history, no matter how slowly we think it does, because we live so few years on this planet. But would you have thought that anyone in their right mind could have shouted such a slogan before May '68?

True. That really ended Leninism, didn't it?

You mean everywhere, not just our Stalinist CP?

I mean Leninism. After all, he did say "give me a hundred men trained in fighting the police and I will seize Russia." Efficacy! Stalin was the creation of Lenin.

Did Lenin have a choice? Attacked on all sides, "volunteer" armies from fourteen capitalist countries, two formidable White armies, a bankrupt un-

productive economy, no food, no heat, what could he do? Unless he resorts to the efficient criteria, the Bolsheviks are doomed. So the NEP [New Economic Policy], so the Cheka [secret police], so the repressions . . .

. . . and so Stalinism. Once you introduce the criteria of efficiency in the rules of society, the idiot becomes a slave, the genius a dictator.

Which is why the revolutionary thrust must remain a group.

Yet you admire Pierre, who rules the maos as a dictator.

He encourages them to discuss the tactics, the issues, and to vote on the actions they are to take.

But, whatever he claims, his view prevails, always.

I agree. I keep telling him he has to democratize. The maos must become a genuine group-in-fusion.

But they're not, which is why so many are quitting.

Then they will fail.

June 1973

GERASSI: What got into Malraux to be so vindictive against *Les Temps Modernes*? De Gaulle had not yet come to power?

SARTRE: I don't really understand. I think it was because we ran stuff by Victor Serge, and his friendship with Trotsky's wife. Malraux hated Trotskyists, probably because he was once very close to them, and he had no respect for Serge, perhaps because so many intellectuals did.[1] We published sections of his memoirs and some of his letters, including to Trotsky's wife.

And why did Gallimard cave in to Malraux's demands, when *Les Temps,* though not a review well read, was extremely popular with French intellectuals then, especially those who were neutralists?

Gaston [Gallimard, the founder of the publishing house] was terrified of Malraux. Now that Gaston is retired and [his son] Claude has taken over, plus that the old man who owned Julliard is dead, we asked to be taken back by Gallimard, and Claude agreed. He's basically right-wing but couldn't care very much.[2]

Did Claude ever intervene, or just make suggestions?

No, never. After we ran articles by the anti-psychiatrists, he got interested and published Pontalis, [David] Cooper, and [R. D.] Laing.[3]

Did you have a big argument with Pontalis?

No, merely a discussion, and he said he could not stand by that article

247

["The Man with the Tape Recorder"], and quit [the editorial board of *Les Temps Modernes*]. I did not pressure him to quit; in fact, I said he could write all the rebuttals he wanted.

You do have a knack for not alienating the opposition, like those priests, the chaplain prisoners, in your camp. I tried to see Leroy again the other day. But he's in Africa now. He had told me that you were the axis of his life, and that you abandoned him, but then not.

He's a strange fellow. In the stalag, he was very methodical and serious about his role as a priest. Then he began to have problems with his vows over women, left the church, and married, and now is separated.

You made him the commentator in your play *Bariona*. Was that not to anger the Germans?

Not at all. I thought he would make a good actor, and he did. But it wasn't the principal role. That was Bariona of course, who is really Jesus, or Jesus as a rebel. The Germans understood exactly what we were saying, to never give up the fight, but either they couldn't care less, or they thought it might give the prisoners a bit of stamina, which couldn't hurt them considering the situation. Maybe they liked the fact that Bariona dies with Jesus. They came to see the play when we put it on, and seemed to like it.

And the chaplains?

They loved it. It triggered many hours of conversations. After lights were out at 9 p.m., we would gather around a small candle, and argue, pleasantly.

About what?

Everything. I remember one discussion: Where did Jesus pop out? Was it from the vagina, full of blood, tied by the umbilical cord? Or did he pop out of the stomach all clean and rosy? Since neither the Bible nor any of the texts go into that, the conversation was very heated, but with no animosity. Actually the priests liked those "after-hours" sessions, especially any discussion over morality.

Like what?

Well, as you can imagine, the fundamental one was, if god is all powerful, how can man be free?

Ah yes, and that famous one with the cops? The ones who were resisters?

Which one? Remind me.

According to Leroy, when they were thrown into your barracks, they immediately said, OK, let's organize to escape. We can, we must do anything to escape. You said: anything? Yes, they replied. OK, you said, go bugger that disgusting Nazi fat slob over there. He wants it and he needs it. And while you do it, the rest of us will escape. Ah, non, the cops replied. So morality imposes limits to human behavior, you concluded.

I don't remember, but I wonder, because if the Nazi had been young and pretty, one of the typical German krauts, would they have refused? If so, the issue seems more taste than ethics. But it's very possible that we did endlessly discuss such problems.

Every night? Like a ritual?

Yep.

And the priest knew you were an atheist?

Of course. We had settled that when everyone accepted that I write the play.

And was writing and staging *Bariona* what attracted you to the theater the rest of your life?

No, actually, I was already hooked on various forms of stage works by my second year of high school. I wrote stupid little operettas, and one-acters.

In the same style as your early novels? The rebel against the nasty world?

Yep.

Why? I mean, you were a nice little bourgeois kid, more or less granted all your wishes, adored by your mother, catered to by your grandfather. Why did you rebel? Against what or whom? Perhaps we should go back and talk about your nonexistent relationship to your father. What do you remember about him?

Nothing much. Above my mother's bed hung a photo of a naval officer, with a small tight beard, I think, who was supposed to resemble me, except that by then I already had one eye that was running away from the other. "That's your father," I was told. And there was occasional talk at the dinner table about his exploits, but I suspected that they were made up. Otherwise, nothing.

Did you feel abandoned by your father?

No, not at all.

In your *Flaubert* you stress the importance of a person's first six months of life. Not true for you?

Maybe, but that would necessitate an intense analysis. I tried once with

Pontalis, but we both decided to stop, as we were then too close. There's no doubt that an analyst would focus much more on my early relationship with my mother, which was quite incestuous, visually speaking, that is. When I was eleven or twelve, I often imagined her naked, and then having sex with her, without knowing how. Then my stepfather enters the picture, and she sleeps in his bed. That made me jealous. Or rather, the idea that they had sex horrified me. On top, he was much older than she, and the idea of that old worn-out body lying on top of that young attractive one horrified me. But he spent little time with her, he was a chief, told people do this or don't, and that made me hate him. But where did I get this class antagonism, I have no idea. And at home too, he talked like a chief, giving orders left and right. Occasionally, he tried to act like a father, but quickly became a boss again, and my mother often had to intervene. Did his behavior turn me into a rebel? I doubt it. He never did impose his values or lifestyle on me, and if I say I hated him, it's wrong, I just had no respect for him. Now why did I scoff at success, because he was successful during that period of my adolescence, I have no idea, especially because I admired Zévaco's heroes, who were all successful. But their success was in saving others. My mother's propaganda about him was that he was saving others by giving them well-paying jobs, but that didn't influence me one bit.

Yet the end of your trajectory gets you to be a total collectivist, without ever having lived a day in a collectivity, besides prisoner-of-war camp, a convinced extreme Marxist of sorts, a position that demands a particular style of life, deep inside a Marxist-Leninist-Maoist interpretation of class struggle, which demands that its adherents be what they preach, that to call oneself a mao, one must be a mao, embedded in a group which, despite its errors, and god knows they make them by the bucketful, expect that you live what you preach, even if they don't, but they want to, and do try.

Pierre does, to a certain extent.

Aw, come on Sartre, he lives with his wife, nicely separated from his comrades who don't even have his phone number. He's like you: you both go to the meetings, argue out your position, or even better state it, period, then go home, and don't answer your phone, work on your *Flaubert,* which will be read and admired by academicians, but contribute nothing to the revolution. So where is your participation in a group-in-fusion? But I'll grant you that you are a rebel, to the core, always out of sync with the mainstream left, and with the regular Marxist-Leninists. Now, considering that you had a very pleasant childhood, that your mother loved you, that your grandfather catered to you, even if at times he forbade something, where did the rebelliousness develop?

In La Rochelle.

Why, because you didn't belong? Because the group that was already established when you got there was reluctant to let you join? That's typical of all adolescent groups.

Before La Rochelle I was not only pampered, but I was awed, as I lived with a god, who loved me. That tall monster in a white beard, whom everyone respected and feared too, loved me. That was some contrast after that. I mean, that man, when he appeared in church to tell the assembled parishioners that France had won the battle of the Marne, was really as if god had spoken, perhaps even made it possible.

OK, he was perfection, and everyone who thinks rebels against an imposed perfection. Is that the root of your rebellion? Most folks could make the same statement.

But I knew that Charles was not perfect, that in reality he was a poseur; he was a buffoon. Then came La Rochelle.

Where you stole money from your mother to buy cakes in order to bribe the gang to let you join? Any kid in that situation might do the same, but not become a flaming maoist.

Don't forget my stepfather. Not only did I not like him, the way he treated my mother and me, as a boss, but I knew that he was a boss in fact, that he gave orders to people who had to call him "patron," because he paid them to do what he wanted them to do.

Not enough to become class conscious and committed to the class struggle. Rebellion is more profound.

I think my rebellion is linked to literature, since reading was a way of escaping the real to try to find truth elsewhere.

That's no way to get an agrégation; did you retreat into literature at Normale too?

Yes, but I no longer considered it a retreat. At Normale I came to the conclusion that the whole thing was nothing more than a gigantic charade. Remember that I flunked the first time, because I wrote something absolutely original, which later was published as my *Theory of Emotions*, so I had to adapt the second time around. I went to the library, deciphered a pattern of those who came in first for the last ten years, did exactly like they in 60 pages,

then added 240 pages of quotes from the professors and philosophers who were respected in those days—that meant not a word on or by Hegel—came in first, then sneaked into Normale one night and destroyed every copy. No, for me, Normale, except during such stupid exercises, was my last escape, though I didn't realize that until my first crisis, and I made sure to enjoy it to the fullest.

Did Maheu, Guille, Nizan, Aron, think the same way?

I don't think they thought of it in the same way, as the end of the good life, so to speak. Aron was much too serious. He never joined us when we went whoring and drinking. But Maheu certainly did; he was very funny, and as I told you was always fun to be with until he started going up the ladder at UNESCO.

I told you, I think, that when I interviewed him, he was incredibly nostalgic, and while he refused to talk about his affair with Castor, and he knew that I knew he had been her first lover, still when he remembered scenes in which she appeared, his eyes became moist. I liked him a lot. Did your gang change its complexion when Castor joined in?

For me, no, but Maheu was not happy when she told him that Stépha had introduced us to her. Actually, Stépha and Castor were very close, always studying together, and since she was living with Fernando, it was perfectly normal that the four of us started going out together. When we all intermingled, it didn't really work. Fernando and Castor didn't get along too well at the beginning; she was put off by his arrogance, well, at first, until she learned that it was Fernando's cover-up for his insecurity, his endless quest for a god he knew didn't exist, but as you know we all eventually became very close and Maheu sort of lost out.

Did Fernando and Castor end up having an affair?

You should ask her, but you know your father, he had to seduce every woman he liked, but he went after Castor's sister, Poupette, first.

What about Stépha and Maheu? I asked Maheu, but he dodged the question.

Everyone was in love with Stépha, and certainly so Maheu. But as you know, Stépha may not have cared who Fernando slept with but would refuse all suitors on her side.

Do you know the story of Noiditch? I don't know his full name, but he had been Stépha's lover in Vienna, before she met Fernando. One day, he came to Paris, absolutely broke, and Stépha was really anxious and pleased to see him. Fernando gave him money to take Stépha out in style so as to alleviate his guilt. When they met again, Noiditch gave Fernando back his money, saying she had insisted that they go to a student restaurant and refused to sleep with him, saying that she was hooked on that "tyrant." She then apparently added: "Oh, give him back his money; he's also very poor."

Ha-ha ha. Everyone loved Stépha.

You, too?

And how!

Did you manage to seduce her?

Nope. No one did.

So the two groups stayed separate, the foursome on one side, nice respectable bourgeois couples, and the trio on the other, laughing, carousing, whoring, getting drunk, right?

No, first of all, your parents may have come from bourgeois backgrounds, but they were constantly broke. Fernando rarely sold one of his paintings, and Stépha made a living by giving her rich, or better-off, acquaintances facial massages. And the trio was not what you think: Maheu was around but he was married and went home in the evenings. No, the trio was Nizan, Guille, and me. And then Nizan went off to Aden, and the trio disappeared, but Maheu was not in it.

Guille was hooked to someone then too, but he stuck around. Was it that Maheu, coming from a peasant family, felt uneasy with your guys?

Peasant family? Where did you get that? His parents were university teachers.

He told me.

That's because they owned a farm. Ha! He conned you. Well, you have to be a con man to run UNESCO.

And Aron, who claims he came up with the idea of contingency and introduced you to phenomenology?

Yep, another con man. As I told you, "contingency" was an idea I had since adolescence. It accompanied my notion that necessity does not exist except in math, but Castor and I ignored that when we made our pact. As for phenomenology, your father talked to me about Husserl for two years before Aron went to Germany. I even had read a book by [Emmanuel] Lévinas about it. No, what Aron made me want to do is go to Germany, all expenses paid, to have a good time. The problem is that everyone had to invent stories, including me, because I went the year the Nazis were fighting the Communists in the streets of Berlin, and I was dancing and whoring in cabarets.

Did you at least study some? How about Hegel?

Are you crazy? Who goes to a new country, full of history and culture, to read Hegel, of all people?

So where did you get, or get and change, your notion of in-oneself and for-oneself?

In my own brain.

You never read Hegel's *Phenomenology of Spirit* back then?

Sure, after the war, in 1945.

What? '45? After you wrote *Being and Nothingness*?

Yep. And what I didn't know, I learned later from Hyppolite's book. I didn't have access to his work while a prisoner.⁴ But when I read it I added some chapters to *Being and Nothingness*. The real Hegel I got to know after reading Marx, who made Hegel known throughout the world.

Which explains why in the *Critique* you seem very close to Hegel, but not in *Being and Nothingness*.

Exactly.

So the myth that Aron stimulated you into writing the concepts you elucidate in *Being and Nothingness* is just that, a myth? He himself claimed that he was the originator in my interview with him.

He had absolutely nothing to do with *Being and Nothingness* or my philosophical views. I didn't discuss anything with him. One can't: he immediately interjects his ideas about anything you talk about. No, indeed, I remember very well how I began to develop my ideas in 1940 in the army, before becoming a prisoner. I remember that during the Phony War I was given a leave and called Castor; she met me at the station, and I immediately started telling her about my ideas. We talked, or I mostly talked, for hours, while we had a long breakfast. Her comments were incredibly helpful. She would say, You jumped too fast to a conclusion there, or That's not very clear, or You better widen that deduction. One could never do that with Aron; he would immediately tell you how he would make that argument and go off on tangents, which you didn't give two hoots about.

I suspect that all the myths about Aron have been created by the media, which loves his pro–United States and conservative political positions.

Absolutely. And of course because he is totally, completely, systematically second-rate, fundamentally a stupid jerk.⁵

November 1973

GERASSI: In *Being and Nothingness*, you had two goals, to get rid of determinism so as to affirm our freedom, and to stress the fullness of that freedom through the creativity and contingency in our actions, and our consciousness of them, which you define as active and call praxis.

SARTRE: Not yet, that's in the *Critique*. I take it you have read the notes I gave you last year of both my ethics and volume two of the *Critique*. Don't forget, neither is ready yet, and won't be for quite a while.

In *Being*, you relied on Hegel's notion of master-slave without giving him credit, and now I know why—you hadn't read him. But your interest was mainly psychological, to show how the master is dependent for his identity on his relationship to the slave to give him validity, thus rendering them both objectified, what you later would define as practico-inert. In your notes for an ethics, which by the way I liked a great deal and hope you decide to publish,[1] and volume one of the *Critique*, your interest has switched from the individual to the group, or rather you argue that for the individual to become intentional, that is historically meaningful, he or she must create a group, that is, become part of a group-in-fusion. But since the individual's need to have meaning remains, Marx's "objective class interests" are not enough to explain historical movement. As a result, there is no guarantee, no inevitability, hence no historical materialism, though class war remains the primary explanation of historical movement and evolution, as you show through your analysis of the French and Russian revolutions.

OK, go on.

OK. There's no guarantee that we are going to win, ever. But we are unwittingly given the tools to try by the enemy that oppresses us. Like your sort of "collective," which charges the Bastille, and unifies into a cohesive and coherent group-in-fusion by intentionally, that is consciously, or to use your term, in praxis, defying the officialdom's actions. OK, the Bastille is seized, what then? A "mediating" party arises within the group creating a dynamic that you call "fraternity-terror" because it is both a threat (by giving orders) and a potential solution to an impasse (by offering solutions). It also allows the individual to better understand his or her position by colliding the self and other. That leads to both the individual and the group redefining their freedom as an act, and therefore organizations and institutions as degrading and alienating, or to use the terms of the *Critique,* as serializing and atomizing. Which means that if we win, or are winning, we can move to conditions where material scarcity is eliminated. But the most important conclusion for me in all that is, no one can be free unless we all are, that our struggles must be through groups-in-fusion, which come from the base, from the people, even if they suffer temporarily from your "fraternity-terror," and that history remains, perhaps not materialistically determined, but intentionally defined as a class struggle. And that struggle—and here is the link between your early work, like in *Being and Nothingness,* and your later opus, like in the *Critique*—frees not only the slave but also the master, hence humanizes both.

What do my notes for *Critique 2* add to that?[2]

What I got out of that incredibly difficult to decipher scribble of yours is a few precisions, which helped me understand the stuff I just said. Like "totalization," though we've talked about that before. I liked your example of the artist-painting, the combination of an imagination with bits of paint, canvas, pebbles, whatever, a combination that is a social entity, a thing-for-itself, which when finished, of course, is then merely a piece of inertia, and begins to deteriorate. It is now a bit of "worked matter," which has been totalized by human activity, and becomes institutionalized by alienating organizations. It's a good way to explain my bus example, the group-in-fusion seizing the bus, then becoming serialized after leaving it, but being permanently changed, thus affecting the state of things. As you said, the group has expressed creative subjectivity expanding its intentional-freedom. So even if it becomes serialized again, it is not a defeat, merely a hiatus in the endless struggle in which freedom expands. I also liked your definition of that fraternity-terror entry, what becomes the "pledged group," which generates that "moment of the trap," causing the passage from creative freedom to institutionalized inertia. Nothing comes easy, does it? In politics as in our consciousness, we are a mixture of in-itself, the sturdy, inert, identity, and the for-itself, the moving, active, dynamic explorer, a perpetual dialectic between our "facticity" and our "transcendence," resolved by plunging us "in-situation" where we are "more," because we are the praxis that seeks to escape constraint and express our freedom. That's what you mean, in the *Critiques* as well as in *Being and Nothingness,* by your statement that we are "condemned to be free."

Good. Arlette will give you the rest of the *Critique*—well, I haven't finished it—but the newly corrected manuscript when she finishes transcribing it. Actually, she corrected it, though she kept asking me to be more precise and tell her what to write. It may be that I shall never work on it again. I am too blind now to write.

What? All I've been doing since I got back is read what you did since I left, all those articles, the speeches. You didn't stop for a moment.

That's not the same. Articles, speeches, even if one writes them down first, and for major political or philosophical conferences one has to, are one thing. Writing is another. They're done mostly by formula. I could even dictate them. But to write . . . I don't understand the Americans who use typewriters. I have to write longhand.

But the American writers I know use a typewriter as you use a pen. They're not trained as secretaries who can type sixty, eighty words a minute without looking at the keyboard. The writers didn't go to school to learn how to type. They use two fingers, like I do, and see every letter they strike.

Still, to me, the shape of words, their configuration, how they look on a page is important. And now with my one eye going to pot, it's getting harder and harder. I end up scribbling.

You have always put them down in such a manner that very few people in the world could decipher them anyway.

Ha! Well, Arlette transcribes what I write, Castor can read it, and so can you, no?

With pain. I remember family sessions at home when Stépha received a letter from Castor, whose handwriting is even worse than yours. We would sit around and say, That's an "f," No it's a "p," and so on. It would take a long time to figure out her letter.

But you can read mine, no?

To tell you the truth, the hardest part of my work with you now is reading your unpublished works, like your 1964 *Morale*. What a job. I'm glad I did it though, because Gallimard's transcription is full of mistakes.

You have an advantage, that you've been around us, even as a child, so you know how we express ourselves, and can guess, too.

But you've tried dictating. The book of exchanges between you, Pierre, and Gavi is all on tape, which Arlette in transcribing. Why not write that way?

Novels?

Sure, like [Georges] Simenon.[3]

Novels maybe, but certainly not careful analyses where every word is crucial.

Plays are OK, though. You speak the dialogue out loud as you write.

But I don't write plays or novels anymore. And for the rest, it's really too hard, as I'm now basically blind.

What can you see? The TV? Cars coming at you? You still go down in the morning to have breakfast alone at the café—how are your eyes for that?

I look at the TV two evenings a week with my daughter. I don't see the people, just vague shapes, but I hear the dialogue, so I can still enjoy some of it. Cars are a problem: I do see motion, but I can't be sure until it is less than ten meters away, and then it could be too late if it's a fast-moving car. As far as writing is concerned, well, as you see I scribble, sometimes one line over the other since I can't see what I write.

What about your Monday column for *Libération*?[4]

I do it as an interview. That is, Pierre asks me questions on the subject I want to write about, then puts my answer into a column form. How does Stépha deal with her affliction? Can she see anything?

Like you, motion at ten meters. She now walks with both a walker and a white cane attached to it. And she still cooks, feeling the ingredients with her fingers. She refuses to stop teaching, so she gets help from two students, one a Russian young woman, who helps her prepare her Russian class, and a guy who helps her with her history classes. She knows the subjects so well that it works. She told me, I love teaching so much, if I have to stop I'll commit suicide. She asked my advice, explaining herself so calmly, I said yes, I understand.

I think you were right.

What I find amazing is the responses of her students. I sat in on some of her classes, without telling her, and the students didn't know who I was. They tell her if they come in late. They identify themselves if they talk. They're totally different than they are in different classes. And she is still a fascinating teacher. Do you continue to refuse to have someone share your apartment with you, to help you?

Well, this studio is too small, but yes, I have lived alone all my life, except on vacations, of course, and I am used to that. But being without a telephone, that was scary.

How did they fix it so quickly? Took me five months to get a phone.

Gisèle Halimi talked to Edgar Faure, and I got it yesterday.⁵

Faure? That reactionary crocodile? Did you know him personally?

In 1958, we were supposed to have lunch together, I don't remember why, when suddenly the alarm went off that Paris was going to be invaded by the mutinous generals coming in from Algeria to seize power. He called me to tell me every able Frenchman was to go sit on the tarmac to stop the generals from landing there. And we did, by the thousands.

Why did that stop the generals? Generals have no respect for human beings—why didn't they plow right through you all?

There's still a lot of debate about that day, who started the rumors, and why. Was it a way to bring de Gaulle to power? Faure joined him eventually. Anyway, two guys came and fixed my telephone. For me to be without it is very risky.

What about the papers? Does someone read them to you?

Castor reads me *Libération* and parts of *Le Monde*.

So you're up to date on the events in Chile?

Exactly as you predicted. The communists refused to arm the people until it was too late, and now they're all going to get executed.

So will the socialists, the MIR [Movement of the Revolutionary Left], all the left-wing groups, even some of the good Christian Democrats, though most followed that bastard Eduardo Frey who supported the Pinochet coup. Tell me, are you still keeping that old schedule of yours?

Pierre most mornings. That's how my politics are kept to date. Then as usual, except I never go to movies anymore. Just the TV with Arlette.

And still Wanda and Michelle as usual?

Yep, and my little Greek friend too, she's in Paris now.

How about Lena? She's also in Paris now.

Oh yes, I see her quite often.

How many years is it since you last saw her?

Ten years maybe. I really enjoy seeing her, though you know, the old feelings are dead, killed by time I guess, for both of us, but we really do enjoy each other's company very much.

Do you speak of old times?

No, not at all.

How about old friends?

The only real old friend was Ehrenburg, and he's dead. Did you like her when you saw her?

Very much.

Did you ask her about those old times?

Sort of, but I felt she didn't want to say too much, except that you had been the most fascinating man in her life. I got enough out of my talk to realize that for her, too, it had been a very intense and very deep relationship.

Certainly. For me too. How does she look now?

She looks very good, very classy, with allure. She's up to date on everything, very well read, and very hip.

Castor told me that she is the most interesting woman she ever met. Neither was intimidated by the other.

And Castor can be intimidating, not like you?

Me?

Let me tell you about Catherine. She was intimidated in advance. Oh my god, I'm going to meet the great Sartre! But she said, fifteen minutes after our first get-together, she was perfectly at ease, joking, even semi-teasing, semi-flirting with you.

I sort of felt that. It was very nice. Now you know why I like to spend time with the young.

OK, but Lena was not that young when you met her.

That was not a flirting, that was serious. What age would you give her?

I'd say forty-five or so. I'm going to see her again next week. I really look forward to that.

Hey now, don't grab her away from me, like you did with Michelle.

Oh my god, Sartre! You're getting possessive in your old age?

Ha-ha ha. And when are you going back to America?

Just after Lena leaves. Ha ha ha! In a few weeks.

With Catherine?

Yes. But she may not stay if I join the Weather folks. If I don't I'll see you in a year.

Good luck.

November 1974

SARTRE: How is Fernando feeling?

GERASSI: I think he knows he's going to die. He asked me to tell the surgeon that he does not want to come out of the operation if he cannot go through to the end of summer without morphine. He can't paint with morphine, he says.

Did the doctor agree?

He called me for a meeting yesterday morning, just before I left the University of Pennsylvania hospital, to go to the airport in New York. There were six of them in the room, the anesthesiologist, his helper, another surgeon, and two other doctors. They asked me all sorts of questions, very probing, very serious; they obviously wanted to know if he meant it. Then when I went to say good-bye to him, he asked Stépha to leave the room, and grabbed my hand and said, "Please forgive me for my whole life with you, forgive me for not telling you that I loved you, for not congratulating you when you did well, like when you were first at the bac, or when you published your books, or when you refused to pay your fine and went to jail. Don't ever do that with your children. Tell them how marvelous they are whenever they merit it." He had tears in his eyes, first time I ever saw that, and so did I, of course.[1]

As I presume you have now, too, but I can't see, though I do see better than last year.

Yes, Castor told me when I called this morning from the airport, and you're planning to go to Portugal, she said.

I wanted to ask you about that. You were there long? Go everywhere? Did you see Otelo [Saraiva de Carvalho]?

Yes to all your questions. I was there in August and all of September, and would have stayed longer if Stépha hadn't sent me a telegram about Fernando. Otelo is wonderful, funny, easygoing, not at all as I imagined a military officer. [Carvalho was one of the leaders, with General António de Spínola, of a left-leaning military coup that overthrew the right-wing authoritarian government of Portugal in April 1974.][2] We drove together to Algarve, where he is living now that he is sort of out of it and Spínola is in charge. I told him you wanted to see him, and he's delighted at the possibility.

Robert [Gallimard] tells me you picked up the finished copy of the conversations with Pierre and Gavi [published as *On a raison de se révolter*]. What do you think?

A lot of reservations. First of all, those two come across as hating each other.

Ha, well, yes, they don't like each other. But Pierre is much softer now, more malleable.

Now that he's unemployed, so to speak, I mean now that the GP has been dissolved and that *La Cause du Peuple* is dead.

It's now dead; they will reissue it, you'll see.

But in the book he comes across as very hard, unpleasant, as does Gavi, for that matter. Both of them talk about I this and I that. Where's their collectivism?

But still, does it not come through from our conversations that we hope that a new movement without leaders, spontaneous, emanating from the base, can emerge in full freedom, where all agree . . .

Sure, until a crisis occurs, like you're all agreed to demonstrate against such a law or action by the government, peacefully, but then the cops charge, and some want to fight back, others want to run, who says what to whom? Who leads, who convinces all to do what?

No one. Each does his thing.

Ha! And that's going to get a real movement going? The road to revolution?

Be serious! You want centralism?

How else are you going to get a unanimous response when the situation changes unexpectedly?

That's our task, to find efficient freedom.

Not in this book!

Don't be nasty. We were trying to set up the decentralized, group-infusions category first, then the manner in which they can be coordinated in action. Now we have to find how to constitute the manner in which goals, or tactics, can be changed with freedom, rather *in* freedom, when the circumstances demand it.

Without leaders? I for one, and, I would venture to say, most of the maos who are my friends, would not want to be led by Benny, by Pierre as you prefer to call him.

I think he understands that. He wants to do another book with me, a dialogue precisely to find how we can act as a collective absolutely freely, since the concept of collectivism changes when one takes it from the point of view of freedom.

And for that you first need a theory. Yet you yourself have claimed that theory comes out of practice.

That's what Pierre and I will try to work out in the next volume.[3]

Forgive me for saying so, but you'll have your work cut out for you, because what is important, it seems to me, is that Pierre gets rid of his intellectualism. It's easy to get down to the level of the group as far as content is concerned. Just a little self-control to say nicely "I'm confused about that," or "I now realize that I don't know how we can do that," and so on. But to stop the style, the air, the swagger, the handshakes, the walk, the looks of a superior being, which all intellectuals exhibit consciously or unconsciously, is extremely hard. That's why we need cultural revolutions. It's not enough for the maos to seize power, if they could; it's even more important that they reflect the angst, the inner doubts, the hopes and aspirations, the genuine expression of real freedom of the masses. More important than contentment, than the good life, than all the slogans invented by all politicians, the left must offer a program of personal and collective dealienation. Can your maos offer that?

No. But unlike the rest of the classic left, they know that's what they must do. But wait, you're taking notes full blast. Let's go back to my flat and use the tape recorder. You've got to get stuff down for your interview for *Playboy* anyway.

What do you think your influence has been on France today, on its ideas, its politics, and what effect do you think it will have—in other words, what do you see as your legacy?

I don't know. I don't even know if I will leave any mark at all.

Surely in philosophy . . .

Oh yes, on philosophy.

And the theater?

Much less. No, what I hope defines my journey on this planet has been my commitment to freedom, that everything I have written or every action I have partaken has always been in my drive to stress the importance of freedom, real freedom, not the superficial kind that your government and mine, your commentators and mine, claim we have—that is, the freedom of the rich to say and do anything they like in the media they buy, or of the vote, which is limited to a rigged system they set up, or the equivalent under central committees, in sum, the kind of phony freedom that limits, or indeed eliminates us as free agents. Such free agents, if we can create a collective in which they flourish, would be totally unalienated.

That kind of free agent cannot exist under capitalism or Stalinism, and your definition of philosophy fits into that perfectly, since you insist that the task of the philosopher is to understand the human being in his era, not to find truth, correct?

To interpret man in his times.

But the times are defined by the freedom at the base.

Exactly.

Which is why your statement "we were never as free as during the occupation" is not a contradiction.

That's correct, because we had very clearly defined choices, to fight back one way or another or to collaborate. In those times, our freedom defined our choices perfectly.

And the fact that there were more collaborators in France than in any other occupied country changes nothing. It demonstrated that the collabos chose to collaborate as their free choice. But that clear-cut situation does not exist today.

Commitment of oneself as a totality is still the issue, it always is.

But the choice of what kind of commitment entails doubt today.

Doubt does not stop decision.

But there was no doubt in 1942. When you told that man who wanted your help in deciding whether he should stay in France to help his aging mother or go to London to fight with the Free French, that he was free to choose, it was an easy answer for you. Today, the situation, hence the choices, are much more fluid. To decide what to do is much harder.

True, in 1942, a choice to fight the Nazis entailed one's whole life, even if one could imagine or hope that the Germans would eventually withdraw. Today there is no such clear-cut situation. But one's commitment is total, in each situation. What that means is that the choices come up faster. But always within that commitment.

OK, let's use our previous example, the group made up of folks who are totally committed and who decide as a collective to go to the demonstration together, and who bring their children because they have defined their participation as peaceful. But the cops charge, flailing their vicious clubs every which way. Some decide to run, some stay and fight back. The unanimity, the collective stand, is lost, and those who decided to fight, feeling abandoned, lose some of their verve and are crushed by the cops. Yet you say, each made a free choice, as a collective? A contradiction, no?

No. The free choice as a collective to oppose the government's whatever action by joining the demonstration was right. What went wrong was to think, as individuals, that the collective could determine the character of the enemy, and hence they misread what would happen. Whether a demonstration ends up peaceful or not is never, never, decided by the demonstrators. Yes, of course, the press always blames the hooligans, because they throw the first rocks, or whatever. That's because the press never understands, or never wants to show that they understand, that governments are by their very essence violent. Cops are never sent to protect lives. Their job is to protect property and defend the status quo, hence are violent in their very nature. The violence of those without power, the poor, the oppressed, the occupied, is counterviolence. Governments and their media always call the opposition terrorists if they resort to violence. But they have to choose against the violence of the government, which is violent even if it is not exerted. The fact that governments have police forces and armies makes them violent by definition, even if they never use the cops or the armies to impose their will. Those who oppose that will have no choice but to be violent, even if they in turn do not use it. So in your example, the collective decision to oppose the government implied their counterviolence, even if they never used it. And the govern-

ment's reaction to the demonstration was violent, even if their cops never once struck the head of a demonstrator with his baton. And to get back to our original issue, the task of the philosopher today is to make that clear, by analyzing the contradictions, the essences of governments, the choices that the people have, living in and under such situations.

Does today's youth understand that?

I think so, not all of course, but those who fought in '68, especially the older ones who remember what France was like twenty years ago. It was then, indeed fifty years ago, thirty years ago, but also when they rebelled, in many ways, in the center of the world, and they know that. Paris was the most stimulating city in the world, with its painters, its writers, its energy, its café life envied everywhere. As great as that was, it made it easy for the alienated to bury themselves in that cultural paradise, to ignore the future, to forget that they were alienated because everyone was. Today, that's all gone. No one has the illusion that we are the center of the world.

Worse. Not only is French culture today derivative, but the French seem to hate each other, making life here . . .

. . . mediocre. Absolutely.

And that makes you an optimist?

Because it has made it clear to our youth, and it will be even more so to the next generation, that France doesn't count anymore, that we are part of one alienated and alienating world, which must be transformed, and that the process of transformation is itself dealienating.

Yet, except insofar as you can barely see anymore, your life as a Parisian is unchanged.

I am a Parisian out of habit, but I have long been convinced that any revolutionary act anywhere is a move to change the whole world.

But your revolutionary commitment is relatively recent. Do you renounce the past?

No, not at all. In fact, the book I feel closer to is still *Nausea*.

Yet back then, and in that novel, your interest was the lonely and alone individual, who asks himself, What is the meaning of life? And that question, ultimately, was your task to answer in philosophy. Now your question is, What is the meaning of action? A tremendous difference.

Action is what carries life, only action. My life is a given, in a situation in which I grow up alienated. The alienation is man-made. I cannot do anything

against the given: that is my human condition. The alienation I can and must fight. That is the only task of my activity. And to dealienate my life must be as part of a collective. Individual action only leads to more alienation.

Yet you get pleasure from knowing that people still read your works, those in which, like your childhood mentor Zévaco, an individual hero saved the damsel in distress, the lost and the weak.

Why not? They were part of my trajectory toward my understanding that our situation is alienated.

So you continue to be pleased that folks read your novels, that your plays are performed, like right now, *No Exit*?

All my plays, indeed all my early work, also exposed our alienation.

Like "hell is each other." But that phrase comes across as a psychological statement.

If it's badly played, yes. It is both psychological and metaphysical. Today, the statement is both political and metaphysical.

You have said that you no longer believe in psychology. True?

Yes.

Yet you were interested enough to write a mammoth scenario on the unconscious.

Did you read it?

The sections that Arlette has, in which you are fascinated by the idea of the unconscious.

No, you misread it; my scenario is about Freud and how he discovers the idea of the unconscious.

But if you didn't believe in it, why write it?

Because [the film director] John Huston offered me 26 million [francs], and I was broke then.[4] Did you see his movie [*Freud*, released in 1962]?

No, but I liked the scenario.

Huston changed so much of it that I had my name taken off. It ended up being a movie about the man Freud and not about his supposed discovery of the unconscious, which has so affected psychology to this day.

You don't think that the way you were raised led to certain behavior patterns or ideas that, without your being aware of them, characterized your life, and that "without your being aware of them" is what we normally call the unconscious? Like the fact that your grandfather never talked about god but about books, pointing to the shelf and in effect saying, believing, that what was on the shelf was immortal, giving you the conviction that if your books got to that shelf you too would be immortal, from which you derived two conclusions: one, that god did not exist, or if he did it had no importance at all, and, two, that you were not afraid of death.

Yes, of course, but that was not unconscious. I loved my grandmother, and she was Catholic. My grandfather was Protestant, at least in name. They both dismissed the other. So who was right? It obviously did not matter. On the other hand, no one disputed the value of those books on the shelf. I never heard anyone dismiss the value of Hugo or Balzac. So I concluded, not "unconsciously," that books are more important than gods.

The significance, psychologically, is that you did accept some sort of all-powerful authority. If you call books god, OK, but the books became a guiding force in your life, proving, the psychologists would say, that all children need authority and . . .

You want to insist that the fact that everyone needs someone or something to look up to is a psychological fact? Why? Does it not show that all kids, perhaps we could say, everyone, needs a value to strive for? But why say it's unconscious? It is part of the situation we are in, which is dehumanizing because it is alienated. Next you tell me that the Oedipus complex is a psychological reality.

And how would you describe it?

As a boy matures and becomes aware, or anxious, about his rising sexual needs or impulses, he turns to the only person he has loved, obeyed, the only person that hugged him when he cried, caressed him when he suffered, and suddenly feels more attraction. Perfectly normal. I had that with my mother. And like all kids I became jealous of anyone coming between us, in my case, my stepfather. No, listen, psychology that deals with your individual problems in hyphenated situations is meaningless. Psychology must develop new tools to deal with the being in-situation in which he too is part.

Like the man with the tape recorder?

Exactly. Both committed. Both in the soup, as we used to say. Both risking. Both equal.

OK, let's say you and I are members of the same collective. And I fall in love with that woman but I can't get an erection with her when we try to make love. I come to you and ask for your help. I explain that I have never had that problem before, with prostitutes or friends, but now that I am madly in love and want to live the rest of my life with her, I can't get it up. What do you say?

First, I have to put myself on your level, not a superior doctor type. I do that by telling you a similar experience that happened to me. Then we start talking about what it means to be committed, until we arrive at the solution, in this case fairly easy, that you are reluctant to totally give up what you think is your freedom. Then we discuss what is freedom. But the important point is that at all stages, I have to be in the soup, risking revealing stuff about me, as you reveal about you. Otherwise you stay alienated. Existential psychoanalysis deals with social problems, never individual.

OK, let's do it now for the '68 generation. The trauma, so to speak, is their saying: "In May 1968 we were promised the moon and we never even got the earth!"

To begin with, the statement is wrong. In '68 they had no idea where they were going, or what they wanted. Cohn-Bendit's statement that they didn't give a damn about the swimming pool, they wanted to make love, shows that they understood that they were totally alienated by their government, the education system, the morals and values imposed on them by the capitalist society, but not how to fight it, what to do about it. They were collectively against, but not collectively for. So when they failed, they fell back into the past, traditional parties, demonstrations, marches, et cetera. What psychologists call regression, but to me was an attitude of defeat.

When you say "falling back into the past," you mean becoming atomized, serialized?

Career oriented. They became doctors, educators, engineers, bureaucrats, striving for their own and doing their own.

Not all, obviously—look at your maos. To them, returning to the past means studying yet again the previous revolutions. But that means not understanding that each situation is total. There can never be a Russian Revolution anymore, nor a Chinese. Why do they call themselves Maoists? They would be better off calling themselves gauchistes, la révolution gauchiste, as the media describes them. Or the Nanterristes or the "nancennistes."[5] There are no models for revolution. Each must be completely embedded in the local situation, as was the Cuban, and as will be the next one. Ours, wherever it comes and whenever it comes, will owe a great deal to May '68 here and the movement in the United States, but not tactics or strategies—rather that commitment we were talking about. I think there is only one absolutely clear characteristic we will manifest: the new revolutionaries will refuse to sacrifice themselves in order to make the revolution. They will make it, because they will want it for them and for their collective. The revolution will not tolerate elitism.

And it will be decentralized. How? We don't know yet. We have been offered a monthly TV program in which we can work that out . . .

Who we?

Castor and I with whomever we want to invite.

Total freedom to say what you want?

We wouldn't have accepted otherwise.

So you're planning to use the system against the system.

The contracts are on the way.

Ha! They feel that strong that they are willing to show the world that they can tolerate any criticism, any call to action?

I guess so. They gave me their word. Pierre and I are already working out the first program. [That first program, as well as two more, were ready to be aired but were never shown. The government-owned television network did not keep its word, and after Sartre died, it canceled the deal.]

Farewell

Sartre died in 1980, at age seventy-five, in great part because of his abuse of drugs. But as he once told me, since he had rarely slept more than four hours per night, in effect he had lived much more than the average person. "Do the arithmetic," he laughed; "at seventy I'm already ninety." For his obituary, the Anglo press gave him a nice send-off but claimed he had become totally irrelevant. *Newsday,* however, asked me to write my farewell. This is what I wrote, which was published intact on April 17, 1980.

WE ARE ALL THE CHILDREN OF SARTRE'S MIND

Some of us may not even know his name. Many of us have never even read his works. But most of us use his language—and feel his thoughts—every day of our lives.

Fail though we may, we try to face our situation and overcome our anxieties by leading authentic lives in committing ourselves to our projects and to our fellow human beings. Understanding that we can never escape our background, our heritage, our time and space in a world that we have neither chosen nor accepted—in a phrase, our human condition—we, nevertheless, continuously try to give meaning to our absurdity through our action, the responsibility for which we reluctantly yet defiantly, painfully yet proudly, proclaim as our own.

When we hedge, when we blame others, when we hide in the dark closets of rationalization or in the gaudy showroom of determinism, we know—deep in our hearts and souls—that we are guilty of bad faith.

Whether we like it or not, we—the three generations of this century—are all the children of Jean-Paul Sartre.

To many academicians, especially in America, Sartre is a bad philosopher. His emphasis on the "I" as a starting point to consciousness of self is too solipsistic, they say. His constant reevaluation of man's situation, forcing a perpetual questioning of our ethical imperatives, is too arbitrary, they complain. His ferocious commitment to the changing complaints of the downtrodden and of the underdog makes him too fickle, they conclude.

True, in the genteel halls of academia and in the carefully manicured gardens of officialdom, Sartre's philosophy could find no home. He posed too many difficult questions without giving permanent palliative answers. He rummaged through too many hidden recesses of the mind to console the complacent. He scoffed at too many dogmas to soothe the tormented. But to the young in age as well as in spirit, he remains their conscience. He told them as he told himself, over and over: The world may be a meaningless fact that you cannot control, your pain and your suffering may be the dictates of gods you can never know, your death may be no more rational than your life, yet you are what you do—and you know it.

Said Sartre: By making this whole absurd conglomeration of contingent events known as "life" your very own, by understanding that whatever you do, you posit it as an absolute moral value for all others, by doggedly seizing existence as your own and tenaciously heralding it as valuable, hence as moral, you are truly alive—and free.

To Sartre—and to us, his children—freedom became defined by its limits. God, who can do all things at all times, and a stone, which can do nothing, are not free. To choose is also not to choose its opposite. Freedom is therefore painful. It generates anxiety. Human beings are thus the only creatures who can give meaning to their existence. For meanings, like childbirth or any creative act, are the result of effort, that is, pain. With every choice we make, Sartre said, we feel the "other." With every act, we establish a human bond. And that bond is what we call morality. Thus by starting with the egocentric "I" human beings discover the social—and, more significantly, the collective—"we."

Sartre lived by what he preached. In each situation be made his choices and acted accordingly. Naturally, therefore, he made mistakes. Some-times the mistakes were awful, as when he sided with the Communists in 1954 and defended the ideology's monolithic iron heel in words (*The Communists and Peace*) and in deeds (by consciously acting as their "potiche," as he said, or front man in their Peace Congress propaganda network). But he never blamed others for his being a fool, and undid his mistakes with equal fervor (as in his book, *The Ghost of Stalin,* in which he attacked Russian communism and criticized himself for his earlier support).

Sometimes, he was alone among intellectuals in standing for his convictions. During the May 1968 "Events"—the worker-student uprising—for example, he, like France's other famous men of letters, was booed by rebellious students; unlike Communist poet Louis Aragon, who reacted by calling the youths "a bunch of punks," Sartre went home to figure out why he had failed to communicate, not why they could not understand. Out of that experience, Sartre concluded that the young would never again opt for a revolutionary party that did not proclaim the absolute worth of each individual. The result, which some have dubbed his "anarcho-Maoism," was a political philosophy of action which, while opposing the stratified and hierarchical bourgeois state, insisted that revolution must be made while fighting for it—in other words, that the end is only justified by the means.

Sartre was an enormously generous man and very modest. Though he earned a great deal of money with his plays, novels, essays, philosophical works, and biographies of Baudelaire, Genet, and Flaubert, he died in debt, having given away most of his fortune to political movements and activists, and to an untold number of struggling intellectuals. To this day, five young writers are receiving monthly checks from Sartre's publisher not knowing their true source.

He was equally generous with his time. Once in 1954, while working on my dissertation on him, I was accompanied by a young friend who told him she did not understand his philosophy. Sartre spent the next two hours talking to her in simple terms—and fascinated us with the depth of his explanation.

He felt that taking this time was nothing special since—always refusing to believe in "talent"—he said that he had simply developed a craft, just like the carpenter or the mason, and communicating was part of that craft. As for inspiration, that, he used to say, "comes with pulling the chair up to the desk."

At his desk after 1968, he spent mornings writing his biography of Flaubert, afternoons and evening dashing off political tracts, and still found the time and strength to participate in literally hundreds of street demonstrations denouncing injustice.

"The role of the intellectuals," he would say, "is to explain the issues and to communicate the battles, not to define them. The people choose battles." But I once asked, isn't spending so much time on Flaubert—three volumes in which Sartre uses the times to explain the man and the man to explain the times—a contradiction for an activist? "Yes, of course," he answered, "but I am both a bourgeois writer like Flaubert, and a revolutionary activist like Babeuf. I assume responsibility for both."

I once showed up at his tiny, book-crammed, but otherwise stark apartment extremely distraught because of a failed love affair. He listened caringly to my sad tale for hours, then said: "As you know, I chose to live my amorous life openly, but such a decision entailed giving up passion. Today, as I look at you, I realize that I have never cried for a woman. I envy you."

Sartre's philosophy is difficult to live. Perhaps because of that, most Anglo-Saxon commentators and teachers, raised on an escape-crammed philosophical tradition of pragmatism, preferred to praise the moral message propagated by Sartre's existential rival, Albert Camus. Since all organized actions lead to doctrinaire authoritarianism, said Camus, all we can do is shout, No!

Bad faith, replied Sartre. What we must do instead, he said, is commit ourselves over and over again. No act is pure. All acts are choices, which alienate some. No one can live without dirty hands. To be simply opposed is also to be responsible for not being in favor, for not advocating change. To fall back on the proposition that human actions are predetermined is to renounce mankind. No writer can accept the totalitarianism implied by "human nature." If he writes, he wants to change the world—and himself. Writing is an act. It is commitment.

Sartre remained committed all his life. Once he experienced dependency on his fellow fighters during the war and in the subsequent resistance movement, he concluded that our only hope, for each individual one of us, was to understand that there is no "I" without the "we," that as long as one man sleeps on a bed of roses while others collapse on beds of mud each of us remains incomplete—and partly dead in our souls.

That is the message that our generation—and those to come—takes from Sartre, the man and the work. In more than a dozen classes I have taught in the last few years on the philosophy of commitment, I have found that Sartre more than any other writer of our century best reaches the inner depths of the young.

They may think that they belong to the "me" generation. But they are just as angry, just as anxious, just as tormented as we of my generation were. And not only because of their individual fates. The future of those who sleep on beds of mud continues to gnaw at whatever self-complacency they exhibit. Sartre shakes them out of their dogmatic slumber in a way Hume's philosophy never did and never will.

With Sartre, they understand that there are no shortcuts to truth—or to life, love, and revolution. He not only speaks to them directly, he lives inside them. Sartre is not just the century's greatest moralist. He is also its greatest prophet.[1]

Notes

1. Fernando had been talking with friends at the Rotonde Café on Montparnasse on July 18, 1936, when his friend André Malraux rushed in from his office at Agence France-Presse with the news that Franco had invaded Spain as part of a coup d'état to overthrow the republican government. As soon as he heard this, Fernando asked Sartre, who was also there, to take me home and explain to my mother what had happened—and he immediately went off to the Spanish Embassy to volunteer to fight against Franco. At the embassy he was told to wait. Two days later, following a send-off attended by all of the artists and writers of Montparnasse, described by Simone de Beauvoir in her memoirs, he and three friends left for Spain to join the Republican cause.

2. Lacan, the famous post-structuralist psychoanalyst who focused on such Freudian unconscious complexes as fear of castration, was a friend of Sartre, and at one time tried to analyze him.

3. She survived, became a militant, and wrote an important book about the era, called *La Goutte d'Or*, the name of the Algerian sector of Paris.

4. Ripert was a leftist Christian Democrat who served as de Gaulle's minister of planning.

5. The Algerian War for independence from French colonial rule began in 1954. In France, a tripartite coalition that included the left won election in 1956, and the socialist prime minister Guy Mollet sent a French military force led by Jacques

Massu to crush the Algerian rebellion. Massu's troops systematically tortured Algerian prisoners, including the leaders of the Communist Party (graphically described by Henri Alleg in *The Question,* published in 1958). The French minister of justice at the time was the socialist François Mitterrand, who became president years later, and it was he who launched the slogan "Algérie sera toujours française" [Algeria will always be French]. The Algerian crisis led directly to the return to power of Charles de Gaulle in 1958 and the establishment of the Fifth Republic in France.

6. Sartre used the word *merde,* which is much more common in printed intellectual discussion in French than the word "shit" is in English.

7. Lycée Henri IV and Lycée Louis-le-Grand are two of the most demanding public secondary schools in France. Philo was then the year after the end of high school, when students prepared for the extremely difficult *baccalauréat* exam, which was often claimed (erroneously) to be the equivalent of a B.A. Khâgne and hypo-khâgne were the two years of preparatory study required for entrance to the "great schools," such as L'Ecole Normale Supérieure.

8. The Ecole Normale, which is the most advanced and difficult school of social sciences, and for which entrance is by a competitive nationwide examination, is on rue d'Ulm in the center of Paris. Sartre studied there from 1924 to 1929. The *agrégation* is an advanced doctoral degree that requires tough exams and finally a dissertation on an original theme, to be defended against as many as four "inquisitors."

9. Sartre's first dissertation was a very original work that he later published as *A Theory of Emotions* (1939). For his second try he read the previous ten first-place finishers, noted the structure they had in common, and applied this formula to his own work. The formula was this: 60 pages on a philosophical theory that closely resembled but was not identical to the prevailing philosophical view by the reigning master of the time, then add 240 pages (dissertations were expected to run 300 pages) of quotes, résumés, and debates about that prevailing view, always making it win over all objections. After he finished first in the agrégation, Sartre and his best friend, Paul Nizan, snuck into the school library, rounded up all the copies of his second dissertation, and burned them.

10. Sartre began his teaching career in Le Havre in 1931. Since all of Les Grandes Ecoles, the great schools, of which L'Ecole Normale is among the most prestigious, are state-sponsored schools, totally free, the government demands that its graduates teach, at prevailing market wages, in state schools for ten years after graduation. One can pay back the education's costs, prorated, at any time, as Sartre did after his first best seller, *Nausea,* in which Le Havre is called Bouville (Mudtown).

11. The philosopher and political scientist Raymond Aron became friends with Sartre at L'Ecole Normale. As a well-known social democrat, he became an "established" thinker and was loved, and still is, by the mainstream media. Fernando, who explained phenomenology to Sartre, had studied philosophy first with Kurt Cassirer

in Berlin, then with Edmund Husserl in Freiburg. He was in the same class with Martin Heidegger, and they both ended up as teaching assistants (*privatdozent*) in the local *gymnasium* (upper high school) as they prepared their dissertations. Fernando had actually finished his (on "the phenomenology of thinking"), but had not yet defended it, when he happened to hear a lecture by the art historian and philosopher Heinrich Wölfflin. Fernando thereupon abandoned philosophy, followed Wölfflin to Munich and then to Zurich, where he joined the studio of the painter Stanislaw Stückgold, and decided to be an artist. After spending a couple of years copying the paintings of Velázquez at the Prado in order to "gain the skill," he came to Paris in 1924 and ended up living with a Ukrainian émigré, Stépha Awdykowicz, who was studying at the Sorbonne in the same class as her best friend, Simone de Beauvoir, who was also preparing for her agrégation and often studied with Sartre. (Beauvoir placed second, behind Sartre, in 1929.) Beauvoir had a short affair with her classmate René Maheu, who "deflowered" her (as she told me, although she did not say this in her memoirs), after which she and Sartre became lovers. Stépha and Fernando were married in 1929, and the two couples often vacationed together.

DECEMBER 1970

1. The 1968 rebellion began on March 22, 1968, at one of the University of Paris branches, Nanterre, when the local prefect came to inaugurate a swimming pool that the government had built. At the commemoration, a student named Daniel Cohn-Bendit yelled, "We don't give a fuck about your swimming pool, we want to make love," and demanded that restrictions on women's dorms be decided by the occupants rather than by administrators.

"Danny the Red," as he was quickly dubbed both because of his politics and his red hair, was a French-born German Jew whose parents had come to France to escape Hitler in 1933, but had returned to Germany after the war, hence giving him a German passport, which gave the authorities the excuse to deport him, temporarily, when he became popular with students across France. In a speech attacking the bourgeois students who would inevitably become exploiters of workers after they graduated, the Communist Party head Georges Marchais scoffed at "that German Jew" as a spoiled troublemaker. That got a million students marching through Paris chanting, "We are all German Jews!"

The students were quickly supported and organized by leftist but anti-communist militants, particularly the young instructor Alain Geismar, student union leader Jacques Sauvageot, and Trotskyist agitator Alain Krivine. They condemned the whole French political system and specifically attacked the educational system, which forced students to compete against one another through a series of tests—as Sartre, Nizan, Aron, Beauvoir, and most of the government officials had themselves gone through—that guaranteed an alienating political structure. As the movement

NOTES TO PAGE 29

gained more and more followers—5 million students from high schools and universities had joined the marches by mid-April—the Communist Party began to backtrack. By May 3, workers all over France had occupied their factories and were demanding, like the students, self-determination (*autogestion*). At the Rouen shipyards, communist workers helped students distribute leaflets condemning the CP for its participation in the political system. At Sud-Aviation, workers went on strike against union orders, demanding more of a voice in their lives.

The leaders of the unrest, including Geismar, Krivine, and Cohn-Bendit, had been influenced by their teachers, their reading, the intellectual ferment bubbling in the cafés and academia and the journals of the day. At the forefront was *Les Temps Modernes*. Sartre himself had broken with the CP for refusing to condemn the Soviet invasion of Berlin, in 1953, and then of Hungary in 1956. His book *The Ghost of Stalin* had shaken youth's hope that the CP would lead the struggle against the new capitalism. André Gorz, political editor of *Les Temps Modernes* and Sartre's disciple, had been refining a new ideology, soon known as existential Marxism, which basically claimed that all old notions of a materially exploited proletariat no longer applied. In advanced industrial capitalism, Gorz said, workers would be more and more highly trained and skilled, hence well paid, but more and more alienated from their work. Socialists, he predicted, would have to demand more self-management, a restructuring of the work center to allow for more worker creativity. As early as 1957, Gorz had written in *The Traitor*, which was prefaced by Sartre, that there can no longer be a unified revolutionary class, and in his 1964 book, *Strategy for Labor*, he foreshadowed the emergence of a new working class, which would be much more spontaneous, anarchistic, and basically white-collar.

On May 8, Sartre, Gorz, Beauvoir, and their group signed a declaration carried in *Le Monde* supporting the students. On May 12, as 5 million took to the streets of Paris, Sartre approved their methods in an interview on Radio Luxembourg. The communists continued to define the students as spoiled brats. Claude Lévi-Strauss lamented the death of structuralism and "that all objectivity has been repudiated." He blamed Sartre, and his followers blamed Marcuse. Cohn-Bendit set the record straight: "Some people have tried to force Marcuse on us as a mentor; that is a joke. None of us have read Marcuse. Some of us have read Marx, of course, Bakunin, Althusser, Mao, Guevara, Lefebvre, and all of us have read Sartre." Cohn-Bendit had studied with Henri Lefebvre, a communist philosopher who advocated a revolution through dealienating festivity, for which the CP reprimanded him. Geismar had studied with Louis Althusser, whose Marxism offered no voice to spontaneity. When Althusser showed up at the Odéon, the Paris bastion of culture that had been seized by the students, he and Louis Aragon, the communist poet, were jeered. Lefebvre, too, was booed, despite his support, simply because he tried to tell them what to do.

But when Sartre entered, he got a standing ovation. Asked why he was there, he answered, "To learn," which prompted another standing ovation. He told me in an interview for the *New York Times Magazine* (October 17, 1971): "I did learn. I understood that what the young were putting into question was not just capitalism, imperialism, the system, etc., but those of us who pretended to be against all that as well. We can say that from 1940 to 1968, I was a left-wing intellectual, and from 1968 on I became an intellectual leftist. The difference is one of action."

On May 25, de Gaulle reached an agreement known as the Grenelle Accord with the CGT, France's largest—and communist—union confederation, granting workers unprecedented material benefits. Yet laborers throughout France refused to return to work. When Georges Séguy, head of the CGT, tried to address his members who had occupied the Renault car centers, he was booed. By that night, 10 million workers were on strike.

By May 29, Cohn-Bendit had snuck back from Germany, and all of France was virtually paralyzed. De Gaulle went to Baden-Baden to ask General Massu, head of the French forces occupying its sector of Germany, to invade France and restore order. Massu refused. When it became clear that the government was about to fall, de Gaulle offered French workers a 10 percent wage increase. The Communist Party gave in, promising an alliance with the Socialist Party and other leftist groups, and a platform that would fight alienation and try to establish self-management in industry. The workers began to return to their jobs. The educational reforms were canceled. The revolution was over. That didn't save de Gaulle, however; in a plebiscite later he was voted out of office. The CP never came through on its vows, and it gradually lost its power in French politics. Once the biggest individual party in France, it now struggles along on 9 to 12 percent of the vote.

Cohn-Bendit became a politician and is currently a German Green Party deputy to the European Parliament. Krivine became head of the Trotskyist League, and ran for president of France numerous times, not in the hope of getting elected, but in order to explain his views, since French law provides for equal media time for all candidates during a campaign. Geismar became a supervisor of the educational system.

2. *Fesse à fesse*, in French; literally, "ass-cheek to ass-cheek," meaning very close and dependent on one another.

3. Beauvoir had affairs with both Olga Kosakiewicz and Bost (their threesome formed the basis of her novel *She Came to Stay*). Sartre also famously tried to seduce Olga for as much as two years. Olga was supposed to star in his play *No Exit*, but didn't, probably because she refused to have an affair with him. Bost and Olga became romantically involved with each other, and eventually married. Bost remained a loyal friend of Sartre's all his life.

4. Wanda Kosakiewicz, Olga's younger sister, became a longtime Sartre lover (the character Ivich in his novel *The Roads* was partly based on her). At one point Sartre proposed marriage to Wanda.

5. Arlette Elkaïm was a nineteen-year-old Algerian Jewish student of philosophy when she became Sartre's mistress in the 1950s. He legally adopted her as his daughter about a decade later.

6. Michelle Vian (born Michelle Léglise) was married to the writer and musician Boris Vian, who died in 1959. She became one of Sartre's mistresses in 1949, and remained very close to him until his death.

7. At the time of this conversation Sartre was renting a studio at 222 boulevard Raspail; Beauvoir's apartment was on rue Schoelcher, very nearby. Sartre had bought an apartment when his mother moved in with him, at 42 rue Bonaparte, but he got rid of it when she died, and always rented after that. Beauvoir, whose books always hit the best-seller list and made her a lot of money, bought her apartment. The other three were purchased by Sartre, who was very generous. When I decided to buy an apartment, he lent me thirty thousand francs (about twenty thousand dollars then). Later, when I sold it, I gave him a check to repay the loan; he looked stunned, asked what it was. When I reminded him, he said, "Well, I don't remember," and tore it up. Sartre made most of his money from his plays, although Gallimard, his publishing house, never refused to send him money whenever he asked, no matter how much was in his account. One reason he adopted Arlette, he told me, was because she was very methodical and would never forget to send his monthly "allowance" to his various former mistresses, which she did, meticulously.

JANUARY 1971

1. Schools in France are closed on Thursday and Sunday, not Saturday.

2. While in his twenties, Nizan wrote a book called *Aden, Arabie* (1931) about a trip he made to the Middle East, followed by a slew of political novels. During the Spanish Civil War he was a correspondent for *Ce Soir*, a communist daily. He quit the Communist Party after the Nazi-Soviet Nonaggression Pact, joined the French army, and sent his party card to Jacques Duclos, a communist senator and the Comintern's top foreign ideologue. He was killed in the battle of Dunkirk in 1940.

3. These works were published posthumously by Gallimard in Michel Contat, ed., *Sartre's Youthful Writings*, in 1990.

4. La Gauche Prolétarienne (GP), the Proletarian Left, was a party of young ultra-leftist Maoists, whose activism was a bit weird by usual political standards; it was very moral. The GP did things like seizing unoccupied buildings and opening them up to the homeless, inviting important intellectuals, like Sartre, Michel Foucault, Jean Genet, and Claude Mauriac, to help forestall attacks by the police. At this time I was teaching at the University of Paris VIII, Vincennes, because I had been blacklisted in the United States as a result of my participation and jailing in a 1966 student antiwar protest at San Francisco State College, which, like all universities at the time, encouraged war research. The teachers' union lawyers fought that blacklist de-

cree and eventually won, in 1976, whereupon I was hired by the University of California at Irvine.

5. In *Sartre par lui-même*, edited by Francis Jeanson (Paris: Seuil, 1969), a compilation of autobiographical quotes by Sartre.

6. Jeanson was the organizer of a network that actively assisted the Algerian independence fighters. The declaration, released in 1960 and originally signed by 121 well-known French intellectuals and cultural figures opposed to France's colonial war, advocated sedition against the French state, calling on the French people to aid the FLN by giving them not only medicine and money but also arms, ammunition, and intelligence, and wherever possible to carry out sabotage against the French effort. The manifesto, de Gaulle said later, did more to persuade him to grant Algeria full independence than the FLN's constant attacks.

7. The title means something like "In the Shadow of the Execution Wall." It has not been translated into English.

MARCH 1971

1. Guille's parents were actually teachers who owned land.

2. A compound in the 14th arrondissement of Paris set up by the French government for advanced students, both French and foreign.

3. An aside at this point between Gerassi and Sartre reads:

> GERASSI: You know that changed radically in '29. Fernando's parents, who had been extremely rich, lost all their fortune when the Atatürk government [of Turkey] confiscated the holdings of foreigners in 1927. They came to Paris broke and told their sons, OK, we paid for your life until now, so it's your turn to reciprocate. Fernando and his brother, Alfredo, a pianist, tossed a coin and Alfredo lost the first round. Two years each, they had decided. So Alfredo went to work as a salesman for some Hungarian electrical company. But in '29, he went back to his music and told Fernando to take over. He did, and so well that the company offered him the top job in Madrid. He did so well there too that he rented a huge house, had two maids, staged huge parties at which the intelligentsia flocked, and when all Spaniards took their siesta, from four to eight, he painted. At eight o'clock he returned to his office, like everyone else.
>
> **SARTRE: I remember very well. It was at those parties, when Castor and I visited him, that we met Neruda, Gonzalez, Alberti, Dalí, even Picasso, who used to stay with Fernando and Stépha when he came to Madrid, right?**
>
> No, that was in Barcelona. Fernando was so successful that he asked to establish the firm's headquarters in Barcelona, which he greatly preferred to Madrid. Do you know that it was because he was poor that Stépha hooked up with Fernando in the first place?

In Berlin?

No, she disliked him then. In 1925, she was living with Alban Berg, who had gone to Berlin from his native Vienna because his opera *Wozzeck* (completed in 1922) was finally going to be performed (in December 1925). She had first met him in Vienna when she was released from jail for having written and distributed feminist tracts. Berg was staying in a sort-of reserved-for-musicians mansion, where Alfredo was also staying. And Fernando came to visit him. "They were both filthy rich," she told me, "but at least Alfredo was not ostentatious about it. But your father was an incredible dandy; I couldn't stand him." When she ran into him in 1927 in Montparnasse, however, he was completely broke. "He couldn't even afford a belt; he held his pants with a rope. But he was the same dandy. This time, I liked him."

And so she became the breadwinner of the Gerassi family.

Until the end. After he was discharged from OSS [Fernando worked for the U.S. Office of Strategic Services during World War II], he made a sort of living by doing translations. But when he decided he had to paint again, in 1946, she went to work, off the books because they didn't have work permits, in a shoe factory, ten hours a day, then did the shopping on the way home, then cooked. I hated him for that, and I also lost respect for my mother.

Is that why you ran away from home, at fifteen?

A week before my sixteenth birthday. I slept in the park that first night, it was in July, then I got a room in a boarding house for five dollars a week. You know what had happened. I came home from school for dinner that day, and Stépha served us the same concoction we had had for three days. I remember it very well, a sort of creamed stew on bread, what in the army we called "shit on a shingle." And I said, Not again? Fernando jumped: "How dare you criticize the food, you're not even a paying guest here." I got up and went to pack. I heard my mother, I swear, not my father, my mother, I still can hear her, say to my father, "Go in there and patch it up. He's too young to go on his own." And I heard, I still hear, my father say, "Let him go. It'll be good for his character." Well, it was the reverse. They both told me so later.

Boy, what a woman! No wonder I was so . . . And she kept financing him, didn't she?

Yep, three years after they were hired to teach at the Putney School in Vermont, he quit to paint full time, and she kept teaching. When she was forced to retire at sixty-five, she went to work for Rudolph Serkin's music school in Philadelphia, and came home every weekend to prepare food for Fernando for the week. Even when she was operated on for breast cancer with two radical mastectomies, she went back one week later and cooked him his week's food. I asked her once why did she give up her own desire to write. She said, "I decided he was a better painter than I was a writer, so . . ."

4. Zaza was the third of six children in a very Catholic upper-middle-class family. As a result of her friendship with the Catholic but already doubting Simone de Beauvoir, whom she met in school at age eleven, as well as the Russian Orthodox but then agnostic Stépha, Zaza began to have her own doubts about her faith. She was ecstatic about her impending marriage to Merleau-Ponty, also a Catholic but by then an atheist. When he broke his vows as a result of her family's blackmail letter, she fell into a depression that, according to Beauvoir, caused the encephalitis that killed her at twenty-one. She was called Elizabeth Mabille in Beauvoir's *Memoirs of a Dutiful Daughter.* See also *Zaza: Correspondance et carnets d'Elisabeth Lacoin* (Seuil, 1991).

5. Maurice Merleau-Ponty was teaching at the prestigious Collège de France when he died of a stroke, in 1961, at age fifty-three. *Sens et non-sens* has not been translated into English.

APRIL 1971

1. I was an observer at the latter representing the Revolutionary Contingent, the name of the chapter of Students for a Democratic Society at the Free University in New York. The university flourished for a while on Fourteenth Street, attracting antiwar militants from all over New York and across the country. American delegates at OLAS included a delegation of Black Liberation fighters, headed by Stokely Carmichael.

2. Padilla was an award-winning poet who was arrested and imprisoned for writing critically about the Cuban revolutionary government and then forced to publicly recant his "subversive writing." He became the subject of international controversy when writers and intellectuals, including Sartre, protested his repression.

3. Rousset was a political activist and writer in the late 1940s and 1950s and part of Sartre's Third Force movement until it fell apart. He then argued that neutralism was nevertheless the only respectable position to maintain, even if it might not save the planet. Sartre ridiculed him as the editor in his play *Nekrassov.*

4. Following de Gaulle's resignation in 1969, Georges Pompidou was elected president. He reversed de Gaulle's policy of vetoing the United Kingdom's application to join the European Economic Community (a forerunner of the European Union), leading to British membership in 1973.

5. Böhme was an early-seventeenth-century German Christian mystic, known as "the servant of god." Eckhart, a German mystical theologian of the late thirteenth–early fourteenth century, was charged with heresy by Pope John XXII. Thomas à Kempis was an important German Christian theologian of the fifteenth century.

Ignatius of Loyola was an influential sixteenth-century Catholic theologian and the founder of the Jesuit order.

6. "Slum" (*un taudis*) is an exaggeration; we lived in a three-floor walkup under the Third Avenue El (the aboveground rail line that has since been demolished) in Midtown Manhattan.

7. Fernando was still painting, and walking every day the two miles to a little red schoolhouse that the town of Putney, Vermont, rented him for the ridiculous sum of thirty-five dollars a year—a purely symbolic gesture, because the school, though abandoned, was required by law not to operate at a deficit, and someone had calculated that the cost of keeping the driveway open at that spot cost thirty-five dollars. Everyone knew him, with his black beret and his faithful chow at his side. At first they would stop to offer him a ride, but as he refused politely ("I have to walk for my health," he would say), they learned just to slow down and wave. He died of cancer in 1974 at seventy-four.

8. Sartre had visited the United States in 1946 as a reporter for *Combat*, a newspaper edited by Albert Camus, and was shepherded around the country by some publicity organization. He never traveled to the United States again after that.

9. There were two problems, actually. The first was when he visited in 1946. Fernando at one point asked him if he had collaborated with the Nazis. Sartre jumped, shocked at the question. Fernando quickly explained that he had heard that Sartre had put on his play *The Flies* at the old Sarah Bernhardt theater, named for the great French actress, but changed by the Germans because she was Jewish. That was true, but I did not dare bring it up. The second was after my parents finally gained American citizenship (helped by Robert F. Kennedy), and they went to Vienna to see Stépha's mother, who was still in a displaced-persons camp, to arrange better living conditions for her. They phoned Sartre, asking him to meet them in Milan, where they had been invited to stay free. Sartre refused, insisting that they come to see him in Rome. But my parents could not afford the detour and the hotel stays that would be required. I reminded him of that issue.

10. In French, *la drôle de guerre:* the first eight months of World War II, following the German invasion of Poland, when no fighting on the Western Front was taking place. Sartre was then in the meteorological service with nothing to do. So he started writing.

MAY 1971

1. General Ridgway, of Korean War fame, was appointed head of NATO military forces in Europe in 1952. The French left reacted angrily, staging huge protest demonstrations that featured signs reading "Ridgway Go Home!" The standoff was not resolved until de Gaulle made his coup in 1958 and ordered NATO forces out of France.

2. Blum ordered the French border with Spain closed in obedience to a directive from the Non-Intervention Committee created by the League of Nations, despite the fact that Nazi Germany and Fascist Italy and, to a lesser extent, Soviet Russia were violating the committee's arms embargo.

3. Jeanson had become a key editor of *Les Temps Modernes,* and eventually became chief editor. Lanzmann was a good friend of Sartre's and was Beauvoir's lover for years. He produced and directed the hugely successful film documentary *Shoah* (1985), and then an awful one on the Israeli Defense Force. (He and I were once friends, but we fell out over my support of the Israeli Socialist Organization and a Palestinian state.) Both Jeanson and Lanzmann fought in the resistance during the war, but neither was considered by Sartre and Beauvoir a member of "the family," which mostly included prewar students and friends. My so-called membership in the family was because of my parents.

4. I did interview Jeanson and his wife, and liked them tremendously. Jeanson has written or edited various works on Sartre, notably *Sartre by Himself* and *Sartre's Ethics.*

5. *The Condemned of Altona* (1959), which is rarely performed anymore, is about a Nazi German industrialist and his family. One of the main characters in the play envisions a future in which a race of crabs sits in judgment of humankind.

6. Fernando had escaped from Franco's forces at the last minute on the last plane to leave Barcelona. Because the French were then arresting all Spanish Republicans, he parachuted over the French Pyrenees and made his way to Paris, where he obtained a work permit by sticking up the prefect of the 14th arrondissement with a pipe in his pocket. When the prefect saw him take it out and put it in his mouth, he told him he would now be arrested, but Fernando apparently said: "You want the press to know you got held up by a pipe?" Whereupon the prefect accompanied Fernando to the door and quipped: "I am honored, my general." Fernando was then denounced by the Russian émigré artist Nicolas de Staël, who earned his living as a police informer. Fernando was sent first to Fresnes, the central police holding station where later eighty thousand French Jews would be processed for Nazi extermination camps, then told he would be freed if he joined the French army. Fernando said only with the rank of colonel and his own brigade, which he commanded near Les Vosges. During the debacle, he got all his Jewish soldiers into Switzerland, then returned to Paris and the exodus with Stépha and me.

OCTOBER 1971

1. The French call September *la rentrée,* the return, as if everyone had gone and then returned. Of course, this is true only of those who can afford a vacation. Certainly not the poor Algerians and Moroccans, or the blacks from former French colonies in Africa.

2. In general assemblies at the university, everyone who might be affected by any decision or policy being considered was invited, not just students but also teachers, administrators, cleaning workers, even the rector of the university. The administration and rector of Vincennes were then communist, and opposed to any movement that gave decision-making power to the base, to an unorganized majority. One consequence was very significant. The cleaning staff, mostly illegal Portuguese immigrants hired by a company contracted by the rector, went on strike to demand better pay. Some teachers, including me, immediately supported the strikers, telling our students that class would he held on the picket lines. An AG was then called, where the vast majority voted to support the strike. By day four, almost no classes were held. The rector then called on his party to help, and on day five we were attacked by the *service de l'ordre*, the order service, meaning the enforcer goons of the CP, all tough steelworkers ready to bash our heads with metal pipes. But because of the press, alerted by some of the most famous professors then teaching at Vincennes, including Gilles Deleuze, Lacan, Foucault, and Sartre, we were able to hold on and the cleaners won a new contract. What we got was the rector's promise that all decisions affecting the university would thereafter be submitted to the AG. It didn't last, of course, as the CP gradually and quietly forced out the anti-CP leftists (*gauchistes*), including me two years later.

3. In *The Cell*, two men, one a torturer for the prerevolutionary Cuban regime of Fulgencio Batista and the other an intellectual opponent of Castro's revolution—the former clearly recuperable, the other not—are awaiting execution. It was produced at New York's Judson Memorial Theater in 1961 and various times in Cuba.

4. *Tout* [Everything], a new-left nondogmatic Trotskyist street newspaper, took its name from the 1968 student protest slogan, "What do we want? Everything!"

5. The New York chapter of Students for a Democratic Society (SDS) started a Free University in 1966 above a fast-food joint on Fourteenth Street that attracted not only hundreds of students, even from out of state, but also some "name" professors, like Conor Cruise O'Brien, Noam Chomsky, Isaac Deutscher, and Eric Hobsbawm, among others. We also published a review titled *Treason*, edited by a revolutionary named Sharon Krebs and influenced by Jeanson and Sartre's seditious stand against the war in Algeria. My play *The Cell* first appeared in this review.

6. Which, nevertheless, he did do during the May '68 strikes.

7. *Mauvaise foi*, usually translated as "bad faith," although the concept has nothing to do with faith. It means fooling oneself, refusing to acknowledge reality, but where reality is the situation, not something metaphysical.

8. That is what indeed happened. Soon after the Liberation, de Gaulle was installed as France's provisional president. But soon he was denouncing the system as moribund as it had been before the war, with a constant rivalry among scores of parties, from the CP, which was the biggest, to tiny provincial parties. In 1946, de Gaulle

got fed up and quit, saying that when France was desperate, the French would call him back. Which is what Gaullist historians claim happened in 1958, but in fact, de Gaulle staged a coup d'état and established the Fifth Republic, giving the president—himself—near-autocratic power. In 1946 he had obeyed the constitution and offered the presidency to Maurice Thorez, head of the largest political party, the Communist Party. Thorez said no thanks. He knew very well that should he take over the presidency of a country still suffering economically from the war and still dominated by U.S. troops, he could only discredit communism as a way of life, then get overthrown.

9. An FBI officer from Kansas, Mitrione was trained as a CIA expert in explosives and then torture, and was sent to various countries in Latin America to teach the local police how to torture without leaving traces. As correspondent A. J. Langguth documented, first in the *New York Times* in 1970, then with specific details in his book *Hidden Terrors,* published by Pantheon in 1978, Mitrione became especially adept at the use of the *picana,* an electric cattle prod, to deliver extremely painful shocks to torture victims. He was eventually kidnapped by the Tupamaros, Uruguay's resistance movement, and tried in an underground people's court in 1970. He was taped confessing with such precise details that there could be no dispute about the facts, and was then executed. The CIA has steadfastly refused to admit that it furnished friendly Latin American police forces with implements used for torture.

10. Sartre believed but had no proof that Moulin's decision to work with the communist underground, which he did after consultation with de Gaulle in London, led a right-wing Gaullist member of his unit to betray him. Moulin was tortured to death by Klaus Barbie, the "butcher of Lyon."

11. This part of the story is called "Drôle d'amitié," or Strange Friendship, and was published in *Les Temps Modernes.*

12. *Dirty Hands* is about a lowly communist, Hugo, sent to be secretary to the most respected leader of the party, Hoederer, with the task of assassinating him because the other leaders are against his policy of cooperating with noncommunists. After Hoederer is killed, Moscow orders the party to cooperate with noncommunists, and Hoederer is turned into a hero.

13. Or, actually, refused to sleep with him.

14. Boris Vian was an acclaimed novelist and jazz musician. He was married to the actress Michelle Léglise, who later became one of Sartre's mistresses. Vian died of a heart attack in 1959, at age thirty-nine.

15. *Salt of the Earth* (1954) was directed by Herbert Biberman, produced by Paul Jarrico, and starred Will Geer (as the sheriff), who had all been blacklisted in Hollywood during the McCarthy-era witch hunts, featured the real-life miners of a New Mexico zinc mine and their wives, plus the Mexican professional actress Rosaura Re-

vueltas. *Queimada* (1969), released as *Burn!* in the United States, is an Italian film directed by Gillo Pontecorvo, starring Marlon Brando, about British neocolonialism and revolution in the Caribbean in the nineteenth century. Pontecorvo's best-known film, *The Battle of Algiers* (1966), is actually shown to American soldiers bound for Iraq, since it explains so well native insurgency.

16. A Portuguese-trained agricultural engineer from the Portuguese colony of Guinea-Bissau, Cabral led the independence struggle against Portugal until he was assassinated by a CIA operative who had infiltrated Cabral's African Party for the Independence of Guinea and Cape Verde, barely a few months before the country won its freedom in January 1973. At the Tricontinental Conference in Havana in 1966, Cabral developed the theory that in Third World anti-imperialist struggles, revolutionary leaders must commit class suicide.

17. Benny Lévy, an Egyptian Jew born in 1945, came to France illegally with his family as a child, studied philosophy at the Ecole Normale, and got involved in the May 1968 events. As a Maoist and editor of the GP's *Cause du Peuple,* he went by the names Pierre Victor and Pierre Bloch. When Sartre became blind and hard of hearing in the 1970s, Lévy became his personal secretary, and would read him the newspapers every day. Thanks to the intervention of Sartre, Lévy was eventually granted citizenship. Influenced by the Talmudic philosopher Emmanuel Lévinas, Lévy became a serious student of the Talmud, moving "from Mao to Moses," as the joke went.

18. Drieu la Rochelle and Brasillach were first-rate prewar writers, influenced by the monarchist, reactionary, and anti-Semitic essayist-poet-critic Charles Maurras, a member of the Académie Française. All three were tried for treason after the war and condemned to death. De Gaulle refused to commute the sentences of Drieu, who committed suicide, and Brasillach, who went to the gallows shouting "God bless France, despite!" He did commute that of Maurras, who had opposed actual collaboration and who stayed in jail until 1952, a few weeks before his death.

19. The Barbouze was a top-secret French police force composed of agents from France's foreign intelligence service, which systematically tortured "enemies of the state."

20. I met the Mailers when I was fifteen and working as a gofer after school for the International Literary Bureau, and fell madly in love with Norman's sister Barbara, who unfortunately was much older and didn't requite my attentions. I don't remember how it happened, but one weekend when I was driving to Vermont to see my folks, I took along an old Trotskyist pal of Fernando's, the French writer Jean Malaquais, and Norman Mailer. Malaquais and Mailer were so taken by the area that they rented a house nearby, which is where Mailer wrote *Barbary Shore,* which he dedicated to Malaquais. Mailer and Fernando became good friends.

21. Sartre did attempt a comprehensive ethics through various works, most of

which have now been published. Besides his massive though unfinished second volume of the *Critique of Dialectical Reason*, they include his lecture at the Gramsci Institute in 1964, his notes for his canceled 1965 lecture series at Cornell, and his posthumously published *Notes for an Ethics*, written on and off from 1960 until his death in 1980. Together, the works combine Existentialism and Marxism to establish an ethics of authenticity, commitment, and socially founded decision making, grounded in historical context, hence constantly evolving and changing, which explains its difficulty.

DECEMBER 1971

1. Salacrou was one of France's most popular prewar playwrights, whose greatest successes were staged by Charles Dullin, the same director who made Sartre's play successful. After the war, Salacrou mixed his ferocious denunciations of social injustices with an all-pervasive anguish at the absurdity of death.

2. Vavin is the basic Montparnasse stop, site of Le Dôme, La Coupole, La Rotonde, and Le Select cafés; Saint-Germain is where Le Flore and Les Deux Magots still flourish.

3. Louis-Ferdinand Céline, whose real name was Destouches, published his brilliant first novel, *Journey to the End of the Night*, in 1932, introducing a streetwise language that influenced most French and Western writers who followed him. A physician by trade, Céline then wrote various pamphlets attacking Jews and praising the Nazi attempt to rid the world of them. Branded a collaborator, he escaped jail by fleeing first to Germany, then Denmark, and returned in 1951 when he was pardoned. He wrote more novels but survived mainly as a physician, and died in 1961.

4. Roger Garaudy had a very strange politico-philosophical life. He was a prisoner in Algeria during World War II. Later he attempted to reconcile Marxism and Catholicism, waging enthusiastic debates with prominent writers of both sides, including Sartre. In 1982 he abandoned both to become a Muslim, taking the name Ragaa. In 1995 Garaudy published a treatise on the Holocaust denying that Jews were killed in concentration camps; he was charged with "Holocaust denial," which is a racial slur under French law, and was fined $40,000—which was partly paid by the Iranian government—and went to live in Spain. His book was widely translated into Arabic, Persian, and various African languages.

5. Duclos, a longtime prewar French communist deputy, was a renowned leader of the resistance, then a senator after the war. He ran for president in 1969 and got 21 percent of the vote. He died in 1975.

6. At first a communist, then an independent leftist deputy, Rossanda, a brilliant writer, editor, and journalist, was one of the founders of the daily *Il Manifesto*, which is still published today.

7. Vanetti, a journalist of Abyssinian and Italian descent, had lived in France

until 1938, when she immigrated to the United States to marry an American doctor. In 1945, when Sartre came to the States and Fernando introduced her to him, she was working for the propaganda bureau of the Office of War Information, as was my father, after he was discharged from the OSS. Sartre and Dolores became lovers, and she showed him America very thoroughly.

8. Creole was a subsidiary of Standard Oil (now Exxon-Mobil).

JANUARY 1972

1. The novels *Aurélien* and *Cheval Blanc* were typical communist tearjerkers.

2. Lukacs, a Hungarian Marxist literary critic, was billed by communists all over the world, and many bourgeois commentators as well, as a brilliant analyst and philosopher. He survived all purges and died in 1971.

3. Conditions at this prison, where many of the militants of the time had been interred, were so outrageous that not only Sartre and Foucault but also Mauriac and other intellectuals denounced them, forcing the French government to undertake some basic reforms.

4. The title of Zola's famous attack, written in 1898, on the controversial condemnation of Alfred Dreyfus to Devil's Island. Sartre wrote his own "J'accuse" about the repression carried out by the government, which became a famous poster prominently displayed on university walls.

5. These attacks caused Sartre to feel dizzy for a few minutes. His doctors said they were caused by his excessive consumption of speed for most of his life.

6. Sartre refused the French Legion of Honor and the Nobel Prize for Literature.

7. Yuli Daniel and Andrei Sinyavsky were tried in 1966 for writing parodies of the Soviet system and smuggling them out of Russia. They refused to go into exile and survived.

FEBRUARY 1972

1. Generals Edmond Jouhaud, Maurice Challe, and André Zeller, with the support of General Raoul Salan, were the official leaders of the March 1961 coup against the de Gaulle government, which had decided to negotiate with the Algerian National Liberation Front after the French voted overwhelmingly for Algerian self-determination in a national referendum. After the coup's defeat, mainly because soldiers refused to obey the generals, the putschist brass launched the OAS, which bombed scores of pro-Algerian intellectuals and assassinated loyal officers and civil servants. The OAS was dismantled in 1963, and the generals, including those who had taken refuge in Franco's Spain but had been turned over to the de Gaulle government, were tried and condemned to various years in prison, with Salan getting the death sentence. Some of the real OAS leaders, mostly colonels and right-wing

civilians who were found guilty of murder, were executed by firing squad. The OAS torture experts escaped to Argentina, however, and taught the military there how to torture during the "dirty war," in which thirty thousand were "disappeared" and tortured to death. Jouhaud, Challe, and Zeller were amnestied in 1968 and eventually reintegrated into their services.

2. Maria Casares Quiroga, the daughter of a Spanish Republican prime minister, grew up in France and became one of its great stage actresses, starring in plays by Ibsen, Synge, and Camus himself. She is still heralded for her movie roles in Marcel Carné's *Children of Paradise*, Robert Bresson's *The Charterhouse of Parma*, and as death in Jean Cocteau's *Orpheus*.

3. Lazareff was a journalistic genius who turned *Paris-Soir*, then *France-Soir*, and other magazines like *Elle*, along with TV news programs, into huge successes. More sensationalist than political, he would often forget his right-wing sympathies for a hot story, right or left.

4. Wanda Kosakiewicz played under the name Marie Olivier, subsequently as Wanda Olivier.

5. Both Dominique Desanti and her husband were powerful communist political essayists during this period.

6. Literally, the Great Sartrienne, but in French street talk it was more like the Great Sartriod or Sartroush.

7. Robert Gallimard, a son of the founder of the publishing house, had become a good friend of mine.

8. Karol, Rossanda's live-in partner, was a journalist who often wrote for the non-CP leftist weekly *Le Nouvel Observateur*, and also wrote an excellent analysis of the Cuban revolution in a book titled *The Guerrillas in Power*.

MARCH 1972

1. Marty refused to plead guilty to any of the charges during the party trial, saying he was too old to remember what he had said, and died in 1966 supposedly heartbroken.

2. Over the years I told Sartre about many of my adventures in North Vietnam with a team investigating war crimes, and he always wanted to hear more. One was about my stay in Nam Dinh, which the United States claimed had never been bombed, but the *New York Times* correspondent Harrison Salisbury, who had been there before us, said that in fact it had been heavily bombed. One day, two U.S. planes flew overhead. Salisbury had written that the city was completely defenseless, but when the alarm went off, antiaircraft batteries sprang up out of nowhere. Every tree seemed to open up, every roof parted to a cannon. It was an amazing sight. Later, after the all-clear, the mayor, a woman who had fought the French and spent eight years in jail, toured the city with us to view the damage from the four or five bombs the

planes had dropped. I told her that Salisbury had written it was a defenseless city, and she laughed. Then I said, But I prefer it this way, seeing how well you defend your city. She came over and hugged me. That's when Sartre quipped: "Just how a proud French mayor would have done."

Incidentally, when my book came out, with my pictures of Nam Dinh and its mayor, Salisbury called to tell me that I had made him realize he had been blind. Our team was invited to meet with Pham Van Dong, and later Ho Chi Minh. During our talk with Pham, I asked him if he entertained the possibility of accepting international brigades, like in Spain. He answered that if it would lead to uniting all socialist forces against imperialism, perhaps. Then, rather brashly, I said, "Could you say yes before Friday?" Why Friday? he asked. Because, I said, we are supposed to leave Friday, but if you would accept internationals, I would stay and be the first American brigadier. Pham was a man of steel who had spent all his life fighting French colonialists and sixteen years in a French prison. Up to that moment, our talk was very formal. But then, when I made my stupid remark, he jumped to his feet and rushed across the room and embraced me. We all laughed and from then on our discussion was full of banter, jokes, teasing, and fun.

APRIL 1972

1. Just after the battle of Guadalajara, one of the rare Republican victories, Fernando, who had taken over command when General Máté Zalka, known as Pavol Lukács, was killed by one of Mussolini's Capronis, ordered all the civilian political commissars who went around giving orders but didn't actually fight to be put under tent arrest for the duration of the next battle. Fortunately that battle, Huesca, was also a victory, yet the representative of the Comintern, André Marty, still wanted Fernando executed. He was saved by Malraux, who had raised enough money to bring a whole air wing, L'Escadrille Lafayette, to Spain, but told "Comandante Luis," Vittorio Codovilla, the Argentine Communist Party chief who also represented the Comintern, that if they executed Fernando, he would not bring the planes and would denounce the CP's torpedoing of the Loyalist war effort. Malraux was extremely well known then, having written one of the greatest novels of the twentieth century, *La condition humaine* [Man's Fate]. Comandante Luis caved in, and sent Fernando to defend Barcelona. (The complete story is in Henri Godard, ed., *André Malraux* [Paris: Gallimard, 2001].)

2. The word he used was *crapule*, which is much stronger than scum. Koestler had also been very close to the CP, and was trusted by its militants, but when he turned he revealed everything he knew.

3. The CRS was hated by opponents of the government. Signs painted on walls in 1968 routinely read "CRS = SS."

MAY 1972

1. Pierre Mendès-France was a moderate socialist and part of the government of prewar Popular Front prime minister Léon Blum. He escaped from a Vichy jail in 1942 to join de Gaulle in London and was economic minister in his provisional postwar government. Favoring government control of the economy, he quit when de Gaulle opted for market economics, was repeatedly elected a deputy, and formed the "peace government" in 1954, which ended the French war in Indochina. He then agreed to Tunisia's independence, but lost power when he also wanted to grant Algeria its independence. The Mendès-France bow tie was worn by his followers supporting an end to French colonialism in Algeria in 1956, but with a million French "pieds-noirs" voting, he lost the election. He opposed de Gaulle's 1958 coup, but supported his negotiations with the FLN, which eventually gave Algeria independence. He then retired from politics and died in 1982.

2. Nikolai Bukharin, one of the original Bolsheviks, was jailed, exiled, then elected to the Soviet Central Committee and Politburo, appointed editor of the party daily *Izvestia*, and made head of the Comintern. The originator of Lenin's New Economic Policy, he opposed Stalin's collectivization program, and was the main writer of the 1936 Soviet constitution, which guaranteed freedom of speech, press, assembly, religion, and privacy of the person, home, and correspondence—all of which was then ignored by Stalin, who had Bukharin executed for treason in 1938. He was rehabilitated by Gorbachev in 1988.

3. Communist senator Jacques Duclos, who trained homing pigeons in his garden, was arrested and charged with using them to send secret information about France's defenses to the Soviets, giving rise to a massive witch hunt against French communists in the early 1950s. Unlike the trials in the United States, where the population always tends to believe government lies and propaganda, in France the cases were laughed out of court by its more sophisticated juries.

4. Because Picasso pleaded his case directly to Stalin, London was not executed.

5. I went to plant coffee trees in the Isle of Pines that year, the Isle of Youth, as it got to be known. And one day, I think in my second week, some cadreman comes up to me, hands me a rifle and five bullets, and tells me, "It's your turn to pull guard duty tonight." But, I said, I'm a gringo, an enemy. He said: You work with us, you eat with us, you play with us, you pull guard duty with us. And so I did.

6. Matzpen, the Israeli Socialist Organization, was created in 1962 by the left wing of the Israeli Communist Party. Following the Six-Day War in 1967, it opposed Israeli occupation of the West Bank and Gaza Strip. When I visited Israel, Sartre arranged for me to be shown "the real Israel" by Matzpen members, one of whom, to my surprise, had been my student at NYU in 1966.

7. Lanzmann has since become the director of *Les Temps Modernes*.

8. The anarchists inevitably showed up for all demonstrations against the government.

9. The Communist Revolutionary League was the most important Trotskyist party in France, long headed by Alain Krivine, one of the leaders of the May '68 events. He was a member of the European Parliament from 1999 until 2004, and resigned from the LCR's political bureau in 2006.

10. To me, the center of the play is Valerra, the conman who claims to have escaped from Russia with a list of who will be shot when the Russians occupy France, and who sells space on the list to the ambitious Red-baiting bosses of the newspaper for which Palotin works.

11. Husserl, the founder of modern phenomenology, insisted that experiences must be analyzed as "things-in-themselves"—"bracketed off"—and not with metaphysical speculations. Heidegger, his onetime student who replaced him as professor of philosophy at Freiburg University, pushed that analysis to consider being (*Sein*) in its temporal and historical context, and *Dasein*, from which Sartre derived his notions of in-itself and for-itself, and in-situation.

12. Both Ehrenburg and Simonov spent years as war correspondents, and both wrote very popular novels. But Simonov, who also wrote very popular poems and plays, often made into movies, toed the line much more skillfully and was decorated with Lenin and Stalin prizes, and was made head of the Union of Writers of the USSR. Ehrenburg died in 1967, Simonov in 1979.

13. Osip Mandelstam was one of modern Russia's greatest poets; repeatedly arrested and freed, he finally died in a "transit camp" in 1938. Nadezhda Mandelstam, his wife, wrote about his ordeal in two extremely moving memoirs, *Hope Against Hope* and *Hope Abandoned*.

14. Gide, who won the Nobel Prize for literature in 1947 after publishing such gems as *La symphonie pastorale* and *L'immoraliste*, joined the CP in 1930, visited Russia, and then quit, denouncing its totalitarianism.

JUNE 1972

1. The Tupamaros were extremely popular in Uruguay as long as they kidnapped high government officials and released them only on condition that their corrupt deals with U.S. capitalists were exposed on the front pages of their newspapers. They remained popular even after they executed the CIA torture expert Dan Mitrione, after revealing his taped confession that he had taught the Uruguayan police how to torture prisoners. Once the dictatorship fell, the people voted for a nonviolent leftist party.

2. Born in Algeria and raised as a practicing Catholic in Marseilles, Louis Althusser was a brilliant though erratic student whose thesis on Hegel at L'Ecole Nor-

male got him appointed there as an instructor. He was captured during World War II, and then began to focus more and more on Marx, joined the CP in 1948, and remained a ferocious though controversial communist, often criticized by party bigwigs, until his death. His various works focused on Marx's epistemology and reinterpreted *Capital*, concluding that the distinction between object and subject is an illusory ideological concept from which man cannot escape without destroying the bourgeois state. Plagued by periodic mental disorders, Althusser strangled his wife in 1980, spent three years in a mental hospital, and died at seventy-two, in 1990. Many of his students were in the forefront of the May '68 rebellion, and his works are still studied avidly by leftists and Marxists all over the world.

3. Carpentier, a novelist, essayist, and musicologist, was one of the founders of the Cuban Communist Party and a lifetime leftist even after he quit the party. Not comfortable under the Castro regime, which decided to send him to Paris as its cultural attaché, he remained a loyal supporter of the regime until his death in Paris in 1980.

4. Dedijer was an early Yugoslav communist and extremely courageous partisan during World War II. He was elected to Tito's Central Committee and often represented Yugoslavia at the United Nations. Ousted from all official positions for siding with Milovan Djilas's criticism of civil-liberties abuses, Dedijer remained an active, if controversial and independent, communist, writing history and Tito's biography, with Tito's acquiescence and collaboration. He served on Russell's War Crimes Tribunal; he died in 1990.

OCTOBER 1972

1. Glucksmann dedicated himself to helping the "boat people" and eventually turned so pro-Israel that he ended up on the far right, which gained him huge popularity as a leader of "the new philosophers" in the pro-U.S. media.

2. Geismar abandoned politics, called himself a petit bourgeois, and joined the Ministry of Education.

3. Twenty-five militants from Jeanson's network of "suitcase carriers" for the Algerian resistance movement went on trial for sedition on September 6, 1960. Among those who had escaped capture were Jeanson and Henri Curiel, an Egyptian Jew who fought for Third World independence from the age of fourteen until he was gunned down in front of his apartment in 1978 by Israelis who objected to his call for peace talks between Israel and Palestine. One day before the trial began, the Manifesto of the 121, calling for open sedition and refusal of draftees to fight in Algeria, was published and, despite government seizures, censorship, and arrests of distributors, widely promulgated. The immediate result was a huge student rally against the war, but because neither the CP nor its affiliated unions supported Algerian independence, and although neither the network nor the manifesto changed govern-

ment policy, the mood in the country slowly shifted, as story after story of French torture became publicized. Marcel Péju, one of the network's main organizers and a longtime anticolonialist agitator, and also the editor of *Les Temps Modernes* after Jeanson went underground, once congratulated Ahmed Ben Bella, the first president of independent Algeria, for its courage and tenacity in gaining its freedom. Ben Bella replied: "And congratulations to France's intelligentsia, which stimulated that courage and tenacity with its own."

4. Alleg's book, published in 1957, was immediately banned because it gave details on the torture by the French army of him and Algerian rebels. In spite of the censorship, more than two hundred thousand copies of the book were sold, and it inspired Gillo Pontecorvo's film *Battle of Algiers*. After he was jailed for sedition, Alleg escaped to Czechoslovakia. After Algeria won its independence, he returned and rebuilt his old daily, *Alger Républicain*.

MAY 1973

1. Sartre and I had both been traveling during the winter, and when we met again in May he wanted to know what I had learned and my reaction to the folks I had met. The following is part of our exchange on the day we got together again.

> **SARTRE: Castor tells me you had a talk with [Salvador] Allende [of Chile]. What did he have to say?**
>
> GERASSI: He expects a military coup soon. We actually had a big argument over that. I said that since he was so sure, he should distribute arms to the *cordones,* that's the rings of workers who live near the factories, grouped just outside the capital, Santiago; the workers have organized defense committees, but they have no arms.
>
> **What did he answer?**
>
> He said that if he distributed arms to the workers, the Communist Party would quit the government and not support it.
>
> **So what? There are no communist parties in the world that still want to wage revolutions.**
>
> That's what I said, but he insisted that in Chile, revolution is impossible without the communist workers, and they will hesitate as long as the party does not tell them to go. When the coup comes, he said, we have to survive three days, because the workers won't wait more than that to join the fight. And in a civil war, he said, the Americans will send not only arms but also so-called expeditionary forces to join the military if the workers are armed right away. We have to wait until the whole world knows that the military is trying to overthrow democracy, he insisted; we need Argentina and Peru, at least, openly on our side. But wait, I'm here to ask you about your trips, to Japan, Egypt, Israel, where else?

In a moment. First tell me, what did you respond to Allende? You knew him well, no? You could talk frankly?

Oh, yes. I toured the country with him, and that great socialist leader Salomón Corbalán, during the '64 campaign. Corbalán was head of the party then, a really fantastic guy, who died of a heart attack at thirty-nine. Oh, so, yes, I told Allende that the United States will back a coup that they organize, not one that's off the wall by some general, and the one they back will never give Allende three days. But he insisted he couldn't risk it.

Do you think he'd get support from Argentina and Peru?

Absolutely not. Héctor Cámpora, the president [of Argentina], might want to, but [Juan] Perón will tell him not to. [Juan] Velasco Alvarado, the nationalist-populist general in charge in Peru, might send some military aid if Allende can hold out a while. But when the United States decides to bring him down, it will be quick, and they'll probably kill him. Did you know that in my book on Latin America I predicted that Perón would never return to Argentina? Ha! He'll be president again within a year, you'll see. Takes care of my crystal ball.

You sound like you like the Peruvian?

Velasco? Guardedly. He was head of military intelligence during the war against the leftist guerrillas, so to understand them better, he read everything they wrote, and it convinced him that they were right. So when he came to power by a coup, with other nationalist generals, he carried out many of their reforms, like nationalizing the oil and banks, enacting an agrarian reform, he even freed Héctor Béjar, the head of the major guerrilla group who had been caught and jailed, and put him in charge of an outfit called the Conscientization of the Masses. My book sold a lot in Peru, so when he heard I was going around asking questions, he invited me for dinner. We talked quite a bit, but not very openly since there were three or four other generals around the table. I don't think he's that solidly in power. There are other generals around who are not as suspicious of the United States as he is.

So no revolution there either in the offing?

Nope.

How about Venezuela? Castor tells me you saw [Rafael] Caldera twice, once privately.

He's a Christian, a believer, not just a member of the Christian Democratic Party, and tries to be moral. He tries to overturn what that pig [Rómulo] Betancourt did before him, like he recognized the Soviet Union and its satellites, raised the taxes on the oil company profits, stuff like that. But Venezuela is so completely dominated by the United States and its pro-U.S. ruling clique that he can't do much. No one can. That's one country that desperately needs a revolution, a revolutionary leader that can grab the oil away from the clique and use the revenue to help the poor. But enough on my trip. Now yours.

2. Giscard d'Estaing did run for the presidency and win in 1974, and he did arrange then for Cleaver to get a French temporary residence permit. Cleaver, who was under indictment in the United States for the murder of a policeman, had split with Huey Newton and the Black Panther Party a couple of years earlier, gone to Cuba, then China, and finally Algeria, where Ahmed Ben Bella gave him, and various other Panthers who advocated armed struggle, residency and immunity from police searches (for drugs, not weapons). I went to see Cleaver in Algeria, and when I returned I told Sartre that he was officially completely in agreement with the maos in France, but was really a flake and a drug-head in private. Nevertheless, when he came to Paris illegally, before Giscard arranged his stay, I put him up in my apartment, where Catherine Yelloz was also staying and with whom he had an "unpleasant," she said, affair while I traveled to Latin America. Catherine and I had an open relationship, but Cleaver couldn't face me when I returned, and he moved out to stay with another ex-Panther. Cleaver returned to the United States in 1975, in a deal supposedly arranged by Giscard d'Estaing and the FBI wherein he would plead guilty to pending charges and receive probation. He then became disillusioned with everything, joined the Moonies for a while, then switched to the Mormons, supported Reagan for president in 1980, and died in 1998.

3. The book, *On a raison de se révolter* [We Are Justified to Revolt], was published by Gallimard in 1974. It has not been translated into English.

4. Miliukov and Kerensky were liberal leaders of the government after the fall of the Russian tsars and before the Bolsheviks came to power; both honored Russia's commitment to the Allies during World War I, which was extremely unpopular, but both also tried to respect all civil liberties.

5. Deleuze and Guattari, philosophers and academic militants who were greatly influenced by the May '68 events, collaborated in developing a theory of "schizoanalysis," which claimed that schizophrenia was a neurosis maintained by capitalism as a way of perpetuating itself. To combat capitalism, or these insidious "societies of control," they said, such nonviolent "swarming" of hierarchical structures by "leaderless resistance," what they called "rhizomes," will eventually succeed. Sartre rejected their theory. Deleuze and Guattari both died in the 1990s.

JUNE 1973

1. One of the genuine prewar revolutionary idealists, Serge was jailed many times in France, Belgium, where he was born, and Russia, both before and after having joined the Bolsheviks and worked for the Comintern as a propagandist. Originally an anarchist, he thought of himself as an anarcho-communist and openly criti-

cized Lenin as part of the "Left Opposition" until repression became too strong under Stalin, who had him arrested and tossed into a dungeon. A French campaign to free him got him released. He ended up in Mexico, where he wrote various political novels, helped Trotsky's wife with her memoirs, and died in 1947. His *Memoirs of a Revolutionist*, which reveals him to have stayed a libertarian communist until the end, is brilliant and fascinating.

2. In 1990, after Claude Gallimard died, his sons fought for control of the publishing house. The most political, and rightist, Antoine, won. Claude's brother, Robert, with whom I had always dealt and who was socialist, quit. *Les Temps Modernes* is still being published by Gallimard. It has stopped being revolutionary-left since Lanzmann took over after the death of Sartre and de Beauvoir, but except on the issue of Israel, it is still more or less socialistic.

3. Pontalis was a strong advocate of anti-psychiatry. Cooper, who first used and defined the term "anti-psychiatry," and Laing, who did not like the term, both were extremely prolific, writing not only about their attempt to show that schizophrenia was a social disease, but also about politics, claiming, like Deleuze and Guattari, that capitalism is the principal cause of all contemporary social maladies. Laing started Kingsley Hall, a safe house where doctors and "mental" patients lived together in an attempt to "cure" schizophrenics, generating a whole battery of fascinating books, pro and con, about his methods.

4. The philosopher and Germanophile Hyppolite graduated from L'Ecole Normale, translated Hegel's *Phenomenology of Spirit* into French in 1939, then published *Genesis and Structure of the Phenomenology of Spirit* in 1947, which influenced his younger colleagues, including Foucault, Deleuze, and Sartre. Hyppolite became head of the Normale in 1955, was given a chair in 1963, and died in 1968.

5. Aron and Sartre made a show of reconciling at the end of their lives in order to sponsor financial help and immigration permits for the "boat people," the thousands of Vietnamese who fled the communists when the United States abandoned them following the Vietnam War.

NOVEMBER 1973

1. Written in 1947–48, they were published in one volume in 1982 by his daughter.

2. This unfinished work was published in 1985.

3. Simenon was known as the world's most prolific writer, with a total of 550 published books, including more than 200 novels, 75 of them starring Inspector Maigret. Simenon could dash off 60 to 80 pages a day, and once he got used to tape recording he could write a whole novel in one night. He died in 1989.

4. Sartre helped found and finance the new daily newspaper *Libération*, which began publishing in 1973. He served as the "responsible editor" until May 1974, dur-

ing which time all employees, from the actual editor to the janitor, were paid the same. It was transformed into a regular daily with a "normal" pay system when Sartre stopped being responsible, and began to take ads in the early 1980s, allowing private investors to come aboard—although this was apparently not enough, as it closed for three months in 1981. Reorganized and reformatted, with Serge July, a former Maoist who had helped get it started, as its director, "Libé" stayed on the left, opposed all parties, left or right, and claimed to combine counterculture and radicalism, but gradually lost its fire and edged into mainstream.

5. An opportunistic politician, known as the Weathercock because he changed political affiliations with the wind, Faure served in various governments, including as prime minister and foreign minister, and in 1973 as president of the National Assembly. During World War II he fought in the resistance, then made his way to Algiers to join de Gaulle; he was France's prosecutor at the Nuremberg Trials and represented France at the Geneva Conference meant to end the war in Vietnam. He died in 1988.

NOVEMBER 1974

1. Fernando survived this operation, but he died two nights later.

2. Carvalho was a career soldier born in Portuguese-occupied Mozambique, and in 1974 his boss was Spínola, both of them being then in charge of repressing the independence movements in Portugal's colonies. Their coup overthrew the dictatorship of Marcello Caetano. When the homeland army was ordered to crush the coup, the people of Lisbon and elsewhere started placing carnations, then in full bloom, into the barrels of their rifles, hence giving the movement the name the Carnation Revolution. In 1975, the extreme left within the military tried another coup, but Spínola denied his backing and Carvalho did not support it either, though he sympathized with the left's position. Accused of helping terrorists, he was jailed temporarily but quickly freed. He ran for president on the far-left ticket in both 1976 and 1980, but lost, and retired to Algarve.

3. This volume was never finished. Sartre became incapable of reading again not long after this, and Pierre Victor became his secretary. Victor eventually reverted back to his real name, Benny Lévy, got his doctorate, taught philosophy, discovered his Jewish ethnicity, learned Hebrew, went to Israel, joined a yeshiva, and became a rabbi and Talmudic scholar. The interviews he did carry out with Sartre after he went blind portray the old man as recognizing that he was affected by the Talmud; commentators scoffed that Lévy had turned Sartre into a Jew, and Simone de Beauvoir denounced the interviews as a fraud. To me, when I saw Sartre the last time, six months before his death, he quipped that scandals keep the public's interest, hence "my books being read." Lévy died of a heart attack, at fifty-eight, in 2003.

4. The amount was worth almost half a million dollars at the time.

5. The University of Paris X, Nanterre, is the campus where the 1968 student leftist movement began, and the University of Paris VIII, Vincennes, is where it quickly gained the support of both the students and the intellectuals teaching there, like Foucault, Deleuze, and others. "Nancennist" would be a combination of the names Nanterre and Vincennes.

FAREWELL

1. When his body was taken to the Montparnasse Cemetery, the cortege was followed by 250,000 people, and 50,000 stood with heads raised high, "as he would want," said the student next to me. "We are not mourning, we are praising." Simone de Beauvoir fainted almost into the tomb. When she died six years later almost to the day, she was buried with him. Every day since, folks place flowers or mementoes on the tomb. In July 2006, I photographed a used Métro ticket on which is scribbled: "On gagnera la prochaine fois" [We shall win next time].

Acknowledgments

Obviously, I am most indebted for this book to the team of transcribers in Paris, but especially to Catherine Yelloz, who went over each transcription, corrected the mistakes, explained to me many of Sartre's references, made me look up the folks he talked about, and took notes of my numerous restaurant conversations with Sartre. Subsequently, as I started editing the two thousand single-spaced pages of the transcriptions, many friends tried to help me focus on what was crucial and what had to be said but also explained. Among those in America, the best were Peter Manicas, former chairman of the philosophy department at Queens College, CUNY, where I still teach in the political science department, and now director of liberal studies at the University of Hawaii at Manoa, and Leonard Weinglass, a great people's lawyer and personal friend. In France, I was often well guided by Claire Etcherelli, a wonderful novelist and for years the manager of Sartre-Beauvoir's magazine, *Les Temps Modernes*. But it was my literary agent, Linda Langton of Langtons International Agency, who really made the book possible, by spending hours pushing and encouraging me when the task seemed too formidable, holding my hand when I was depressed, and constantly reminding me that I was privy to the mind of one of the greatest thinkers of the twentieth century and not to waste it.

Index

Sartre, Jean-Paul (*continued*)
76, 187, 203–4, 229; on death, 7–8, 15–16, 17, 148–50, 152, 160–61; death of, 272, 303n1; and drug use, 62–63, 193–94, 223; early childhood of, 249–50; early education of, 2–5; early philosophical development of, 41, 50–54, 64–65, 69–70; early reading habits of, 1, 2, 9–10, 22–23, 30; early writing efforts of, 1, 2, 10, 23–24, 38–39; on education system, 60–61; on equality, 11–12; on ethics, 120–21, 290–91n21; on freedom, 34–35, 41–42, 45, 72–73, 78, 162–63, 248–49, 256, 265; on freedom of choice, 122–23, 129, 145, 265–66, 273–74; on Freud, 128, 129, 268; on de Gaulle, 77, 78, 82, 232; and Fernando Gerassi, 5–8, 24, 27–28, 40–41, 76–77, 82–84, 111, 138–39, 278–79n11; financial circumstances of, 282n7; generosity of, 274; John Gerassi's biography of, xi, xiv, 211; John Gerassi's relationship with, ix–xiv; and his grandfather, 1, 3–5, 8–11, 14, 20, 22, 251; on guilt, xi–xii, 16; handwriting of, 257–58; on happiness, 27, 28, 29, 30, 35, 146; health problems of, 150, 238, 292n5; on humanism, 13–14, 46, 60, 104; on imperialism, 133; on individual responsibility, 114–15; influences on, 49–50, 52–54; insecurity of, 11; on intellectuals in society, 74–75, 101–2, 119–21, 275; as "judge" of culpability in mining incident, 35–36, 95–96; in La Rochelle, 2, 3, 4, 9, 14, 16, 21–22, 24, 27, 29–30, 47–48, 251; legacy of, 265–68, 272–76; in Le Havre, 24, 39, 70; love affairs of, 30–31, 32–33, 154–55, 220–23; on martyrdom, 38; on Marx, 52, 255–56; on meaning, 81–82; medication required by, 21; on men of action, 7, 8, 59, 267–68; and Merleau-Ponty, 72; on money, 74; on moral gestures, 96–97; and his mother, 8–9, 20–21, 24, 25, 47, 250; on his mother's remarriage, 14; operettas by, 45; on philosophy and action, 178; as prisoner of

the Germans, 41, 78, 104–5, 114–15, 248–49; as professor, 70, 78; on rationalism, 50–51; rebelliousness of, 250–52; on relationships, xii–xiii; on religion, 42; on revolution, 46, 94–104, 240, 263–64, 270–71; on revolutionary morality, 99–100, 119–21; in Russia, 154–55, 200–203; Russian novelists as influence on, 58–59; on security, 129–30; self-analysis by, 250–51, 268–69; and his stepfather, 9, 20–22, 24, 48–49, 60, 250, 251; on suicide, 17–18; as supporter of student rebellion, 280–81n1; as teacher, 24, 39, 70, 91, 278n10; and the Third Force movement, 80, 108, 115, 127; on trust, 237–38; on violence, 45–46, 206; vision problems of, 258, 302n3; women supported by, 163–64, 240–41; on women versus men, 78–79, 85; on writing, 16, 17, 33–35, 39–40, 53, 140–42, 143–45
—works by: *The Age of Reason*, 59, 66, 83, 127; *Bariona*, 248, 249; *Being and Nothingness*, 43–44, 47, 72–73, 86–87, 109, 114–15, 133–34, 179, 200, 254, 255, 257; *The Communists and Peace*, 44, 157, 161, 167, 182–83, 274; *The Condemned of Altona*, 15, 90, 91, 210, 222, 287n5; *Critique of Dialectical Reason*, 51, 86–87, 121, 134, 193, 212, 254, 255–56, 257; *The Devil and the Good Lord*, 161, 162, 167, 177; *Dirty Hands*, 107, 159, 289n12; "L'enfance d'un chef," 24, 61; "Erostrate," 8, *The Family Idiot: Gustave Flaubert, 1821–1857*, 16, 74, 113, 140, 144, 147, 162; *The Flies*, 108–9, 111, 114, 286n9; *The Ghost of Stalin*, 161, 197, 274, 280n1; *The Henri Martin Affair*, 167; *In the Mesh*, 198; "J'accuse," 144, 292n4; *Les jeux sont faits*, 115, 126; "The Legend of Truth," 47; "The Liberation of Paris," 122; *Materialism and Revolution*, 153; *Men Without Shadows*, 127; "Merleau Vivant," 179, 182; *Nausea*, 52, 74, 81, 267, 278n10; *Nekrassov*, 161, 168, 197; *No Exit*, 11, 108, 110, 268, 281n3; *Notes for an Ethics*, 291n21; *On a*